RUSSIA AND THE IDEA OF EUROPE

The end of the Soviet system and the transition to the market in Russia has brought to the fore the centuries-old debate about Russia's relationship with Europe. In *Russia and the Idea of Europe* Iver Neumann discusses whether the tensions between Romantic nationalist views and Europe-orientated liberal views can ever be resolved. The issue of nationalism is examined as one of the most powerful and alarming of Russian responses to the pressures exerted by European models.

Drawing on a wide array of Russian sources, Neumann outlines the argument as it has unfolded over the last two hundred years, showing how Russia is caught between the attraction of an economically, politically and socially more developed Europe, and the appeal of being able to play a European-style imperial role in less-developed Asia.

Neumann argues that the process of delineating a European 'other' from the Russian self is an active part of Russian identity formation. The Russian debate about Europe is also a debate about what Russia is and should be.

This book will be of great interest to students of Russian studies, European studies and international relations, and to any reader interested in the concepts of nation and identity.

Iver B. Neumann heads the division for foreign and security policy at the Norwegian Institute of International Affairs.

D1532060

THE NEW INTERNATIONAL RELATIONS
Edited by Barry Buzan, *University of Warwick*, and Gerald Segal, *International Institute for Strategic Studies*, London

The field of international relations has changed dramatically in recent years. This new series will cover the major issues that have emerged and reflect the latest academic thinking in this particularly dynamic area.

INTERNATIONAL LAW, RIGHTS AND POLITICS
Developments in Eastern Europe and the CIS
Rein Mullerson

THE LOGIC OF INTERNATIONALISM
Coercion and accommodation
Kjell Goldmann

RUSSIA AND THE IDEA OF EUROPE

A study in identity and international relations

Iver B. Neumann

London and New York

First published 1996
by Routledge
11 New Fetter Lane, London EC4P 4EE

Simultaneously published in the USA and Canada
by Routledge
29 West 35th Street, New York, NY 10001

Typeset in Palatino by Florencetype Ltd,
Stoodleigh, Devon
Printed and bound in Great Britain by Mackays of
Chatham PLC

British Library Cataloguing in Publication Data
A catalogue record for this book is available from the
British Library

Library of Congress Cataloguing in Publication Data
A catalogue record for this book has been requested

ISBN 0-415-11370-9 (hbk)
ISBN 0-415-11371-7 (pbk)

Believing, with Max Weber, that man is an animal suspended in webs of significance he himself has spun, I take culture to be those webs, and the analysis of it to be therefore not an experimental science in search of law but an interpretive one in search of meaning.

(Geertz, 1973: 5)

There are difficulties also with the view that places culture, and in particular, domestic culture, in the system's position as the principal guide to the interpretation of international politics. In the first place, when Adda Bozeman decided that the future was not bright for law in a multicultural world, her main source material was the doctrine of the several cultures rather than their practice of co-existence. And just as *The Soviet Design for a World State* seems more alarming when put together from Marxist-Leninist texts than it does when mixed with the historical record, so might a textual approach give a harsher view of the clash of cultures in world politics than is justified by the reality of their mutual recognition.

(Vincent, 1980: 259)

To Ingeborg, Ida and Linka

CONTENTS

CONTENTS

SERIES EDITOR'S PREFACE

This is a book in the series on the 'new international relations'. We began the series in large measure because we recognised that the end of the Cold War marked a major change in the pattern of international affairs, and that there should be a place where authors dedicated to understanding the new features could find a congenial platform. Of course, the reason for the end of the Cold War was the collapse of communism and the collapse was in return the result of a recognition in Russia that they could no longer sustain their empire. Thus, a series on the new international relations that did not include a major analysis of Russian attitudes and policies leading to the collapse would have a gaping hole at its heart. We were fortunate to have attracted one of the bright young stars of European analysis of the former Soviet Union, Iver Neumann, to turn his dissertation on how the Russians adopted and adapted the idea of Europe, into a major book.

Iver's effort can and should be read through different lenses. For the historian, there is a fine summary and analysis of the evolution of the Russian state and its relationship with Europe. This is a study of both the idea of Europe in Russian debates, and also a broader understanding of European ideas that helped shape Russian politics. Thus, for the more specific historian of political thought, there is an even more detailed and subtle analysis of how Russia learned to think about itself and its relationship with European ideals. Inevitably, this was a messy process, and its very complexity leaves much open for Russian leaders who came later.

For those with stronger interests in current affairs, Iver's analysis offers a thick soup of ideas on where Russia might be going. It is now almost a cliché to note that Russia, like much of Europe, risks going 'back to the future'. As Barry Buzan has noted elsewhere, the lifting of the Cold War overlay uncovers many aspects of Europe's old history. Iver explores these ideas and suggests the basis on which new and old European ideas are likely to become hooked into the Russian political debates. So much of the current Russian discussion about the future concerns an assessment of Russia's roots, that students of current Russian foreign policy will find new twists to an already complex fabric. Russian history and its relationship with Europe remains a messy set of intellectual strands, but it is on these threads that the future Russian relationship with Europe and the wider world will be built.

There is even much for the student of the wider fabric of international affairs, especially those with an eye for potential clashes among civilisations. Is Russia really part of European civilisation? This is a question of the highest and most current policy, for a positive answer might suggest the need for Russian membership in both NATO and the European Union. The fact that the answer seems to be No, has encouraged many Russians to see their foreign policy options as lying elsewhere. The basis for exploring Russia's Asian identity or the notion of something distinctly, Eurasian, lies in these debates about Russia's true civilisation. The battle between Westernisers and others in turn plays a crucial role in shaping the domestic politics of Russia.

The battles are in fact only just joined. Thus, the analysis of the ideas and arguments involved in Russia's relationship with European ideas is likely to be with us for some time. Because the arguments involve very old ideas, and because the debates will run for some time, this is in a sense a book about how the old international relations shapes the new. As a result, the series editors are happy to welcome it as the epitome of the series and the kinds of intellectual challenges that we all face.

Gerald Segal
International Institute for Strategic Studies, London

PREFACE

Although Europe played a key role in Russian identity formation at least since the late seventeenth century (Rogger, 1960),
this book picks up the story about a century later. The revolution in France in 1789 utterly changed the setting for the Russian
debate about Europe. The military challenge to Russia which
grew out of the French Revolution had a political parallel which
was no less challenging. Once the revolution had removed
enlightened despotism in one country and so demonstrated that
this regime type was man-made rather than inevitably given,
debate about its legitimacy could be expected in other countries
too. The introductory chapter discusses these matters in more
detail.

Chapter 2 focuses on the Decembrist uprising and the Russian
reactions to it. The Decembrists saw Europe as a cultural entity
of nations which included Russia. Since Russia was a European
country, they argued, it should evolve along European lines both
politically and economically. For them, this evolution required
constitutionalism. They therefore followed the lead of people like
Speranskiy and forged a constitutionalist position which was to
hover on the margins of the Russian debate about Europe until
1917. The Decembrist uprising demonstrated to the state that it
could not dominate the Russian debate about Europe simply by
reiterating a legitimist position, and by keeping other positions
from being formulated. Other Russians, such as Prince
Odoevskiy, saw the Decembrist uprising as an example of how
seemingly positive European ideas could slowly corrupt Russia's
best and brightest. Their reaction was to set store by a variant
of Russian Messianism where the Christian idea of Moscow as
the Third Rome was played down, but where the Christian

historicism underpinning this idea was retained. Inspired by German idealism, they elaborated on the organic nationalist thinking of the 'Russian tendency' and established a Romantic nationalist position in the Russian debate about Europe. A third reaction to the Decembrist rising was to start doubting whether the economic and political gulf that was opening between Russia and Europe would ever again be bridged – whether Russia's status as part of Europe was not in jeopardy. This was the main topic of Chaadaev, publicised in his first 'philosophical letters'.

Chapter 3 focuses on how Chaadaev's letter forced the debate about Europe to the centre of the public political space and added to the pressure on the state to formulate a clear position on Europe. It rose to the challenge by formulating a doctrine of 'official nationality', which enshrined autocracy – one of the key assets of Europe's *anciens régimes* now largely abandoned by European states – as part of the basis for the Russian state. The tsar, by on the one hand setting himself up as the defender of 'true' European values now largely abandoned by the rest of Europe, and on the other presenting his relationship with the other monarchs of Europe as one based on Christian fraternity, created an unresolvable tension in the state's position. Chaadaev's letter also sparked the Romantic nationalists to develop their argument in favour of an immediate rapport between tsar and people as a specific Russian way of life, different from and superior to that of Europe. What permitted them to make a comprehensive position known as Slavophilism was their interaction with the Westernisers. The task the Westernisers had set themselves was to show how Russia was *already* developing along European lines, and how it should try to accelerate that development, despite the somewhat different conditions which prevailed there.

Chapter 4 demonstrates how the debate between Slavophiles and Westernisers changed character when the state, following the European springtime of nations in 1848, severely restricted public political space. In addition, the state tried to withstand the challenge of the springtime of nations by moving in the direction of the Romantic nationalists. That, however, proved to be a short-lived phenomenon, as the Russian state's defeat in the Crimean War forced it to rethink its position yet again. The state moved in the direction of the Westernisers. The Westernisers hoped for radical reforms, and when their hopes were dashed their stance radicalised, and their position split into three: a liberal, a 'Russian socialist' and also an embryonically 'Marxist' position. The liberals wanted to copy contemporary European practices. The 'Russian socialist' position – which during the 1860s was to be radicalised and changed into a populist position – advocated a specifically Russian, non-industrial developmental path. The embryonically Marxist path wanted industrialisation on the European pattern. As the state implemented Westernising reform, the Romantic nationalist position changed from a Slavophile, isolationist line towards a pan-Slavist, proselytising line which advocated confrontation with Europe.

In 1881, Tsar Alexander II was assassinated and the state constricted public political space considerably. Chapter 5 demonstrates how the Romantic pan-Slavist nationalists dominated the debate almost by default in the 1880s, only to be marginalised by the resuscitated debate between populists and Marxists in the 1890s. In addition, the Romantic nationalist position branched out into a xenophobic wing and a more spiritual wing, with the latter advocating Russo-European partnership in Christ, and the former isolation or confrontation. The Marxist position split into a Menshevik position and a Bolshevik position in 1903. The break between the Mensheviks and the Bolsheviks concerned how thoroughly Russia should copy European models and how squarely one should delineate a 'progressive' Europe from a 'stagnant' Europe. There also existed a third, marginal Marxist position. To Trotskiy, it was simply impossible to abstract Russian developments from European ones, but he felt that Russia might lead Europe's surge towards socialism.

Chapter 6 shows how the First World War set the nationalist cat among the social democratic pigeons, inasmuch as their supra-national in-group – 'true Europe' – came under immediate pressure as an active agency. The question of the relative importance of national and class identities created immediate confusion as to who the social democratic 'we' actually referred to. Yet the social democrats were not the only ones to grapple with this problem. When the tsarist regime fell in March 1917, the problem of delineating the in-group also hit all those who saw Russia as an autocratic project. This problem was further aggravated, and was, moreover, extended to all non-Bolshevik groups, once the 'liberal moment' in Russian history came to an end with the Bolshevik coup in November 1917. The non-

Bolsheviks had to face up to no less than a reassessment of what Russia and Europe meant to them once the Russian state apparatus had fallen into Bolshevik hands. As the Bolsheviks defined the state's position, the only position which survived in the debate for some time was the Romantic nationalist one. As the 1920s wore on, however, the Russian debate about Europe was further reduced to a debate about the state's position, with Bolsheviks fighting it out between themselves as to whether Russia's relationship to Europe should be one of economic integration or isolation and how 'true Europe' should be delineated from 'false Europe'. By the 1930s, the Russian debate about Europe was reduced to the question of how far it was possible for the state to contract public political space and the group of persons who were represented as embodying 'true Europe'. During the Second World War, public political space expanded somewhat, yet the Russian debate about Europe was suspended to give way to debates about wartime allies and fascism. In the early post-war years, public political space reverted to its interwar shape, as did the state's position on Europe, yet nationalist sentiment served to underline the moral superiority of Russia over Europe even further. Europe's position as the supreme Other to the Russian self was, however, seriously challenged by the imposing role of the United States in the international system.

Chapter 7 discusses how de-Stalinisation involved a shift in the state's position on the West away from seeing it as a singularly hostile 'camp of imperialism' towards seeing 'the capitalist system' as an entity which remained morally inferior, but which was not wholly other. De-Stalinisation also made way for a resuscitation of debate about the state's position in the form of a professional debate between foreign affairs specialists, the *mezhdunarodniki*. These debates did not call into question the basic framework within which Europe was seen, and the debate about moral judgement was limited to a question of how much less advanced capitalist Europe was as compared to the socialist bloc. The focus was rather on how to interpret the relations between Western European states themselves, and also those between Western Europe on the one hand and the United States on the other, as well as on what kind of relationship Russia should have with Western Europe. Following the ousting of Khrushchev in 1964, however, there was a steep increase in the number of writings disseminated at the margins of the public debate, the *samizdat* or privately manifolded literature. While the foreign affairs specialists concentrated on the position of the state, it was left to *samizdat* writers to resuscitate the old Romantic nationalist position – complete with a xenophobic and a spiritual wing – and to attempt the resuscitation of other positions as well. While the images thus presented were seldom original – they were more often explicitly lifted from or latched on to the views of Russian tsarist and/or *émigré* authors – they nevertheless had an original impact, since the Russian debate into which they were reinserted was rather different from what it had been at the time when these images were first presented.

Chapter 8 discusses how, under Gorbachev, the state's position changed, moving away from seeing international relations as a zero-sum game between classes and towards seeing it as a potential positive-sum game between states. Accordingly, Europe was seen as a potential partner. Furthermore, the state's expansion of public political space made it possible for the Romantic nationalist position to go fully public and for a liberal position not only to establish itself, but to become the dominant position in the Russian debate about Europe. The state cut some of the moorings of the Bolshevik position and let itself drift in the direction of the liberals, but it never left all the central tenets of the Bolshevik position behind. As the Soviet state disintegated and the communists lost their grip on the state, however, the new Russian state under Yel'tsin was to adopt a number of the tenets of the liberal position, and the Russian debate about Europe was once again to take pride of place in Russian public political space. However, in the very moment of seeming liberal victory, the Romantic nationalist position was making itself ever more strongly felt in the debate. The content of the Romantic nationalist position hardly changed as a result of the collapse of the Soviet Union. Yet, by seemingly confirming the xenophobic wing's view of the Russian liberals as the errand-boys of the West whose dirty deeds could only serve to split the Motherland, the collapse broadened their appeal. Moreover, a number of communists who found themselves without a position in the debate soon took up the Romantic nationalist one.

Throughout 1992 and 1993, the bearers of the Romantic nationalist position attacked the state's position more and more vigorously. When, in the autumn of 1993, people like Vice-President

Rutskoy and the Speaker of Parliament, Khasbulatov, joined their all-out attack on the state's position, the state moved to redefine public political space. By literally shooting out and closing parliament, putting a new constitution before the electorate and closing down the main printed conduits of the Romantic nationalists, President Yel'tsin's state tried to strengthen the liberal position by weakening the Romantic nationalists. However, since the use of force was not sustained – for example, newspapers were soon allowed to reopen – Romantic nationalists found their way back in parliament after the December elections. They were also able to continue publishing, and made their presence ever more strongly felt throughout 1994. Thus, the state's attempt to redefine public political space proved to be a failure, and the continued strength of the Romantic nationalist position a fact.

The debate continues to be defined by a liberal and a Romantic nationalist position, yet whereas the latter is fairly stable, the former has lost a lot of its radical Westernising quality. The state, moreover, has slid away from the liberal position and is trying uneasily to poise itself closer to the Romantic nationalist position. Although the Romantic nationalist position may not succeed in taking over the state, it seems strong enough to draw the state even closer than is presently the case.

ACKNOWLEDGEMENTS

This book started life as a doctoral thesis in Oxford University, and so my main debt of gratitude is to my supervisor Dr Alex Pravda and St Antony's College. Catherine Andreyev, Pavel Baev, Helge Blakkisrud, Barry Buzan, Robert Bathurst, Yuriy Borko, Timothy Dunne, Thomas Hylland Eriksen, Julie Glidden, Daniel Heradstveit, Richard Kindersley, Olav F. Knudsen, Pål Kolstø, Neil Malcolm, Sergey Medvedev, Heikki Patomäki, Gerald Segal, Harry Shukman, Peter Normann Waage, Ole Wæver and especially Jennifer M. Welsh offered helpful comments on chapter drafts. So did members of the Oxford University Russian History and International Research Seminars, Hilary Term 1992, and participants at the panel on European foreign relations, Inaugural Pan-European Conference in International Relations, Heidelberg, 16-22 September 1992. Series editors Barry Buzan and Gerald Segal and their referees commented extensively and helpfully on a previous draft. I thank Tore Gustavsson, Dagfrid Hermansen, Karsten Korbøl, Gordon Smith, Eilert Struksnes, James Whiting, Jackie Willcox and Caroline Wintersgill for their assistance.

I gratefully acknowledge a British Council Fellowship for the academic year 1987/8, the Norwegian Oxford Scholarship for 1988/9, a third year's funding from the Norwegian Research Council, and an Overseas Research Scholarship. I also thank the Norwegian Institute of International Affairs, Oslo, for granting me leave during the academic year 1991/2; the Institute of Europe, Moscow, for a spell as guest researcher in 1990 when I had the chance to carry out a dozen structured background interviews; the Institute of the US and Canada, Moscow, for hospitality and the Norwegian Foreign Ministry for travel money 1992/3.

NOTE ON THE TEXT

All insertions in quotations are marked by brackets. In transliterating names from the Russian, I have used y to denote both Й and Ы, ' to denote Ь and " to denote ъ (deleted in cases of old spelling). Spelling is retained in quotations as well as in author names, so that, for example, an 'Aleksandr' is Aleksandr when transcribed from the Russian, but Alexander if that spelling appears in an English source. Only in one instance have I given up the attempt at being consistently inconsistent and stooped to common usage: Instead of 'El'tsin', I have used Yel'tsin.

1

INTRODUCTION

Debate about Europe is a traditional staple of Russian intellectual life (Berlin, 1963). Indeed, the idea of Europe is the main 'Other' in relation to which the idea of Russia is defined. This book demonstrates how Russians, when they set out to discuss Europe, also discuss themselves. Identity does not reside in essential and readily identifiable cultural traits but in relations, and the question of where and how borders towards 'the Other' should be drawn therefore become crucial. The making of Russian policy is dependent on what sort of political project its politically leading citizens want Russia to be. Since the fight about this is conducted as a question of how it should relate to Europe, ideas about Europe emerge as a key background determinant for both domestic and foreign policy.

The last decade has seen this debate heating up once again. After the Soviet hiatus, under the present regime Russia is in the midst of an intellectual and structural adjustment to Western models. The questions of to what extent and at what speed the market, the multiparty system and other creations of European history should be adopted in Russia, is an overriding issue of the day. For the student of international relations, this makes the Russian debate about Europe a practical concern. From a Western European viewpoint, moreover, it may be a timely reminder against triumphalism to show that the Russian debate about Europe is highly unlikely to end with a burst of Westernising enthusiasm which would do away with the Russian–European dichotomy altogether. The Russian state spent the eighteenth century copying contemporary European models, the nineteenth century representing the Europe of the *anciens régimes*, which the rest of Europe had abandoned, and the twentieth century

1

representing a European socialist model which most of the rest of Europe never chose to implement. Periods like the present, when the Russian Westernisers have the upper hand in the debate, have in the past been superseded by a turn away from the concurrent political life of Europe. The existence of a pattern does not necessarily translate into recurrence, yet it would be an equally grave mistake to deny its relevance altogether.

If nothing else, the Cold War may awaken the West and Western Europe to the costs of defining oneself partially by means of an enemy image. It is a matter of practical importance to demonstrate to a Western European and Western readership first, that Russian identity is actually caught up in the relationship with Europe, and second, that it is immediately relevant to the course of Russian political development how Western Europe chooses to define itself in relation to Russia.

This book tells the story of how 'multiple alien interpretations' of Europe 'struggle, clash, deconstruct, and displace one another' (Ashley, 1987: 409–10; Foucault, 1977: 156; Der Derian, 1987: 69–70). 'Europe' is seen as a speech act; it is talked and written into existence. Russian interests in 'Europe' are not postulated as one given 'national interest', but are investigated where they are formulated, namely, in discourse (Wæver, Holm and Larsen, forthcoming). Following Tzvetan Todorov ([1982], 1991), three questions are asked of each text: What is the framework of knowledge within which the European Other is seen? What moral judgement is made of the Other? What relationship is proposed between Russia and the European Other? The enquiry is limited to written primary material. The focus is on the debate as such, with its constituting elements and permitted scope, rather than what, for the sake of contrast, could perhaps be called its 'vessels' – particular individuals, particular movements, particular texts, particular journals and publishing houses. The preoccupation is not with Russian participation in a debate crossing borders, but is, on the contrary, confined to Russian debates conducted in Russian, directed at Russians, concerning Europe and, by the same token, the Russians themselves.

Two kinds of events have decided the periodisation of the chapters. One is war; the other is change in the top leadership of the state leading to a change in the state's position.

The problem of which texts to use as source material was not an easy one to tackle. As noted above, although in principle finite, the number of Russian texts about Europe is for practical purposes endless. That in itself is no problem, since I am only looking for the major constitutive elements of the debate which exist at any given time. Elements can be considered major if they are new – not having previously appeared in print – since any new element, even one made at the extreme margin of the debate, may at some later stage move towards its centre. Although not necessarily of any immediate great significance, they have a major potential. Similarly, an element is major if it is already occupying a central place and is thus part of a frame of reference which is widely shared. If one concentrates on books, journals and newspapers which have been widely reacted to in print, it is likely that one can approximate all these elements. In this sense, there *is* such a thing as reading enough.

Where the new elements are concerned, however, one may miss those which never occupied the centre stage in the debate. I have no guarantee that I have not overlooked some of these. To the contrary, it is likely that some such elements have indeed slipped through my fingers. In his work on literary genres, the semiotician Yuriy Lotman (1990) draws attention to how it is *always* possible to find distant precursors for a 'new' genre once it is firmly embedded at the centre of the debate. The reason he gives for this is that elements which are too different from the predominant texts when they are introduced tend to be over-looked by contemporary readers. Ideas may simply be *too* new and different, quite literally so 'far out' of the ongoing debate that they are not even noticed, or are mistaken for something else, or taken to be so incomprehensible as to be worthless. If this is so, it suggests that debates can only evolve gradually, that quantum leaps are only discovered with hindsight. And if so, then discursive moves need not be deep, profound or even wholly original to have an impact; on the contrary, depending on the speed with which the debate moves, they may stand a better chance of having an impact if they are not too *outré*.

Discursive elements come in packages, such as the (unusually sharply defined) Bolshevik package. I will use the more defer-ential word 'position' to denote such packages. In imposing such classification on the debate I have elaborated on the system of classification used within the debate itself. Positions vary as to the number and disparity of their constitutive elements. Similarly, the number of positions making up the entire debate is, as a matter of principle, in eternal flux. Yet one position is a fixture, because it is not, like the others, perpetuated by volunteers. This is the position of the state. The state arrogates to itself the fixation of the limits of public debate, and can bring a range of power resources to bear on the debate itself, from censorship of texts and publication channels, through bestowing of positive and negative incentives onto other participants, to physical extinction. The state's power to define the limits of public political space warrants particularly close scrutiny of its role in the debate. The state does not in any way stand as it were 'above' the debate, nor does it provide the matrix on which that debate will necessarily take place. Yet, by allowing certain positions and crowding out others, and by moving its own position between them, it does seem to aspire, not only to defining the limits of the debate but also to defining and occupying its centre. That is to say, it attempts to define the limits of the debate in such a way that its own position takes up the centre. In the 1930s, the aspirations of the Russian state even went beyond this and towards setting up shop as the political equivalent of the astronomer's black hole, sucking all other political life into itself and making it disappear from public view. Yet, such a collapse of all positions into one single 'general will', that is, the *end* of debate, can hardly take place. Not only all positions, but all texts carry within themselves internal contradictions which will, even without the intervention of other debates, in and of themselves generate new debate (Foucault, 1974: 151). Similarly, a history of the present can have no unquestioned beginning. The main period under discussion is the last two hundred years. The periodisation stems from the double revolution which took place in Western Europe at the end of the eighteenth century. The French Revolution ushered in new ideas about the state and citizenship, and the industrial revolution opened up new ways for man to dominate both his environment and his fellow human beings. At the same time, philosophers conversing in German initiated a new debate concerning man, society and the state. The political categories which congealed at this time were to play an important role in European debate for years to come. It was also the time when Russia, due to its military potential, became a fully fledged Great Power within the European-based state system. For all of these reasons, I take the Napoleonic Wars as the starting point for my investigation of the Russian debate about Europe.

4

However, since the coming to power of Ivan the Terrible or Peter the Great could well have been substituted for the Napoleonic Wars as a starting point, the rest of this introduction will be taken up by a short 'prehistory'.

The earliest written sources on the first East Slavic state formation, Kievian *Rus'*, describe how it was founded by Vikings (*varyagi*; Thomsen, 1877). The twelfth-century *Chronicle of Nestor* sets out how the local Slavic tribes invited the Vikings or Varangians to take on the rule of the land in the 860s:

> And they went over the sea to the Varangians, to the *Rus'*, for so were these particular Varangians called, as others are called Swedes, others Normans, others English and Gotlanders. The Chud, the Slavonians, the Krivichi and the Ves said to the *Rus'*: 'Our land is large and rich, but there is no order in it. Come and rule and reign over us'. And three brothers were chosen with their whole clan, and they took with them all the *Rus'*, and they came.
>
> (Nestor, 1950: 18)

The duality between the land and the ruler employed by this chronicler can be retraced in other sources from the same time, notably the twelfth-century *Lay of the Host of Igor*. For our purposes, it is significant that the word 'Russian' is tied to the land (*zemlya russkaya*) rather than to the invited Norman rulers. During the time of the 'Tartar Yoke', when the land was ruled by nomadic Mongols from a tent capital in Saray, the separation of land and rulers persisted. However, during the fourteenth century, and particularly after the victorious Battle of Kulikovo against the Mongols in 1390, a change can be detected in the language of the surviving written sources. On the other hand, the duality between land and ruler persists. Nevertheless, where the land was formerly the main symbol of Russianness, this role was now taken over by the ruler. The change in emphasis from the land to the state may be interpreted as part of the Russian state-building project (Cherniavsky, 1958).

Rus' had been Christianised by two Greek monks in 988, and the Russian Church paid allegiance to the Patriarch of Byzantium throughout the period of the Tartar Yoke. Although the Russian contacts with the rest of Christendom were weakened during this period, they were never severed. In the course of the fifteenth century, however, it was Byzantium's turn to come under increased pressure from a non-Christian culture.

Throughout Christendom the challenge of the Ottoman Empire was viewed with apprehension. A church meeting was called in Ferrara-Florence in 1438–9, and an attempt made to consolidate the forces of all of Christendom. For the Byzantine Church, to which the Russian Church paid allegiance, this involved accepting the primacy of the Roman Pope. In this attempt at overcoming the split between Eastern and Western Christendom, the Byzantines had the backing of the delegates from Moscow. The Russian Metropolitan Isidor was an active participant throughout the meeting.

Having acknowledged the primacy of the Roman Pope, Isidor returned to Moscow, where it became immediately apparent that his ecumenical interest clashed with the interests of the state as formulated by the Grand Duke of Muscovy. For the Grand Duke, the Russian state-building project was to some extent hampered by the existence of the Byzantine Empire. To him, it was not obvious that Constantinople should be supported in the name of Christian solidarity, to the detriment of state interests (Neumann and Welsh, 1991). Isidor was arrested, and the church union to which he had been a party never materialised.

When Constantinople fell under the Ottoman onslaught, there were some Muscovites who expressed regret and maintained that Russian support for the Byzantine Empire could perhaps have saved the city for Christendom. One the whole, however, they were marginalised by the state. The line of the state church was that Constantinople's fall was God's punishment of the Greeks for their union with the Roman Church, and their acceptance of the Roman Pope. At the risk of over-interpreting the data, one can detect an early incidence of debate about Europe here. The marginalised minority position may be restated as follows: as part of Christendom, Muscovy had a moral responsibility to defend that Christendom in its entirety. By failing to contribute to the defence of Constantinople and the Byzantine Empire, Muscovy carried part of the responsibility for its downfall. Against this position stood the official one, which rested on the premise that Muscovy was not part of one unitary Christendom, but rather was wholly distinct from Roman Christendom. Furthermore, it was held, Muscovy was in fact the unique embodiment of historical truth. Therefore, moral responsibility

did not entail Christian solidarity. On the contrary, the impera-
tive was for Muscovy to keep its true and only Christianity
unsoiled by Roman heresies. In short, the official position
stressed that Muscovy was unique, and morally superior, and
that it should therefore keep itself aloof.

Byzantium's fall removed a threat to the Russian state-
building project. More importantly, it was to strengthen that
project by investing the ruler with new symbolic power. In 1472,
Ivan III married Sofia Paleologue, the niece of Byzantium's last
emperor, Constantine. The marriage immediately gave rise to the
idea that Russia was Byzantium's historical successor, thereby
transferring some of the greatness of the fallen empire onto
Russia. In fact, the idea was taken even one step further, to assert
the doctrine of Moscow as the Third Rome. This doctrine was
to play a central role in subsequent Russian political debate. The
crucial move was made by the monk Philotheus (Filofey) in 1520,
in a letter to the Grand Duke Basil III: 'And now, I say unto
thee: take care and take heed, pious tsar; all the empires of
Christendom are united in thine, the two Romes have fallen and
the third exists and there will not be a fourth' (Strémooukhoff,
1953: 94).

The doctrine of Moscow as the Third Rome did not change
the framework within which the West was seen. Neither did it
change the moral assessment of the embryonic Westernisers. It
did, however, strengthen that assessment in two ways. First, by
explicitly making Moscow the site of the only *living church*, the
ruler's claim to rule the Russian lands was strengthened.
The ruler and the ruled did not merely make up a political and
religious unit; rather, they *were* God's church. One can hardly
think of a more effective way of boosting 'group feeling'. To this
spatial uniqueness given to the Russian state was added what
may be called the temporal uniqueness. Moscow was a living
church, present in time. The two other Romes, the two branches
of the Roman Empire symbolised by their capitals in Rome
and Byzantium, were phenomena restricted to history, and
were therefore dead. The temporal uniqueness thus conferred
on Moscow is bolstered by its strong association with the idea
of apostolic succession. Moreover, the imagery of Christ as
redeemer and bringer of a new epoch echoes in the assertion
that there will never be a fourth Rome. From now on and in
eternity, the spatial dimension of God's church is fixed. The

official position had already assessed Westernisers as being morally inferior and out of God's grace. With the emergence of this doctrine of Moscow as the Third Rome, this claim was capped with the cloak of irreversibility.

The doctrine's explicit statement of the relationship of Russia to the West in temporal terms – the idea of Russia as successor – was not matched by a statement about spatial relations. In other words, the borders of Moscow the Third Rome, that container of God's living church, were not clearly defined. Here, the link between Christian imagery and the Russian state-building project can be seen to have an external as well as internal dimension. The internal significance of the doctrine is to equate the ruler with divine history on earth. The external dimension concerns the relationship to the Other, to the former areas of the Roman Empire. This is surely asymmetrical, inasmuch as the Other has been abandoned by God in favour of Moscow.

The doctrine of Moscow as the Third Rome was bolstered in 1547, when the ruler adopted the title of tsar after the Roman caesar. This step further underlined the idea that the succession of Christendom's capitals was matched by a succession of *rulers*. Hence, the notion that the ruler equalled, not only the state but also divine history, was solidified. At the same time, the boyars, the Russian noblemen who had until this time been able to sustain themselves as an alternative power centre to the ruler, were being divested of their independent status.

This development holds a special interest, since it was probably the debate of the boyars which gave rise to the next key development in Russian political debate. Michael Cherniavsky has suggested that it was the boyar opposition which came up with the idea of Holy Russia, and that this idea was part of their counter-hegemonic thrust, directed at the reigning doctrine of Moscow as the Third Rome.

Holy Russia is first mentioned in a letter from Prince Kurbskiy, one of the leaders of the boyar opposition, to Tsar Ivan IV ('the Terrible') at the end of the sixteenth century. In this letter from exile, as well as in eight other places in which Kurbskiy uses it later, the phrase 'Holy Russia' is intended to stress how the ruler performs his evil deeds on the holy Russian lands. That is, the stress is on the holiness of the lands as such, and, by implication, on the unholiness of the tsar. To Kurbskiy and other members of the boyar opposition, Ivan was simply a usurper who had abrogated to himself the land which was for all of the princely clan to rule. 'Perhaps Prince Kurbskiy began to construct that myth of the nation that he found necessary to oppose the myth of the ruler', that is, the myth of the Third Rome, Cherniavsky speculates (Cherniavsky, 1958: 621). One need not support Cherniavsky's apparent view that this was the first instance of proto-nationalism in Russia to note that the onslaught on the nobility was detrimental to state–society relations in Russia, a relationship whose significance for the debate about Europe in the nineteenth century is immense.

As Russia entered its Time of Troubles at the beginning of the seventeenth century, the Poles took advantage of Russian weakness to occupy Moscow in 1611. Even in this time of hiatus between two tsarist lineages the invader from the West was still repulsed. Two years later, in 1613, the Zemskiy Sobor elected Mikhail Tsar, and relations between the new ruler and the ruled were intended to be put on a new footing. Whereas 'Holy Russia' had come into use in the previous century as a counter-hegemonic move to conflate the tsar's claim to be at one with the people and the land, the term's significance was now successfully altered. 'Holy Russia' came into common use to denote 'the people'. Significantly, it soon came to include tsar, state *and* people. This seems to indicate a conception of the state as an extension of the tsar, the little father, married to the Holy Russian Motherland. A marriage is a metaphor for unity, but unity between two distinct entities. In this case, the two entities are the state and the nation.

The crystallisation of state and nation becomes clear when we examine the role of the liminal Don Cossacks, who resided outside the borders of Muscovy. The Cossacks were of Orthodox faith, and were therefore considered to be Russian. However, the Don Cossacks were always anxious to preserve the right to enter Russia. Cherniavsky (1958: 624–5) draws attention to the way in which Moscow saw its boundaries as those of the 'political' Muscovite state and ordered the Cossacks not to allow freemen to enter 'Russia and the upper [River] towns'. The Moscow government as well as the Cossacks acknowledged implicitly the distinction between, or the nonentity of, the Muscovite state and 'Holy Russia'.

So, whereas the doctrine of Moscow as the Third Rome was

still part of the official position, the state now made other moves which acknowledged that there was no automatic confluence between the abode of the living church (that is, people of Orthodox faith), and the territory of the Russian state as such.

These differing conceptions of the Russian state and the Russian nation around the Time of Troubles were intimately linked with different positions on Russia's relations with the West. In this regard, attention centred on the Western invader, the Polish-Lithuanian Commonwealth. On the one hand, a number of people continued to see the Poles and the West in terms of an Orthodox Christian framework. They were held to be a Western variant of the Tartar Yoke, a godless mass of people spiritually inferior to the Russians, with whom one should have a minimum of intercourse. Others, however, started to see the Poles and the West in terms of another framework. Some Russians saw the question of relations with the Poles less in terms of their Roman Christianity and more in terms of their economic and political organisation. Not infrequently, written statements were made to the effect that the Poles were superior to the Russians in this regard. These embryonic Westernisers surmised, therefore, that backward Russia had something to learn from the Poles and other Europeans. Those who took up such a position were behind an attempt to make Władysław of Poland tsar of all the Russians.

The debate between these two parties is already a fully fledged Russian debate about Europe. As noted by the contemporary Ivan Timofeev, differing perceptions of Europe made it impossible to forge a common Russian identity. Russians, he wrote, were 'turning their backs to each other. Some look to the East, others to the West' (*ovii k vostoku zryat, ovii zhe k zapadu*) (Zen'kovskiy 1955).

The view that the West was a place from which one could learn lost ground during the seventeenth century, perhaps not least because of the Thirty Years War. At the end of the century, however, it began to pick up again. 'The need to move along a new path was acknowledged', the Russian historian S.M. Solov'ev was later to sum up the mood in a famous understatement (quoted in Platonov, 1972: 133). With the coming to power of Peter I, the entire Russian political debate changed radically. Szamuely ([1974] 1988: 125; also Riasanovsky, 1985) goes as far as to see it as 'a new beginning', and holds that the whole history of Russian political and social thought can be seen as the history of the development of contrasting views of the Petrine Reform.

The importance of Peter's views and exploits for the Russian debate on and relations with Europe can hardly be overestimated. First, Russia became a factor of some importance within the European states system. The waging of the the Thirty Years War had merged the two partially discrete states systems focused on the Baltic Sea and the European Continent respectively. It was Peter's victory in the Great Northern War, and especially the victory over the Swedes and their Ukrainian allies at Poltava in 1709, which made Russia the predominant Baltic power. And further, it was because of this predominance that Russia became a factor to be reckoned with in the European states system at large (Watson, 1984). It was no coincidence that Peter's window on the West, St Petersburg, was situated on the Baltic.

Second, Peter's modernisation of Russia from above involved the introduction of a number of Western technologies, practices, beliefs and personnel. These changes also affected the language of state. The title of the ruler was changed from tsar to *imperator*. The significance of the doctrine of the Third Rome for the ruler was weakened as the capital was moved from Moscow to St Petersburg. This slight, but very significant, movement away from seeing the tsar as the only possible expression of the state can also be seen in Peter's alteration of the object of military devotion from being 'the interests of His Tsarist majesty' to 'the interests of the state' (Riasanovsky, 1976: 13). Arguably, given the state of relations between ruler and ruled, Peter's innovations in this field had the immediate effect of increasing the schism between ruler and ruled. In addition, the modernisation drive came on top of the state's onslaught against the segments of the Orthodox Church which refused to submit to the discipline of the state-church, the so-called schismatics (*raskol'niki*).

The bulk of opposition to Peter's Westernising reforms was based on religious views according to which Germans, and indeed anyone who wore Western clothes, were heathen, and therefore inferior and to be treated accordingly. Nevertheless, Peter was to a large extent able to marginalise such views from the public debate (Schafly, 1988). The language of discourse changed in the most concrete of ways, as Russian gave way to

French as the preferred medium for communication among the upper classes. Religiously based opposition to the West was only found among merchants, the *raskol'niki*, and the masses, none of whom took part in official political discourse. As Vasiliy Zen'kovskiy ([1929] 1955: 13) of the Orthodox Theological Institute in Paris was to comment some two hundred years later: 'The eighteenth century's passion for the West makes it fully possibly to say that the Russian soul was indeed taken prisoner by the West'.

Throughout the eighteenth century, Russia engaged in what can only be termed 'region-building' *vis-à-vis* Europe (Neumann, 1994): The Russian state formulated, disseminated and insisted upon a geographical definition of Europe as stretching all the way to the Ural mountains in the east, thereby incorporating the most populous parts of Russia. The idea that Europe ends and Asia begins at the Urals was first presented by a Russian geographer. Having been charged by Peter the Great with the task of drawing up a new geography for his new empire, Vasiliy Tatishchev argued in the 1730s that instead of drawing the border along rivers, 'it would be much more appropriate and true to the natural configuration' to use the Urals – or the great belt (*Velikiy poyas*) – as the boundary (quoted in Bassin, 1991: 6).

The dogged insistence with which the Russian state – within eighteenth-century international debate as well as in the domestic debate – repeated that the Urals made up Europe's eastern border, and the repeated protestations that Russia was a European power, suggest that this was far from obvious to the contemporary observer. 'Russia is a European power', Catherine the Great announced programmatically in 1766, yet at around the same time she admitted in a private letter to Frederick the Great that she was like the raven in the fable, which adorned itself with the feathers of the peacock (Wittram, 1973: 61; Anderson 1970; for a dissenting view, cf. Raeff, 1964).

The revolution in France in 1789 utterly changed the setting for the Russian debate about Europe. The military challenge to Russia which grew out of the French Revolution had a political parallel which was no less challenging. Once what was seen as the 'natural' regime type in France – enlightened absolutism – was overthrown and so became the *ancien régime*, the question of the ruler's legitimacy was bound to enter the debate in other countries also.

2

THE NAPOLEONIC WARS AND THE DECEMBRIST UPRISING

The Russian debate about Europe in the first third of the nineteenth century was dominated by the Napoleonic Wars and their aftermath, the Decembrist uprising. That uprising, which erupted in 1825, sprung out of the debate about Europe, and was to prove of key importance to its further course: once it had folded, the reactions to it would constitute the next stage of the discussion.

Three main positions regarding Europe can be discerned in this period. First, there was the state's position, which was legitimist in the tradition of the *ancien régime*. This position, which I will call 'conservative nationalist', saw the ongoing European developments away from enlightened despotism as a betrayal of ideals once commonly held by all the monarchs of Europe, and by their dependents. For Russia, the answer to this betrayal should be to carry on as before. Second, there emerged a Romantic nationalist position, which was formed under the influence of German Romanticism and shared most of its ideals and pursuits. However, since most of its proponents saw Europe in an Orthodox Christian framework, this position was soon to take on an autochthonous flavour. The Romantic nationalists were anti-modern, and were against what they saw as the etatisation and bureaucratisation of the tsar's rule. Finally, there was a constitutionalist position, which held that political and economic models should be adopted from Europe and adapted to Russian conditions.

The Decembrists were the most visible of the constitutionalists. Another, however, was the tsar's key adviser Speranskiy, who already in 1809 had endeavoured to draw up a constitution for Russia. To Speranskiy, this seemed the eminently reasonable response to the pressure exerted by European developments. However, not everybody saw the question in these terms. The tsar's sister, the Grand Duchess Ekaterina Pavlovna, was among those who held such an adaptation to the political ways of Europe to be the greatest of perils. In response to Speranskiy's move, she prevailed upon one of the regular visitors at her salon, the historian Karamzin, to write a reply. Karamzin's reply, subsequently published as *Memoir on the Old and the New Russia*, is a good starting point for an enquiry into the Russian discourse on Europe, because it formulates the previously mentioned official theme of the Russian state as the extension of the person of the tsar. 'An old nation has no need of new laws', Karamzin states. 'In Russia, the sovereign is the living law. He favors the good, and punishes the bad. [. . .] In the Russian monarch concentrate all the powers: our government is fatherly, patriarchal.' If Russia was given a constitution and the monarch refused to follow it, he continued, the situation would become intolerable: 'Two political authorities in one state are like two dreadful lions in one cage' (Karamzin, 1969: 187, 197, 139). According to Karamzin, the idea of adopting a European-style code of law, foreign to Russia, is symptomatic of the misguided attitude of modern Russia. It is worth quoting Karamzin's complaint at some length:

Imitation became for Russians a matter of honor and pride [. . .] it must be admitted that what we gained in social virtues we lost in civic virtues. Does the name of a Russian carry for us today the same inscrutable force which it had in the past? No wonder. In the reigns of Michael and his son, our ancestors, while assimilating many advantages which were to be found in foreign costums, never lost the conviction that an Orthodox Russian was the most perfect citizen and *Holy Rus'* the foremost state in the world. Let this be called a delusion. Yet how much it did to strenghten patriotism and the moral fibre of the country! Would we have today the audacity, after having spent over a century in the school of foreigners, to boast of a civic pride? Once upon a time we used to call all other Europeans *infidels*; now we call them brothers. For whom was it easier to conquer Russia – for *infidels* or for brothers? That is, whom was she likely to resist better? [. . .] We became citizens of the world but ceased in certain respects to be citizens of Russia. The fault is Peter's.

(Karamzin, 1969: 123-4)

Thus, while Speranskiy and others look to Europe for ideas to improve the Russian political order, Karamzin argues that they are actually weakening Russia, since it is dangerous to tamper with ancient political structures. Russia, he points out, has been in existence for a thousand years, and not as a savage horde, but as a great state. Yet 'we are being constantly told of new institutions and of new laws, as if we had just emerged from the dark American forests' (Karamzin, 1969: 155; also Thaden, 1990a: 179-201).

Karamzin therefore presents the Russian state as the bulwark against 'a savage horde'. In this way, he evokes an image of Russia's enemies throughout the ages, first and foremost the Mongol invaders, but not only them. Those such as Peter the Great and Speranskiy stand accused of being the hand-maidens of Russia's ancient European enemies. By weakening the Russian state they weaken the Russian people, which should be the extension of that state. The key statement comes in the last sentence, where the pronoun 'we' refers to the Russians and the 'they' left out by means of the passive refers ostensibly to both Speranskiy and the Europeans. It is they who hold up new Europe as a new civilisation to the Russians, as if the latter 'had just emerged from the dark American forests'. Europe and its Russian handmaidens, Karamzin implies, try to treat Russia as Europe has already treated the American Indian; trying to change the Russian way of life and encroach upon its territory.

For their part, the ancient Russians had an extra line of defence against this: they identified the Europeans as 'infidels', as wholly Other. Since Russians after Peter insisted on partially seeing themselves in this Other – seeing them as 'brothers' – they could no longer close ranks against the Other with as much ease as before. Nevertheless, they were still able to defend themselves against the European challenge. Karamzin insists that the Russians are *not* like the American Indians, because they can withstand the European onslaught under the leadership of their ancient institution – the state. Hence, he argues, Russia should be isolationist, and keep its distance from Europeans and European institutions. To Karamzin, then, the Russian form of government is simply not compatible with European ideas about a *Rechtsstaat* of the kind peddled by Speranskiy. It is, in fact, morally superior to it.

Defence of autocracy in the face of the challenge from the revolution was also the main preoccupation of a circle known as the 'Russian Tendency'. Already at the turn of the century, this circle had tried to halt the foreign policy feelers which were occasionally put out towards the French. This was one of the means by which they hoped to preserve the absolute power of the tsar. What makes them particularly interesting, however, is the way in which they went about strengthening the specificity of Russia *vis-à-vis* Europe and the unity of the tsar and his people. They engaged in a search for the specifically Slavonic roots of the Russian language and culture, and presented their findings as facts of immediate political relevance. To the 'Russian Tendency' it was a *political* matter whether the elites continued to use the French language between themselves or whether they turned to Russian. Similarly, it was not politically irrelevant which form of Russian should be used. The more Russian linguistic and cultural practices were, the stronger Russia would be. Thus, whereas conservative nationalists like Karamzin read Russian history as the history of the state, and saw the state as an extension of the tsar's person, the 'Russian Tendency' began to look to what they claimed were the *ancient cultural practices of the people* to define what was Russian and what was Russia. In the name of previous practice, they distrusted the further bureaucratisation of the state, because, by increasing the distance between tsar and people, this way of strengthening Russia would prove counter-productive.

The soldiers and intellectuals of the circle presented the fight against French cultural practices – including the use of the French language – and a stemming of French revolutionary practices as two sides of the same coin (Riasanovsky, 1965: 1-6). At this point, the significance of the move away from the state and towards the cultural practices of the people as the focus of Russianness was not particularly marked. The leader of the 'Russian Tendency', Admiral A.I. Shishkov, was president of the Russian academy and sometime Minister of Public Instruction. Like many a conservative nationalist, and like Speranskiy the constitutionalist, he was a man of the state. Before long, however, the cultural bias exerted by people like Shishkov became the cornerstone of what was considered then, and will be considered here, a separate, Romantic nationalist position. 'Romantic' is used to indicate that the view of the nation as an *organic* entity was central to this position.

In order to see the immediate implications of the Russian debate for domestic politics, it might be instructive to compare the Russian reaction to that of Edmund Burke. Superficially, Burke's arguments are similar to those of Karamzin, inasmuch as he argues against the regicides in the name of the time-honoured French institutions and argues that France is 'outside herself'. However, Burke's concern is not primarily with Great Britain as such, but with the survival of what he calls the Commonwealth of Europe: that is, with the international society of his day (Welsh, 1992). Karamzin, on the other hand, is solely and singularly preoccupied with the consequences for the Russian state and nation. Shishkov and his circle do not make a distinction between the French state and the French nation, but fight possible French influences tooth and nail. In Russia, it was left to *the state* to formulate a position similar to Burke's.

The 'Russian Tendency' had to face defeat when, in 1815, Tsar Alexander I presented his concept of a Holy Alliance. To Alexander, the question of 'Russianness' and 'Frenchness' did not enter the political picture in the way the Tendency thought it should. With Napoleon defeated, France was invited to join the Alliance. Alexander presented the Holy Alliance as the cornerstone for the international order which was expected to emerge after the Congress of Vienna in 1815. The main problem was, however, that the Holy Alliance was politically and rhetorically out of step with the social and political landscape on which the other heads of state intended to base the new international order. Built on the 'sacred rights of humanity' and dedicated to 'the Holy and Indivisible Trinity', Alexander's text made even Francis of Austria, himself hardly a liberal, exclaim that here was the final proof that Alexander had gone over the top (Palmer, 1974: 334).

Private doubts like these notwithstanding, the legitimist fear of revolution and the reliance on intervention to check any revolutionary tendencies, were embraced not only by Alexander I and his successor Nicholas I, but also by Francis himself. This shared fear was strengthened after the stirrings in Greece and Italy in the 1820s and the events in Paris and Warsaw in 1830.

17

It was not simply a fear of ideology, or of ideological contamination; there was also the question of French revanchism to take into consideration. A revolutionary France would attempt to overthrow the 1815 settlement, and had every opportunity to join hands with the rebellious Poles against Russia. Considerations such as these formed the impetus for treaties such as the Convention of Berlin, signed on 15 October 1833, where the Emperor of Austria, the King of Prussia and the Emperor of All the Russians recognised that

> each independent sovereign has the right to call to his aid, in case of internal troubles as well as in case of an external threat to his country, every other independent sovereign whom he would consider as most appropriate to render this aid, and that the latter has the right to offer or deny this help according to his interests and circumstances.
>
> (Riasanovsky, 1959: 243)

However, they specified that what they had in mind was not a free-for-all intervention scheme, since 'in the case of such aid being accorded, no power not appealed to or invited by the threatened state has the right to intervene either to interfere with the aid which had been requested and offered or for counteraction' (Riasanovsky, 1959: 243–4).

Alexander's diplomatic moves concerning the Holy Alliance were reflected in the Russian debate about Europe at this time. Hence, for example, the text of the Holy Alliance was read from every Russian pulpit and published in Russia. Interestingly, however, the version disseminated was not the final text, the compromise reached through intricate negotiations and numerous corrections. It was rather Alexander's original draft of the Alliance. This illustrates clearly the more general link between international and domestic debate in general, especially the state's greater potential to manipulate domestic debate. In addition, the contrast between the two versions brings out the difference between Alexander's and many of the European monarchs' frameworks for assessing international relations. One aspect which disappeared from the final version was Alexander's strong emphasis on the brotherhood of monarchs, the feature which perhaps most clearly brought out his legitimist position. Alexander's Europe was indeed a commonwealth of European monarchs, united in Christ and therefore morally equal, and acting in concert to stem the revolutionary tide. Incidentally, the changes clearly indicate to what extent Alexander's views on international order were hardly consistent with those of European conservatives such as Metternich (Kissinger, 1957).

Although Alexander's legitimism and the defenders of autocracy dominated the Russian discourse on Europe, opposition was formulated in the small bands of officers which had served in the Russian army. During the victorious military campaign in Europe, these men had formed expectations of social and political change in Russia. In their view, Russia needed without further delay to approximate what they perceived as the more advanced social and political patterns in the rest of Europe. Those future Decembrists often proclaimed their Europeanness, but also harked back to the ideas of the so-called 'Russian Enlightenment' which had begun during Catherine the Great's reign. Thus, for example, they held popular sovereignty to be a desirable tie between the nation and the state. None the less, ideas such as these could enter the public discourse only indirectly; they were too far removed from the legitimism of Alexander for the state to allow them out in the open. As a result, the societies where these ideas were formulated took on a conspiratorial character. This was far from being a unique Russian development. The closest parallel is perhaps the *carbonari* of Italy, a parallel which further underlines the opposition between these groups and the legitimist ideas of the Holy Alliance.

For most members of secret societies, Europe was a cultural entity of nations which included Russia. Since Russia was a European country, it was argued, it should also politically and economically evolve along European lines. For them, this evolution required constitutionalism. Therefore, members of these groups, like Speranskiy before them, set about drawing up new constitutions for Russia. However, for such constitutions to be put to the test, there had to be a willingness on the part of the state to consider some kind of check on the arbitrary execution of power. Since such a willingness did not exist, the societies planned an uprising, which occurred in December of 1825. It proved to be wholly ineffective in military terms, and was immediately put down by loyalist troops.

Despite these failures, the Decembrist movement was of key importance to the Russian debate about Europe. It firmly established a constitutionalist position which was to hover on the margins of the public discourse for the next eighty years. But, more importantly, the state's reaction to the Decembrist uprising redefined the parameters of the debate and clearly indicated the constraints on political action (Gershenkron, 1962: 164). Furthermore, it showed that the state could not dominate the political field simply by repeating the legitimist position and by keeping other positions from being formulated. In short, the discourse on Europe changed radically.

Three reactions to the Decembrist uprising stand out. Some Russians saw it is an example of how seemingly positive European ideas could slowly corrupt Russia's best and brightest. Others saw it as positive proof of the economic and political gulf that was opening between Russia and Europe, and fretted that Russia's status as part of Europe was no longer secure. Finally, the state reacted by establishing a doctrine of 'official nationality'. Taken together, these three reactions congealed the available range of opinion into three increasingly distinct positions. The rest of this chapter will explore each of these in turn.

One reaction was to hold that Europeanism had led the Decembrists astray, and that Russia needed a new and different moral assessment of Europe from its former apprentice-like attitude. Moreover, the people who made up this position also formulated a new variant of Russian Messianism. As mentioned in the introductory section, there existed an old belief that Russia had a special mission in the world. This position had always sprung from a *religious* framework. Indeed, even for the 'Russian Tendency', which stressed the importance of language and cultural mores, Orthodoxy still held a very privileged place among the characteristics of Russianness.

In reaction to the Decembrist uprising, those such as the Wisdom-lovers (*lyubomudrie*) put forward a variant of Russian Messianism where the Christian idea of Moscow as the Third Rome was played down, but where the Christian historicism which underpinned this idea was retained. The Society of Wisdom-lovers was inspired by German idealism. To Vladimir Odoevskiy, the Society's president, Europe was ahead of Russia in technical skills but had lost touch with what he referred to as its 'instinctive powers'. From this vantage point, he saw it as Russia's great task to reinfuse these powers into Europe. In an instructive case of reversed imagery, Odoevskiy used Peter the Great's vitalisation of Russia by means of Western models as a metaphor for how Russia was now about to vitalise Europe. As the first among European nations, he wrote, Russia's mission was to save Europe from ossification. 'The nineteenth century belongs to Russia!' were the words he put into the mouth of a character in a later novel (Odoevskiy, 1975: 149). The words are the summing up of a key monologue in the epilogue to the novel itself, where the character called Faust has predicted that old Europe may 'be covered by the same layers of immovable ashes as the enormous buildings of the forgotten peoples of ancient America'. The role as caretaker of civilisation has moved from the Jews to Egypt to Greece to Rome to Christianity – 'that people of peoples' – and is now about to descend on young and fresh Russia (Odoevskiy, 1975: 145-9).

Odoevskiy therefore grabs the moral high ground by appealing to a Russian virility, that is, to a Russian *cultural* trait. Out of this claim grows a proposal for a relationship of domination. By grabbing the moral high ground, Odoevskiy also *shifts* the ground. He concedes European superiority in the organisation of political and economic life, but maintains that this is not the ground which 'really' counts. The 'real' ground – the cultural ground – as defined by Odoevskiy, is also the ground where Russia, in his view, happens to be morally superior. Neil Cornwell (1986: 115) sees Odoevskiy as the founder of 'the idea of Russia's messianic mission', but this claim seems exaggerated. Although the Wisdom-lovers were critical of Shishkov's 'Russian Tendency', Odoevskiy and his followers are clearly elaborating on Shishkov's writings. What *is* beginning to emerge more clearly here is a Romantic nationalist position, where the point of departure is the nation defined in cultural terms. This nexus between Russian Messianism and Romantic nationalism would prove to be a lasting and crucial one.

Odoevskiy also elaborates on Shishkov when discussing the nature of the Russian state. Odoevskiy criticises the idea of representative government as a stage prop for 'a couple of merchants or, if you like, shareholders' (Zen'kovskiy, 1955: 35). Where Shishkov had simply criticised the growing bureaucratisation of the state for putting too much organisational distance between the tsar and his people, Odoevskiy brings out the question of who stands to gain and who to lose from such developments. The more bureaucratised the state, he argues, the farther its reach, and the less secure the landed gentry's hold on their privileges. Reform of the Russian state along European lines would serve the goals of 'the merchants'; however, Odoevskiy laments, it would also prove a threat to the dominant position of the landed gentry. It is evident, then, that the debate about Europe was also a debate about the relative standing of different groups *within* Russia. If contemporary European models were approximated, some groups stood to gain, and some to lose.

A second reaction to the Decembrist uprising came from those who still saw Europe in a political and economic framework, and who judged it to be superior in these fields. Their contribution was to question Russia's place in Europe. This doubt was expressed in a number of ways. Nadezhdin, for example, wrote in 1832 that 'we' – that is, the Russians – basically must blame themselves that they

> have nothing, we are nothing, and, by the way, why would we have anything that would be our own? Have we ever made a serious effort really to appropriate Western civilisation, to let it seep in, to *learn*? Oh no, we have been much too lazy, we have been contented with imitation.
>
> (Koyré, 1929: 156)

Others saw the relationship between Russia and Europe differently, and expected the differences gradually to disappear. An example was Ivan Kireevskiy, who in 1832 started to publish his own journal, *The European*. In the first issue, he expressed the opinion that 'Some kind of Chinese Wall separates Russia from Europe, and the air of the West reaches us only through certain breaches' (Kireevskiy, 1911a: 95). Peter the Great's and Catherine's partial success in tearing it down was no guarantee against it being rebuilt. Kireevskiy saw the advocacy of a 'pure national culture' as an attempt to do exactly this, and argued that 'the striving towards nationality (*stremlenie k natsional'nosti*) is nothing but a repetition of undigested foreign thoughts, West European thoughts lifted from Frenchmen, Germans and Englishmen and without pause for reflection applied to Russia'. For Kireevskiy, whereas in Western Europe the search for national roots was a way of approaching the ideas of the Enlightenment, in Russia it only implied uncovering crudeness and ignorance (Kireevskiy, 1911a: 105). To paraphrase, even those like Admiral Shishkov, who set out to uncover the roots of 'genuine Russia', and who held that such a thing existed, did so only because certain texts written by *German* Romanticists had told them what to look for and where to look for it.

Sentiments along these lines were also voiced by people such as Davydov and Polevoy, who initiated Russian philosophising about history around this time. They were also spurred on by questions about Russian identity and whether Russia's destiny was with Europe, or outside it (von Schelting, 1948: 19). Interestingly enough, Polevoy took issue with Karamzin's view that Russian history was the history of the Russian state, stressing instead how the Russian state, like European states, 'had to evolve gradually in interaction with complex historical circumstances over a period of centuries' (Thaden, 1990b: 87). Karamzin had reached his conclusion that Russia's development was different from Europe's by pointing to the specific character of the Russian state and its relationship to society. Polevoy, on the other hand, reached a similar conclusion by pointing to the different relations between state and society which *produced* a state different from those in Europe. Karamzin saw Russian uniqueness and ensuing isolation from Europe as something positive, whereas Polevoy saw it as negative.

Undoubtedly, the most significant variant of this second type of reaction to the Decembrist uprising was Petr Chaadaev's. Throughout the first half of the 1830s, a letter circulated in the Petersburg salons, written in French and datelined 'Necropolis, 1 December 1829'. There was nothing unusual about a letter being copied and distributed among the chattering classes; this was a common way of evading political censorship. The practice therefore created a space for debate which was not really considered public, but semi-private. The writer of the letter, Petr Chaadaev, had as a young man been in contact with the Decembrists. Like them, he was consciously inspired by European, especially French, political ideas. He was also influenced by some of the first theoreticians of European 'civil society', de Bonald and de Maistre. These two Frenchmen had also written on Russia, and stressed its ambiguous geographical position between East and West to explain what they saw as its 'nomadic' character (Walicki, 1988: 87). Chaadaev drew on all of these ideas, and took as his point of departure the argument that Europe had once made up a spiritual whole: Christendom (*Civitas Dei*). This unity made Europe blossom. Although Christendom was subsequently torn asunder by the Renaissance and the Reformation, the Pope remained as a symbol of the unity that was, and that was to be reborn in the future. In contrast to medieval Europe, Chaadaev argued, Russia had made the mistake of following despicable Byzantium, which was not part of 'the universal brotherhood of man'. As a result, it had become an easy prey to the Tartars. When the Tartars left, Russia could have joined the European mainstream, but did not. For these reasons, he wrote, Russia was now like a child born out of wedlock, with no real heritage: 'We are like children who have not been trained to use their brains; when they grow up, they do not have one single original thought'. In other words, all they could do was to copy others. To counter those who clung to Alexander I's victorious escapades in Europe, Chaadaev pointed out that all the Russians had brought home with them were bad ideas which retarded the nation's life – the ideas of the Decembrists. Russia, he lamented, fell between two stools: 'we should unite the two main traits of spiritual life: fantasy and sense, in other words we should create a synthesis of Eastern and Western culture. However, that was not fate's intention'. Further, he continued, Russia was culturally isolated:

> If the barbarian hordes storming towards Western culture had not overrun our country, our names would not have been written into world history at all. In order to attract attention to ourselves, we had to spread out from the Bering Straits to the Oder.
>
> (Chaadayev, 1978: 160-73).

From this, Chadaayev concluded that Russia had no past, no present, and no future. Chaadaev's position regarding Russia and Europe is not so different from Nadezhdin's or Polevoy's. However, he took his argument one step further by explicitly stating that the Russian state seemed not only unwilling, but *unable* to copy Europe creatively. For Chaadaev, this lack of ability meant that Russia had no future. This idea, as will be discussed below, was to become a momentous one.

A third reaction to the Decembrist uprising was the construction of the doctrine of 'official nationality'. The attempted coup of the Decembrists in 1825 indicated to the Russian state that the revolutionary influences exuded by what was seen as a 'new and false' Europe, had started to permeate Russian society as well. The proposed solution to the problem was to increase

Russian society's isolation from the political process. However, a need was also felt to counteract this challenge against tradition. This feeling of restlessness on the part of the state – an example of how conservatism only perceives a need to articulate identity in times of crisis – increased yet again five years later, when revolutionary stirrings in France coincided with the Polish uprising against the Russian state in 1830. In 1833, the Minister of Education, Uvarov, wrote to Nicholas I that

> Given the religious and political conditions in Europe and the widespread propaganda for all revolutionary ideas, it is necessary to attach our country solidly to that bulwark of any nation's well-being, strength and life: We must find and clarify those principles which are typical especially of Russia.
>
> (Riasanovsky, 1959: 134)

In response, Uvarov proclaimed what was to become known as the doctrine of 'official nationality'. The three pillars which were to define official Russia were autocracy (*samoderzhavie*), Orthodox religion (*pravoslavie*) and nationality or nation-mindedness (*narodnost'*). Nicolas Riasanovsky, one of the doctrine's historians, has suggested that although it was presented as being uniquely Russian, official nationality was a variant of the dynastic ideology which underlay all the *anciens régimes* of the old Europe. This may be so, but this interpretation is nevertheless misleading for at least two reasons. First, before the French Revolution, codification of this kind did not exist. Principles like these belonged to the doxa of political life. Only when what was seen as their negation came into being, did there arise a possibility and need to codify them. Second, only the advent of German idealism and the Romantic nationalism it inspired in Russia could have elevated 'nationality' to the status of a separate pillar of official Russia, distinct from Orthodox religion. In other words, although official nationality partially contradicted the main thrust of modern political discourse by denying the principle of popular legitimacy, it was a move which could only have been made *as part of* modern discourse, and no other. In this sense it differed significantly from other conservative ideologies articulated on behalf of the *ancien régime*.

According to B.H. Sumner, official nationality was meant 'to serve as the preservative of Russia as a member of true European civilization against the insidious ravages of false, so-called European civilization represented by the French revolution, liberalism, and secularism'. Sumner goes on to suggest that Uvarov did not condemn the West out of hand, but only the Russian infatuation with the West and the failure to see that there was a 'true' Europe and a 'false' Europe. His conclusion is that the doctrine, like tsarism in general, was an attempt to stand against new Europe in the name of the old Europe of the *ancien régime* (Sumner, 1951: 4; also Raeff, 1964). Sumner's analysis therefore highlights how concepts of Europe and proposed relationships with Europe – what is here called the Russian debate on Europe – were part and parcel of the *domestic* political discourse.

To sum up this chapter, it is possible to identify three main positions in the Russian debate on Europe during the first third of the nineteenth century. At the time of the Congress of Vienna, the debate was dominated by Alexander's legitimism. Alexander's Europe was a Europe of Christian monarchs. In his Europe, Russia was bound to play a leading role due to its military strength and its Orthodox branch of Christianity.

Second, there was a constitutional position, which was to culminate with the Decembrists. Their Europe was a Europe of constitutional monarchies and republics. To them, non-constitutional Russia was politically and economically backward compared to the rest of Europe. It should therefore learn from the West. Texts embodying either one of these positions were produced by intellectuals in and around government. Speranskiy's constitutional projects show that the idea of transforming the state from an autocracy to a constitutional monarchy was represented in the top echelons of the administration. On the other hand, Karamzin's emphasis on the autocratic state as the hallmark of Russianness expressed the traditional self-image of the state.

Finally, there also existed a Romantic nationalist position, which stressed ancient Russian cultural practices, such as the organic tie between tsar and people, as the hallmark of Russianness. The Russian Romantic nationalists held Europe to be morally inferior to Russia because of its godlessness: Russia was to give the highest priority to avoiding its influence. The Romantic nationalist ideal for the Russian state would have made bureaucratisation impossible. But as the state nevertheless continued to develop its bureaucratic machinery to cope with new tasks, the gulf between the Romantic nationalist ideal and the existing state structure expanded. Whereas at the turn of the century an embryonic Romantic nationalist could be the tsar's Minister of Public Instruction, the day was not far off when Romantic nationalist publications would be banned. Thus, whereas the differences between Romantic and conservative nationalists at first seemed to be subtle, they were to prove momentous.

In the mid-1830s, on the eve of what Annenkov and later Berlin have referred to as the 'extraordinary' or 'remarkable' decade of the Russian 1840s, the Russian discourse on Europe was still dominated by these three main positions. Having reacted to what were seen as the false ideas of contemporary Europe and as revolutionary elements under the sway of the false Europe at home, the state's position was summed up in the doctrine of official nationality. This doctrine formulated a view of the state similar to that expressed by Karamzin, adding a dash of culture from the armoury of the Romantic nationalists. The view of what 'true Europe' was like had not changed much since Alexander's day, but the 'false Europe' of revolutionary sentiment was seen as gaining in strength.

The demise of the Decembrists did away with the constitutionalist position and staked out a new position whereby Russia's place in Europe was drawn into doubt. The various groups which adhered to this position shared a similar framework for judging Europe. In essence, they viewed it in political and economic terms, and as a place from which Russia should, but perhaps could not, learn.

The Romantic nationalist position had also changed. Where the 'Russian Tendency' had been quite introverted in its search for the genuine Russian cultural heritage and had resisted close foreign relations with anti-monarchist powers, a shift had occurred in the criteria for comparing Russia and Europe. At the outset of the period, one sees comparisons made on a religious basis: the Russian state and state-church were superior to the order of things in Europe *because* they were closer to God. At the end of the period, by contrast, figures such as Prince Odoevskiy did not explicitly express themselves within a religious framework. Instead, they emphasised Russia's superior spirit and historical vocation to breathe new life into the rigid culture of Europe. The Europe of Odoevskiy and his followers had become an entity which was about to be historically overtaken by Russia.

27

3

OFFICIAL NATIONALITY, 'SLAVOPHILES', 'WESTERNISERS'

As noted in Chapter 2, the Russian state saw the Decembrist uprising as a Russian aftermath of the Napoleonic Wars. The Decembrists embodied the revolutionary thought of the new, 'false' Europe. Consequently, the state saw them as the 'enemy within'. One corollary of such a view is that the Russian debate about Europe, dominated as it was by reactions to the uprising, was still being shaped by a perceived Russian need to come to terms with Europe's double revolution. The introduction of the doctrine of official nationality did nothing to solve this dilemma. The distance between the state's position and the other positions in the debate did not diminish. The most significant development of the 1830s was therefore not the change of positions but rather the way public political space was redefined. The debate about Europe forced its way from the margin of public debate onto centre stage, and became *the* divisive political issue of the day.

Things came to a head in one single event: the publication of a letter by Petr Chaadaev. To this day, many historians of ideas hold this event to be so central that it spelled the *end* of the Russian 1830s and the beginning of what is often called the 'extraordinary' or 'remarkable' decade of the 1840s (Berlin, 1978: 114–209). During this decade, the key development was the crystallisation and polarisation of two positions on Europe. As this chapter will illustrate, the Romantic nationalists gathered under the banner of 'Slavophilism', and those who looked to Europe for political and economic models became known as 'Westernisers'. Whereas in the 1830s the Russian debate floated freely between the main discussion groups, by the end of the 1840s the Slavophiles had established their own exclusive circle and the groups were hardly on speaking terms.

Aleksandr Gertsen, who together with Stankevich was the leading Russian intellectual of the 1830s, once famously called the publication of Chaadaev's letter the 'shot in the dark' which started Russian political thinking. Hyperbole was certainly called for; the splash was indeed ear-splitting. The tsar himself responded by having Chaadaev arrested, declared mentally ill and placed under house arrest. Leonard Schapiro maintains that the reason for the outcry was that Chaadaev had been the first to suggest that Russia might never become like the rest of Europe and that this 'was a startling novelty at the time – if anyone had ever thought of it, no one had ever put it into words' (Schapiro, 1967a: 40). Echoing Schapiro's assessment, Andrzej Walicki asserts that 'After his [Chaadaev's] famous diagnosis Russia's future as a European nation ceased to be self-evident' (Walicki, 1975: 86).

Perhaps Chaadaev was the first to make this claim. Yet, as noted above, similar views had already found their way into print. In 1830, the year after Chaadaev's letter was originally written, Nadezhdin published a piece which pointed in the same direction. Since Nadezhdin was the editor of the journal in which Chaadaev's letter was eventually to appear, it is quite possible that he wrote under the influence of Chaadaev's letter. Interesting as the question of originality and influences may be, the concern of this book lies elsewhere. It is a general point that new ideas need not be deep, profound or even original to have an impact, and that elements which do not latch on to the main texts or positions in the debate tend to be overlooked at the time (Lotman, 1990: 129). Where the Russian debate about Europe as a whole is concerned, the main question is not the originality of Chaadaev's letter. Rather, it is why its impact did not make itself fully felt *before* it was published. In 1836 the letter had already circulated in the salons for seven years, as indeed had Chaadaev himself. But it was only when the letter was published – and so challenged the public political space which the state saw as exclusively its own – that matters came to a climax. Context, not content, was crucial. Before that, the state chose not to take cognisance of the letter, and therefore did not have to rise to the challenge. Once the letter entered the public discourse and the state was shown up as having no means by which to contain it, the discursive field changed irrevocably.

Chaadaev himself was shunted aside; he subsequently changed his views, and it was thus possible for a whole plethora of people to claim him as a predecessor (von Schelting, 1948: 144; Goerdt, 1984: 262–71). In a later work called 'The Apology of a Madman', he reiterated that Russia had no past, whereas Europe certainly had one, and a bright one at that. However, whereas in his first philosophical letter he had assessed contemporary Europe's anchoring in the past as a positive thing, he now held Europe to have lost touch with its past, and therefore to have lost sight of the greater scheme of history. Russia, on the other hand, still had the possibility of borrowing from those ideas, and thus could still find its 'place among the civilised peoples'. In this way, Russia would not only reach par with Europe, but could also at some future stage serve to revitalise Europe. This assertion of Chaadaev's was not new; Odoevskiy had already made it decades before. It does, however, carry some interest inasmuch as it shows how one branch of a Romantic nationalist argument can simply be torn off and implanted on the trunk of a different position. In short, rearrangement of the ideas present in a debate may be as important as the forging of new ones.

The rearrangement of ideas was indeed lively during the 1840s. In the 'thick journals', the two terms 'Slavophiles' (*slavyanofily*) and 'Westernisers' (*zapadniki*) were used more and more frequently. They had initially carried undertones of ridicule, having been used only to refer to the opposition. Now, they were frequently used as terms of self-identification.

Instructively, 'Slavophile' was originally a derogatory term used to refer to Shishkov and his 'Russian Tendency'. This group had devoted itself to purifying the Slav roots of the Russian language. The 'Slavophiles' – that new generation of Romantic nationalists – were clearly the outsiders in the 1830s. The debate about Europe was embedded in a general political debate rife with Hegelian influences, and was therefore heavily universalist. In 1837, for example, Stankevich voiced a widespread sentiment when he wondered aloud why people were 'busying themselves with *narodnost*'' instead of striving towards the all-human and finding one's own form in that very process: 'To invent or think up a character for a nation out of its old customs, its ancient activities, is to wish to prolong for it the period of its childhood' (Schapiro, 1967a: 60).

Stankevich's salvo was directed equally at official nationality, one pillar of which was the principle of *narodnost'*, and at the Romantic nationalists, whose exact concern it was 'to invent or think up a character for a nation'. One notes the similarity between this contemporary Russian critique and the present debate about how nations are invented, imagined, etc. (Anderson, 1983). This work of invention was accelerated in 1841, when self-professed 'Slavophiles' – Romantic nationalists – began to publish their first journal, *Moskvityanin* (the Muscovite). In answer to Chaadaev's charge that Russia had no past, they contended that it was not Russia, but rather industrialising Europe which was without a history. 'What Chaadaev writes about Russia, I write about Europe, and the other way around', already Odoevskiy of the former generation of Romantic nationalists had written to a friend in 1836 (quoted in Meyman, 1975: 275). Thus, in the main article of the new journal, Stepan Shevyrev set out his perceptions of European culture. 'Yes, in our frank, friendly, and close relations with the West', he wrote,

> we have failed to notice that it is like a man who carries within himself a dreadful contageous disease, who is surrounded by the dangerous exhalations of a poisonous miasma. We kiss him, embrace him, share with him the banquet of thought, drain the cup of feeling . . . and do not perceive the hidden poison in the carefree intercourse, and allow the delights of the banquet to mask the odour of decay which he already emits.
>
> (quoted in Walicki, 1975: 51)

The Russian upper classes, he concluded, should turn away from everything European and look to the Russian people for guidance. Shevyrev would intensify rather than add a new dimension to Russian Messianism. The idea of history as a relay race with Russia as the anchorman was present already in the doctrine of Moscow as the Third Rome. When Odoevskiy resuscitated this idea, he played down the religious imagery and substituted the entire people for the tsar as the carrier of history's torch. In this way, he merged the ideas of Moscow as the Third Rome and of 'Holy Russia'. In short, Shevyrev made the addition of insisting that Europe was not only tired and historically *passé*, but already 'rotten'.

Whereas Odoevskiy and Shevyrev had already resuscitated

31

the ideas of Russian history as a conflict between the people or the Land (*zemlya*; also literally the soil) on the one hand, and the state on the other, it was Konstantin Aksakov who was to elaborate on it. To him, it was Peter the Great's work which had taken Russia off the straight and narrow path conceived by destiny. The Land was apolitical, and because it was simply not interested in international conflict, it had the principle of non-intervention in foreign affairs inscribed in its marrow, Aksakov maintained. Moscow was the Land's capital and the living centre of the Russian renewal which Konstantin Aksakov saw in the making. Against Moscow stood Peter's city, St Petersburg. St Petersburg was the state incarnate, a modern Babylon. Aksakov, who happened to be a Muscovite, did not doubt that Moscow would win this fight between Land and state and throw off what he, with a reference to the Tartar exploits in Russia, called the Western Yoke. In this way, Aksakov followed earlier Romantic nationalists in branding the Russian followers of Peter as the errand-boys of Europe. 'Society' (that is, the 'Westernisers') is the representation of the enemy within. Against them looms the hero – 'the Land', 'the people' (that is, the peasants and every other Russian who had withstood Westernisation).

The use made by Romantic nationalists of the old Russian chronicles as well as of ancient distinctions between state and Land was conspicuous and effective. The way this material was used to attack what was perceived as Peter's aberration from the true path of Russia's development could not fail to indict Peter's heir on the throne. The Slavophiles were not anti-tsarist; to the contrary, their critique was targeted against the European-isation of that ancient Russian institution. The tsar should be married to the Land, he should be a patriarch rather than being an *ancien régime*-style autocrat. To put it in Weberian terms, he should preside over a patriarchal, and not a patrimonial state (Kommisrud, 1991).

By pitching their position in direct opposition to Russian contemporary state practice, the Slavophiles also challenged the doctrine of official nationality.[1] The state reacted by repeatedly censoring the publication of Slavophile writings, and by closing journals. The doctrine of official nationality represented the Europe of the *ancien régime* as the true Europe, and condemned contemporary European ideas which strayed from it as expressions of a false Europe. The Romantic nationalists, on the other hand, saw contemporary Europe and Europe of the *ancien régime* as two incarnations of a principle of government which were equally alien to the Russia of the Land. Moreover, they saw the contemporary Russian state – in its aspect of administrative apparatus – as an extension of this alien principle into the organic body of the Russian nation. Indeed, European influence to them was Otherness incarnate – the external and internal Other from which Russia must be saved.

Other Romantic nationalists added to this Russian 'Othering' of Europe. Aleksey Khomyakov's reading of Russian history stressed how national Russian traits, which before the Florence church meeting had coexisted peacefully with the European influences, gradually came into conflict with the European main-stream:

> the enmity only really broke out as a reaction to the insane and deep Russophobia of Sweden, the Hanse, and the Baltic nobility, and even more because of the hostile intrigues of Polish magnates and Catholic priests. Little by little, Russian nationalism took on exclusive and xenophobic traits. The common human spirit (*dukh chelovecheskiy*) was relegated to a very narrow area. This did not square with what is humanly just and true, and with the deepest demands of the Russian spirit. Therefore, it had to provoke a reaction that went to the other extreme.
>
> (Khomyakov, 1900: 154)

This overreaction was Europeanism, which Khomyakov held to have set in at the beginning of the seventeenth century and then, after a hiatus, to have won a complete victory under Peter. Though Russia kept on celebrating Europe, Khomyakov continues, it should have been plain for all to see that Europe was dominated by worthless cultural trends. These trends were rationalism, materialism and egoism, and their modern cause was Catholicism. The real cause, however, was much older and was to be found in what Khomyakov calls 'Kushitism', which dated from prehistoric times. The crippled spiritual outlook which characterised Europe was of a timbre wholly inferior to Russia's Orthodoxy, the only true Christendom.

If Khomyakov is critical of Catholicism, he is equally scathing of that other European corruption of Christendom: Prot-estantism. For Khomyakov, the Protestant principle of freedom without unity resulted in the pervasiveness of bourgeois individualism, and the Catholic principle of unity without freedom transformed itself into atheist socialist internationalism. Khomyakov thus took note of the links between the political organisation of medieval Western Christendom and the contemporary European pan-European ideals of a Saint Simon or a neo-Guelphist.

Khomyakov resuscitated the Christian Orthodox framework for characterising Europe, and in doing so he showed up a blank spot in official nationality. Whereas Orthodoxy was one of the three pillars of that domestic doctrine, the state's preferred Europe was, as discussed above, a Europe of Christian monarch brothers. Perhaps Russia's Orthodoxy could be seen as making it the elder brother. However, the metaphor was still that of close blood relations, not of Otherness. This difference between Slavophile and official views added to the basic difference on the nature of the contemporary Russian state.

Another self-professed Slavophile was Ivan Kireevskiy. Having turned his back on the earlier Westernism which we have seen him profess above, his overriding concern had become the preservation of the Russian national character. He complained that the English, the French, the Italian and the German never ceased being European, always keeping their specific national idiosyncrasies (*osobennost'*). The Russian, on the other hand, 'almost had to eliminate his national personality in order to mingle with the educated West' (Kireevskiy, 1911b: 182).

Kireevskiy now saw Europe in a Christian framework. Contrary to Khomyakov, however, he held European medieval Christendom to be an ideal state, a Golden Age. Where he had earlier regretted Russia's isolation from the Western classicist tradition of rationalism and individualism, he now came to see Russia's isolation as a blessing in disguise. By being cut off from these trends, Russia had not moved as far away from the ideal of Christendom as had Europe. Kireevskiy came to sum up Europe's cultural heritage as individualistic Roman civilisation, the Catholic church and states founded on violence. Against this he set *sobornost'* (conciliarism, rule by a collective mind), faith and the peace-loving Slav tradition. These Russian values, he claimed, could be seen in the way the people of Kievan Rus' had appealed to the Varangians to come rule them, so that they did not themselves have to dirty their hands with politics and violence.

The most interesting of these three signs of European heritage concerns the idea of violence. Kireevskiy passes moral judgement on the European states for being incomparably more violent than the Russian. By comparison to the European states, the Russian state, itself not without strains of violence, is positively *peaceful*. Therefore, he argues, the Europeans can learn from the Russians how to live peacefully. Thus, Kireevskiy's is a new and interesting twist to Russian Messianism, where the main thrust of the argument is to be found in the realm of the spiritual.

The main Slavophile concern was with the cultural nation understood as the Land. The Land's relation with the state was always somewhat knotty, for Kireevskiy as well as for other Romantic nationalists. What they have to say about Russian–European relations is basically confined to 'inter-national' relations in the literal sense of that expression, and not about 'inter-state' relations. Inter-state relations always remained something of a blank spot for the Slavophiles. The rare pronouncements on inter-state relations do not fall within their preferred debate, but latch on to what some of them, sometimes, and then only hesitatingly, acknowledge to be the exigencies of the international system.

As this Romantic nationalist argument unfolded, it moved from the margins of the debate and towards the centre. What permitted it to unfold and to become more dominant, however, was its interaction with Westernising arguments. The task the Westernisers had set themselves was to show how Russia was *already* developing along European lines and how it should try to accelerate that development, despite the somewhat different conditions which prevailed there. One of the most prominent Westernisers was Vissarion Belinskiy. As with so many nineteenth-century thinkers, in Russia and elsewhere, Belinskiy saw the world and Europe in the light of his own historico-philosophical scheme. For him, the evolution of individuals as well as of nations passes through three phases. The first phase is one of natural immediacy. The second is one of abstract universalism of reason. The third phase is characterised by rational reality, where the two first tendencies are transcended and reconciled in a dialectical process. A group of people during their first phase is a people (*narod*); only when it makes the transition to the second stage does it become a nation (*natsiya*). The contemporary relevance of this theory for Russia seemed clear: real nationalism had to transcend *narodnost'*, as formulated in different ways in the doctrine of official nationality and by the Romantic nationalists (cf., Walicki, 1975: 397–403). It follows from this view that only with Peter and the influx of universalistic European ideas were the people 'raised to the level of society', allowing Russia to become a nation. Belinskiy closely followed the Slavophiles in his use of the terms 'people' and 'society'. However, whereas the Slavophiles held the people to be the repository of the immediate, the unsoiled and indeed the holy, Belinskiy saw the people as an undifferentiated, unindividualised, perhaps even tribal mass. For the Slavophiles, society was a sorry mass of atomised, alienated and decadent individuals who had lost touch with their roots in the soil. For Belinskiy, society was the result of inevitable human progress, a hallmark and guarantee of civilisation.

Spurred on by Napoleon's invasion of 1812, Belinskiy argued, Russia had been able to merge universalistic and national ideas, thereby entering the third phase of reason's all-encompassing scheme. As a literary critic, Belinskiy pointed to Pushkin's production to prove his point. Pushkin, he held, was great because he embodied his nation. However, although Russia had already made the passage to the third and final stage of history, it was still at an early point in its development. It could still not claim a central place in humanity's common intellectual tradition. Nevertheless, like all nations, Russia still had its destiny cut out for it, and was a necessary part of history's fabric. To quote,

> Nationhood (*norodnost'*) is to the *idea* of humanity what *personality* is to the *idea* of the human being. In other words: Nations (*norodnosti*) are the personalities of humanity. Without nationalities (*natsional'nosti*) humanity would be a dead logical abstraction, a word without content, a sound without meaning. In this respect I would rather go over to the Slavophiles than stay with the humanist cosmopolitans, because the former are human beings, even if they are mistaken, while the latter make even the truth sound like the embodiment of some abstract logic.[2]
>
> (Belinskiy, 1956: 28–9)

Belinskiy's conception of nations is quite clear. In modernity, they are not only 'the personalities of humanity', but also the entities which confer individuality on to individuals. Incomplete development for the nation entails incomplete development for the individual. 'We are men without a country', he wrote in a moment of doubt in 1841, 'even worse than without a country, we are men whose country is a spectre; can you wonder that we ourselves are spectres?' (Walicki, 1975: 338).

In Belinskiy's thinking, the two seemingly contradictory themes of Europe versus Asia and Europe as the torchbearer of all humanity, come together. They are resolved in his theory of the historical stages of mankind. On the one hand, he exclaims that 'Asia is the land of the so-called natural immediacy; Europe is the land of consciousness. Asia is the land of contemplation; Europe, of will and reason'. On the other hand, he declares axiomatically that 'Everything human is European, and everything European is human' (Riasanovsky, 1985: 127–8, 217).

The way in which Belinskiy stresses the historical mission which providence provides for nations, brings to mind the thought of his Italian contemporary Mazzini. As with Mazzini, Belinskiy's main theme was social relations, and his proposed panacea was nationalism. Although Belinskiy did not follow Mazzini in advocating a confederation of European nation-states, he stressed how the nation was becoming the main social and therefore the main *political* force in the Europe of his time. Like Mazzini, he also stressed how each nation has its own mission. The Russian debate about Europe was different from those conducted elsewhere at the same time, but hardly unique in all respects. Germany and Russia were not the only countries in which Romantic nationalists exclaimed the uniqueness of their nations. And Germany, Italy and Russia were not the only places where attempts were made to reconcile national and universal sentiments.

To Kavelin, as to Belinskiy, individualisation in Russia started only with Peter the Great. His reign marked the transition of the Russian nation from 'physical nationality' to 'spiritual nationality'. Therefore, Kavelin held, pre-Petrine Russian history was hardly more than prehistory. The implications of this view for his assessment of Europe seem quite clear: European development set the historical norm, to which other nations must try to conform. Thus, with their belief in teleological historical parallelism, or 'progress', Belinskiy and Kavelin reveal the European modernist face which dominates Russian Westernism.

Although a teleological view of history was shared by all Westernisers, the debate was not completely dominated by the idea that Russia had to pass through each and every stage of Europe's development. This question of how much, and what Russia should copy from Europe was the issue in an exchange between Botkin and Gertsen in 1847–8. Botkin, a tea merchant, prayed that 'God give Russia a bourgeoisie!', only to be met with a counter-prayer from Gertsen: 'God save Russia from the bourgeoisie!' Belinskiy, in a letter to Botkin declared that 'So far all I have seen is that countries without a middle class are doomed to eternal insignificance' (Gerschenkron, 1962: 164–6). The need for a middle class was something about which the Westernisers, tea merchants and intellectuals alike, were of one mind. Once Gertsen started to deviate from this belief he was no longer treated as a Westerniser by some of his former associates.

To sum up this chapter, as the 1840s drew to a close, the Russian debate about Europe can still be presented as consisting of three basic positions. The three tags, used by the participants themselves, were official nationality, Slavophilism and Westernism. Official nationality and its view of Europe did not undergo much change. Slavophilism amounted to a radicalisation of the Romantic nationalist position. Previously, the moral assessment of Europe had been that of an exhausted predecessor, from which it was wise to keep one's distance. Now, Europe was held to be decadent or even rotten. Some saw redemption for Europe if it could only go to school with Russia; others held that Russia should turn its back and hold its nose while the cadaver that was Europe slowly putrefied. Nevertheless, as acknowledged by Kireevskiy, Slavophilism, like Shishkov's 'Russian Tendency' and Odoevskiy's Wisdom-lovers, adapted a *German* school of thought – Romantic nationalism – to its own uses. As in Germany, the Romantic nationalists set about inventing nationalism in defence of the ancient community (*Gemeinschaft*) against the onslaught of the new society (*Gesellschaft*). Andrzej Walicki (1988: 107) suggests a sociological explanation for this, pointing out that both Germany and Russia were economically backward in relation to the industrialised countries. This meant that the negative sides of capitalism were clear to see for all observers and could be used as arguments against change by conservatives in both countries. He also (1988: 66) traces the geographic roots of pan-

Slavism back to the Pale, i.e., the border areas between Russia, the Ukraine and Poland.

The Russian Romantic nationalists, consciously harking back to precedents in medieval Russian chronicles, denoted their ideal *Gemeinschaft* with terms such as 'Russian Land', and 'Holy Russia'. Like the early Herder, their ideal was the *Kulturnation*, which eschewed the need for a controlling state but which would fuse with the state in a rule of conciliarism (*sobornost'*). Indeed, due to its power connotations, the state was often seen by these authors as a necessary evil. The movement, as with German nationalism, started off as a search for unique roots, especially etymological roots (Riasanovsky, 1965: 1–6). It is a central tenet of German Romantic nationalism that language constitutes nations. The expression 'the Slavophiles' (*Slavyanofily*) actually originated as a derogatory term for those amateur linguists who tried to rid the Russian language of foreign loan-words and sought to revive what they held to be pure Russian speech. Some Slavophiles also copied the German nationalists by collecting local variants of fairytales, songs and so on.

Thus, the paradox is this: the core of Slavophilism was a protest against Russia following the models which emerged in the Europe of the double revolution. Nevertheless, Slavophilism itself was actually an imported cultural programme, an adaptation of ideas whose genesis was inextricably linked to the very same double revolution which the Slavophiles so heartily despised.

Where Westernism was concerned, the main preoccupation was to reconcile universalism and nationalism. Europe's political and economic models were held to be superior, and history itself demanded that they be emulated. The question was how. Before the Decembrist uprising, the trend had been to draw up constitutions for Russia. After the uprising, most Westernisers trusted that the inevitable and inexorable unfolding of history would take care of the politics involved.

Doubts were, however, beginning to emerge. Some incursions from Belinskiy and Gertsen pointed towards a new position, where the point was no longer that Russia had to copy *all* aspects of European development. Rather, the question had become *which* features Russia ought to copy.

4

FROM THE SPRINGTIME OF NATIONS TO THE ASSASSINATION OF TSAR ALEXANDER II

In 1848, the nationalist ferment which had gathered in a number of European states reached a peak. For the Russian state, the ensuing 'springtime of nations' was no surprise, but rather a further confirmation of the sorry state of contemporary 'false' Europe. In foreign affairs, the Russian state reacted by rallying to the side of the Habsburg ruler in his hour of need, and staged a military intervention into Transleithania to crush the Magyar nationalist uprising against him. At home, the state limited political discourse to a minimum. The period of the 1840s, when public political life had been dominated by the conversation of the Westernisers and the Slavophiles, was decidedly over.

The state did more than tightly circumscribing political space, it also attempted to bridge the gap between its own position and the Romantic nationalist one. As a result, official nationality was, for a limited time, adorned with some Romantic nationalist features, as the state attempted to amalgamate itself with the idea of 'Holy Russia'. This dabbling with Romantic nationalism was cut short with the advent of the Crimean War, which the state perceived as a war with Europe. Defeat made the state reassess its framework for judging Europe. The idea of Russia as a bulwark of 'true' European ideals was not discarded, but was left to one side as the new tsar concentrated on reforming Russia along what he saw as European lines. Thus, while before the Crimean War the state had attempted to tie in Romantic nationalism with its own position, in the wake of its defeat it now began to rethink the importance of economic factors for military capabilities. In the process, it made a number of approaches in the direction of Westernism.

The state's new thinking sparked some interesting repositionings among the Romantic nationalists as well as the Westernisers. Where the former were concerned, the military defeat and the state's loss of interest in Romantic nationalism initially made for a period of inaction. Eventually, however, Slavophilism, which had favoured spiritual introspectiveness and Russian aloofness *vis-à-vis* Europe, gave way to pan-Slavism. Pan-Slavism favoured an active Russian foreign policy towards Russia's Western borderlands, and did not shy away from the increased tension with Europe which such a policy would necessarily entail.

The Westernisers, by contrast, had spent the period between the state's crackdown in 1848–9 and the defeat in the Crimean War in the political wilderness. As the state began to implement the kind of reform they had been advocating, their expectations intensified. Subsequently, when the reforms proved half-hearted in both conception and implementation, their position radicalised. In the process, the crack which was already apparent in the debate between Botkin and Gertsen about Russia's need for a bourgeoisie widened into a full split. Two fully fledged and one embryonic position emerged: liberal, Russian socialist and Marxist. First, old-style Westernisers with a belief in constitutionalism and incrementalism conglomerated around the new local government organs, the *zemstva*. They were known among themselves and their opponents as liberals or constitutionalists, and their position will be referred to accordingly. Second, there were those who created a new position, where Russia was to pick and choose from Europe's experience in order to arrive at a specifically Russian socialism. Eventually, the advocates of this position came to concentrate so much on Russia's unique historical potential that they could no longer be referred to as Westernisers. Instead, there developed a position of 'Russian socialism', which, in the course of the 1860s, was further radicalised into a populist position. Although the populists were to become the sworn enemies of the Russian Marxists after 1881, during the period covered in this chapter a number of the people who constituted this position expressed their intellectual debt to Marx. Finally, other socialists continued to hold that history was about to churn Russia through exactly the same developmental stages that Europe had already passed, and then hurl both Europe and Russia into a socialist revolution. Throughout the 1870s, the Marxist hue of this position grew stronger and

41

stronger. It is, therefore, somewhat incongruously and atavistically referred to as the embryonic Marxist position.

The state's reaction to the springtime of nations was immediate. 'We are', Nicholas I exclaimed (using the royal we), 'ready to meet our enemies, wherever they may appear, and, without sparing ourselves, we will, in an indissoluble union with our Holy Russia defend the honour of the Russian name and the inviolability of our borders' (Cherniavsky, 1958: 625). Such exclamations were, it seems, primarily directed towards the Russian Westernisers at home and in exile abroad. Those were enemies who could strike from unsuspected places within, from 'wherever they may appear'. Accordingly, public political space was limited in a degree surpassing even the limitations implemented in the wake of the Decembrist uprising in 1825. The thoroughness with which the state clamped down can be seen in the fact that it issued a special edict which banned the teaching of Western philosophy in Russian universities.

The Westernisers quickly felt this squeeze. Belinskiy had died in May 1848, and his place as the acknowledged prime Westerniser was taken over by Granovskiy. 'There is every reason to go out of one's mind', Granovskiy commented in 1850, and added that 'Belinskiy did well and died just in time' (von Schelting, 1948: 174). However, even Granovskiy doubted whether the European springtime of nations was really a development which Russia should copy. He saw some merit in the fact that Russia, as a 'younger brother', could afford the luxury of standing on the sidelines while its 'elders', that is, the European states, went through this turmoil (Schapiro, 1967a: 80). If this was the attitude of a leading Westerniser who chose to use a fraternal image, it is hardly surprising that a number of people who were more loosely associated with the Westernising position were even more dismissive of what was happening in Europe. Chaadaev, who had always held that Russia had no past and no present, came out strongly against the rebellion against law and order in Europe. In fact, he came very close to the foundation of the state's position when he judged the springtime of nations to be an onslaught on the 'true' Europe which he so highly respected. Chaadaev actually called on the Russian state to intervene in what he now referred to as 'so-called Europe', so that the remaining order could be maintained (von Schelting, 1948: 170).

Chaadaev's reaction was exactly the sort that Nicholas I tried to elicit from his subjects to meet the crisis. According to Michael Cherniavsky, the above quotation contains *the only* official use of the expression 'Holy Russia' made during the nineteenth century (Cherniavsky, 1958: 625). The Slavophiles, however, made frequent use of the term in order to denote their idea of 'the Land' or 'the people' – that is, non-Westernised Russia. When Nicholas saw fit to use it in his proclamation on the European events of 1848, it must be seen as recognition that the situation was one where internal unity in Russia had maximum priority. To reach this end, Nicholas actually overcame his distaste for the Slavophile critique of the nature of his autocratic reign. As already noted, the Slavophiles held bureaucratic rule, which by its very nature disrupted the immediate rapport between tsar and people, to be an unnecessary European abomination. At this juncture, however, the tsar moved to incorporate Slavophile sentiment as part of the state's support. This move towards Romantic nationalism was also a move away from the state's earlier interpretation of official nationality. Among those who noted and criticised this was the conceiver of that doctrine, Uvarov. When he criticised the fervour of the state's nationalist position, he fell out of favour with the tsar and subsequently lost his job.

The implications of the cohabitation of the expression 'Holy Russia' with official nationality were highlighted by Zhukovskiy. In a letter to a friend, he gave a succinct summary of his view of the relationship between Russia the state and Holy Russia:

In the expression *Holy Russia* there is reflected our whole unique history; this name Russia has from its baptism, but its deep meaning it acquired from the period of fragmentation into appanages, when there was one chief, great prince over various subordinate ones, when, together with the great principality there were many small independent ones, and when it all conjoined into one, not into Russia but into *Rus'*, that is, not into a state but into a family where all had the same Fatherland, same faith, same language, the same memories and legends; this is why in the bloodiest civil strife, when there was as yet no Russia [. . .] there was for all the one, living, indivisible Holy Rus'. Russian God, Holy Russia – such names for God and for Fatherland are not possessed by any European people [. . .] Russia has

become a state, the peculiar attribute of the tsar while Holy
Rus' remained as a legend, the common treasure of tsar
and people. *Russia* (*Rossiya*) belongs to the complex of
European states; Holy Russia (*Rus'*) is the peculiar hered-
itary property of the Russian people, confirmed to it by
God.

(Cherniavsky, 1958: 630)

The tsar had simply, in one unique instance, acknowledged the
existence of a 'Holy Russia'. After fifty years, the Romantic
nationalist idea of the nation as a cultural entity in its own right
had inscribed itself into the writings of the tsar himself.
Zhukovskiy, however, goes even further and demarcates two
distinct spheres: the cultural nation and the state. The reason
why this move is so significant is that it elaborates not only on
the tsar's new thinking, but also on a stock Slavophile idea. The
Slavophiles generally, and Kireevskiy especially, had acknowledged that at least *some* kind of state had to exist. Zhukovskiy
is able to upgrade the normative value of having a state, without
entirely compromising the basic Slavophile idea that the tsar and
the people make up an immediate and indivisible spiritual entity.

A corollary of this is that Zhukovskiy's move could potentially have filled in a blank spot in official nationality. There had
always been a tension between the state's insistence on Russia's
privileged moral role as the only Orthodox power on the one
hand, and the idea of Europe being a brotherhood of monarchs
in Christ on the other. That contradiction could have been overcome by assigning the moral superiority to the realm of inter-
national/intercultural relations and the brotherhood of monarchs
to the realm of interstate relations. This corollary was, however,
not made explicit.

Chaadaev's and Zhukovskiy's moves show that the state's
attempt to incorporate bits of the Slavophile position was at least
partly successful. One of the reasons why it was not even more
convincing was that a number of Romantic nationalists failed to
follow Zhukovskiy in championing the role of the state. In 1854,
for example, Konstantin Aksakov wrote in a private letter that
a new path of greatness and power was about to open for Russia.
He saw a great age dawning, 'one of the greatest in world
history', characterised by a lasting alliance of all Slavs under the
supreme patronage of the Russian tsar. Moldavia and Wallachia,

as regions inhabited by peoples 'without any individual significance', ought naturally to be incorporated into Russia. Russia
should also take possession of Constantinople. Moreover,

> since ignoble and ungrateful Austria opposes us, and has
> broken off all relations with Russia, she has released us from
> our obligations and untied our hands. There too Russia will
> fulfil her mission of liberating the ethnically homogeneous
> and largely Orthodox peoples; she will naturally incor-
> porate her former provinces of Galicia and the whole Slavic
> world will breathe more easily under the patronage of
> Russia once she finally fulfils her Christian and fraternal
> duty.
>
> (quoted by Walicki, 1975: 497)

The alliance envisioned by Aksakov is therefore not one of states,
but of peoples. Moreover, it is the Russian people who must
fulfil their 'Christian and fraternal duty', not the tsar or the state
as such. In this quotation, the stress is very much on the concept
of Russia as the Land. Where Ivan Aksakov had consolidated
this understanding of Russia, his brother Konstantin now sets
about specifying where the borders of this Russia are to be
found. The Slavophiles had treated the Russians as God's chosen
people: the Russians were closer to God simply by virtue of
being Russian. This spiritual view had immediate consequences
for the moral assessment of non-Russians – Europeans and non-
Europeans – who seemed to fall beyond the pale. Aksakov builds
on this distinction by adding a missionary perspective to Russian
Messianism. For him, the Russian people is defined as *in vitro*
consisting of *all* ethnically Slav *and* Orthodox groups. This is a
very different matter from the kind of Slavophilism that Nicholas
I tried partially to incorporate into the state's position. Instead,
Aksakov's move can be seen as part of a comprehensive move
away from Slavophilism towards pan-Slavism. He and others
carried the Romantic nationalist position beyond the state's
approaches, and quite literally beyond the pale.

Moves like Aksakov's aside, the tsar could still congratulate
himself upon his handling of the Slavophiles at home. Moreover,
he was in an ebullient mood about Russia's role in the Concert
of Europe and its relationship with the other four Great Powers
of Austria, Britain, France and Prussia. 'The four of you could
dictate to me', he remarked to the French ambassador in 1853,

'but that will never happen. I can count on Vienna and Berlin' (Taylor, 1987: 54). If one sees this statement in the light of Vattel's definition of a Great Power as one to which other members of a states system cannot 'lay down the law' even when banded together, then it immediately becomes clear that Nicholas did not think of Russia as a Great Power in this sense.

Nicholas was soon to find out that he was wrong on this score. When he moved against Turkey the year after he had made the above comment to the French ambassador, the tsar probably assumed the war to be a matter between himself and Austria-Hungary. Before long, however, it became clear that the European great powers would not allow Russia a free hand against Turkey. As he saw the war approach, Nicholas appealed to his Prussian brother monarch in the name of what he held to be the spirit of 'true' Europe:

> Waging war *neither for worldly advantages nor for conquests*, but for a solely Christian purpose, must I be left alone to fight under the banner of the Holy Cross and to see the others, *who call themselves Christians*, all unite *around the Crescent to combat Christendom*? [. . .] now nothing is left to me, but to fight, to win, or to perish with honour, *as a martyr of our holy faith*, and when I say this I declare it *in the name of all of Russia*.
>
> (Riasanovsky, 1959: 265)

The idea of Russia as the only representative of 'true' Europe is indeed strongly present here. Similar claims were made by the Russian state domestically. The Crimean War was presented as a war between Russia the Keeper of the Faith against revolutionary, 'false' Europe. Not everybody was convinced, however.[1] At least some Slavophiles, as well as some Westernisers, thought that a Russian defeat would lead to a new Russian foreign policy which would be more to their liking. Pogodin, who held that the war substantiated his idea that Russia was founded on love and the European states on hate, saw in defeat the possibility for a clean break with Russia's diplomatic past. At one point, he even prayed for a bomb to smother the Russian Ministry of Foreign Affairs.

Russia's defeat did not become a blessing in disguise for the Russian nation in the way Pogodin had expected. Once the defeat was a fact, the state did not break with Europe as Pogodin had wanted it to. Rather, under its new tsar, Alexander II, it adopted a more Westernising practice. 'We cannot deceive ourselves any longer', Duke Konstantin declared, 'we are both weaker and poorer than the first-class powers, and furthermore poorer not only in material but also in mental resources, especially in matters of administration' (Lieven, 1983: 21). Writing to the tsar some years later, the Minister of Finance spelled out the exigences of being a member of the international system more clearly. 'Without railways and mechanical industries', he wrote, 'Russia cannot be considered secure in her boundaries. Her influence in Europe will fall to a level inconsistent with her international power and her historical significance' (von Laue, 1963: 9).(The lack of logic where the correlation between influence and power is concerned, may perhaps be explained by the discursive demands which weighed upon a Russian minister's report to the tsar.)

Thus, the defeat in the Crimean War seemed to have convinced the state that the Westernisers had been right all along. Russia had to see European economic and political innovations not as the twisted outcome of revolutionary mindlessness, but as models to be emulated. Restrictions which had been inflicted in the wake of the springtime of nations were lifted.[2] In 1861, Tsar Alexander II abolished serfdom. In 1864, organs of local government were introduced which were, at least embryonically, representative. The liberals quickly made these *zemstva* a main focus of their activity, and initiated a campaign to forge links between them on the all-Russian level (Starr, 1972; Fischer, 1958). They spent the rest of the century refining their argument as to why Russia should step up the introduction of representative and constitutional measures rather than making qualitatively new moves in the debate about Europe.

Such an attitude of consolidation was not unique to the liberals, at least not for the period up to the end of the 1860s. Whereas the preceding fifteen years had been a period of rapid change and realignments in the Russian debate about Europe, the fifteen years following the Crimean War did not see the same kind of change. The easing of censorship and the concomitant explosion in the number of publications let loose a welter of commentary on Russian foreign policy. But for the time being, that foreign policy was seen as an area of the politically possible, which existed within a given and known framework.

The complacency of the debate should, however, not be over-stated. It has already been noted how the Romantic nationalist position was being radicalised towards pan-Slavism. Although temporarily marginalised by the state's turn towards a more Westernising position, this was to return with a vengeance in the 1870s. Furthermore, the 1860s were notable for the splitting of the Westernising position. Like in most European countries, there was a split along a liberal–socialist divide. A crack also began to emerge between those who wanted a specifically 'Russian socialism', and those who saw little point in stressing the uniqueness of Russian socio-economic conditions relative to European ones.

'Russian socialism' was first and foremost the creation of Aleksandr Gertsen and his associates. As mentioned previously, Gertsen had started to doubt the economic effectiveness and moral superiority of capitalism as early as in 1847. Contrary to the European pioneers of capitalism, Gertsen could observe capitalism at work. The human suffering he witnessed made him ask whether urbanisation and industrialisation was really worth it for Russia, or if it was possible to find some other way to modernise the country. Throughout his life, Gertsen wavered in his answer to this question. But he left his inscription on the Russian debate about it by maintaining that it was possible and desirable to create a specifically Russian socialism. For Gertsen, there existed a true as well as a false Europe. True Europe was pre-industrial, and Russia had the chance to preserve the best of pre-industrial Europe by building on the 'timeless' institution of the village commune. In other words, the transition to socialism could be made without going through a capitalist stage. The Russians' lack of history could therefore be turned to their advantage. The aborted European revolutions of 1848 convinced him that Europe was past its prime, and that humanity's future was not pinned on Western Europe, as he put it:

> If Europe should not be able to lift itself up by way of social transformation, then there are other countries which are ready, and others yet which are getting ready. One is known – I talk about the United States of America; another is full of strength, but also of savagery (*dikost'*) – we know it only imperfectly. [. . .] Before Europe, whose life-strength

was sapped already long ago, stands a people who has just begun to live.

(Gertsen, 1919: 333, 360)

Europe could either succumb to socialism 'like Rome succumbed to Christianity', overcome the challenge of socialism at the price of becoming a flabby Byzantium whose function it would be to keep progress from reaching other countries, or it could give itself over to chaos. Gertsen states squarely that the country in question is Russia, and the people the Russian people. Russia's relationship to Europe should, then, be one of distance and benign neglect. Russia was a world unto itself, with its very own laws of development.

Gertsen's ideas are interesting because, by grafting a number of Slavophile ideas on to an essentially Westernising position, they create a position distinct from both Westernisation and Romantic nationalism. Gertsen's framework is a socio-economic one, where moral assessments are made on the basis of the degree of man's exploitation of his fellow man. In this realm, Russia surpasses Europe. Accordingly, Russia's relationship with Europe should be one of respect, but also one of aloofness. Nevertheless, although Gertsen sees Russia as humanity's torch-bearer, it would be misleading to interpret him as a Russian Messianist (yet cf., Malia, 1961: 290). The way he exalts social relations over strictly national concerns precludes that possibility. His criticism of Mazzini's preoccupation with national self-determination is illuminating in this respect. National self-determination is not an end in itself, he insists, but only a means to realise a new and better pattern of social relations (Herzen, 1968).[3]

Whereas Gertsen stressed the value of socialism as an end in itself, for others it was a possible means whereby Russia could be restored to its former glory as a great power, an answer to the pressure exerted on it by Europe. V.V. Flerovskiy was among those who made this move in reaction to the Russian defeat in the Crimean War. He regretted how Russia 'tailed away' after European civilisation and compared the Russians to the Persians

who, just as we, had had a great State and nevertheless had perished because of their tailing away after the ancient civilization, it comes to my mind that the only way out for

us is the realization of the great idea, an idea which no
other nation as yet ever tried to put into practice.

(Walicki, 1969: 113)

Although it is left to the reader to infer which idea this might
be, the context makes clear that the unprintable word which
Flerovskiy has left out is socialism. The comparison with Persia
is instructive, inasmuch as it shows an awareness that Russia is
not the only state to have been expanded upon by 'European
civilisation'. Flerovskiy admits, moreover, that his desire to turn
away from the old Russian ways and towards European models
emerges not out of respect for their intrinsic value, but because
they seem to be the only means whereby Russia's former greatness can be restored. In this regard, his position is similar to the
state's, even if the state would not approve of, or even understand, his choice of socialism as a means to reach that goal.

The emphasis Gertsen placed on social relations was of
course not idiosyncratic. To the contrary, it was part of the framework within which all socialists saw Russia, and Europe.
Chernyshevskiy, for example, could hardly have been more
explicit when he argued that it did not matter whether there
was a tsar or not, or whether there was a constitution, only which
kind of social relations existed:

It would be best if absolutism could retain its rule over us
until we are sufficiently permeated with democratic spirit,
so that, when a popular form of government comes to
replace it, political power could be handled over – *de jure*
and *de facto* – to the most numerous and the most unhappy
class (peasants + hirelings + workers) and, thus, we could
skip all the transitional stages.

(quoted in Walicki, 1969: 83)

There was nothing particularly new about this move. The
stressing of social relations and the dismissive attitude towards
the liberal preoccupation with constitutions and a law-governed
society were the stock in trade of any socialist. Before long,
however, Chernyshevskiy was to rule out the possibility that
Russia could skip any transitional stages. On the contrary, he
insisted that Russia would have to traverse every single stage
that Europe had gone through before it could reach socialism.
And this move – this mechanisation of Russia's future develop-

ment in the name of history's invariate progress – immediately caused a crack within the socialist position.

Chernyshevskiy's move appeared, appropriately enough, as an attack on Gertsen. Gertsen's flaw, he charged, was to expand the organic imagery pertinent to individuals to embrace entire societies. Societies, Chernyshevskiy held, should not be anthropomorphised. What was at issue here, then, was the question of where the 'engine of history' was to be located. Gertsen, Chernyshevskiy held, made a fatal mistake by seeing the nation as a whole as the engine of history. Instead, history was propelled by class struggle *within* societies, and the nature of that struggle was uniform throughout time and space (Chernyshevskiy, 1987: 249–77). For Chernyshevskiy, assessment of the village commune was a case in point. Gertsen saw the *mir* or *obshchina* as a specifically Russian institution which could prove an important stepping-stone towards a specifically Russian socialism. Chernyshevskiy, on the other hand, saw a universal and primitive institution with no intrinsic value, but which could yet be instrumental in building socialism. To Chernyshevskiy, Gertsen's view of Europe and Russia's relations with Europe rested on an unscientific base. It was a scientific fact, he insisted, that history was a unilinear process which permitted no shortcuts. History itself precluded a specifically 'Russian' socialism, and demanded that Russia should copy the developments which had already occurred in Europe. Once that had been done, however, Chernyshevskiy saw no reason why Russia should not be able to overtake Europe (Chernyshevskiy, 1987). He could even wax lyrical about the possibility: 'History, like a grandmother, is very fond of her grandchildren. *Tarde venientibus dat non ossa sed medullam ossium:* and when western Europe tried to get at the marrow it cut its hands badly on the bones' (quoted in Lampert, 1965: 172). The last shall be the first.

Chernyshevskiy's interventions did not mark an overall turn in the debate. Other socialists continued to represent a non-materialist, anti-industrialist outlook. For example, in 1861, Shelgunov wrote that instead of importing the industrial revolution, Russia should try to find its own special path:

We have already been apes of the French and the Germans, are we now to give ourselves over as apes of the English? No, we do not want English economic maturity [. . .] Why cannot Russia arrive at some new order unknown even to America? We not only can, we must.

(quoted in Billington, 1958: 47)

By the 1870s, the crack within the socialist position opened up by Chernyshevskiy's attack on Gertsen was expanding fast. Those such as Nikolay Ivanovich Ziber, a Marx scholar, could hardly have been clearer in their insistence on the necessity of Russian industrialisation: 'We shall have no sense in this country until the Russian *muzhik* is cooked up in the factory boiler' (quoted in Kindersley, 1962: 98). The majority on the left, however, still preferred their peasants raw. Gertsen's hopes for the village commune were adopted by a number of people who no longer referred to themselves as 'Russian socialists' but as populists. Populism is an important and integral part of the Russian reception of Marxism. Classical populism, writes Walicki,

> was *not only* a reaction to the development of capitalism *in Russia* but also (especially at the beginning) a response of the democratic Russian intelligentsia to capitalism and socialism of the West; after all, it was a traditional preoccupation of the Russian intellectuals to ponder over Russia's future in terms of desirability or undesirability of following the example of Western Europe. From this point of view it becomes highly important to establish what was the Populist *image of Western capitalism*, of its history and its present state. And it is no exaggeration to say that this image was formed under the overwhelming influence of Marx.
>
> (Walicki, 1969: 13)

The life and thought of the Russian peasant were exalted as a model for Russian development at large, and contrasted with decadent European individualism. To give but one example, in 1869 Mikhaylovskiy wrote the following as a comment on the success of CanCan in Paris in 1869:

> Was it not so when the Popes lived in incestuous relations with their mothers and sisters, and maintained brothels? Was it not so when Roman Caesars had public weddings with men? There have always been in society dying elements and these have always led debauched lives. This corruption is one of the sledge-hammers of history. If the comparatively unpretentious Offenbach can spread to all

layers of society and at the same time to all corners of Europe, it is because we are going to have a great amputation. *Novum rerum mihi nascitur ordo.*

(quoted in Billington, 1958: 77)

Also writing in 1869, Tkachev maintained that individualism, as espoused by Russian Westernisers, was first formulated by Protagoras and the Sophists, the ideologists of the urban, bourgeois civilisation of Athens. Against this individualism, he set the anti-individualism of the Sparta celebrated by Plato (Walicki, 1969). 'Decadent Europe' itself also saw a lot of romanticising of the peasant at this time, and people like Mikhaylovskiy and Tkachev in railing against it thus went along with a European-wide trend. As was the case with Russian nationalism itself, here is an example of a Russian variant of a general European phenomenon, but a variant which takes its power from passing itself off as unique. Yet Tkachev's intervention is interesting, not least for the choice of comparative case – in one way it *does* lodge itself in the wider European setting. At this time, ancient Greece was almost universally held to be not only the 'proto-European' phase of history, but also the cradle of European civilisation as such. By choosing this particular point of reference for a comparison of Russia and Europe, Tkachev circumvents the Christian framework for gauging Russian–European relations which was used by most Romantic nationalists, thus forging a new brand of Messianism for the socialists.

Tkachev's move also implies that what is characteristic of contemporary Russia and contemporary Europe is the outcome of historical processes with common roots in ancient Greece. The Russian variant, far from being a poor copy of the European one, is, to the contrary, a morally superior outcome of a parallel historical process.

In the eyes of Chernyshevskiy and his self-proclaimed Marxist followers, moves such as these only confirmed the unhistorical and therefore unscientific nature of the populist position. Their worst fears about populist *naïveté* were confirmed in the spring of 1874, when thousands of populists 'went to the people' to teach and be taught. The failure of this project forced Tkachev to abandon his faith in the people as the arbiter of history, and to place direct action by small, highly disciplined commandos of revolutionaries in its stead:

The people are unable to build, on the ruins of the old world, a new one capable of progressing or developing towards the communist ideal; therefore in constructing their new world it cannot and should not play any prominent or leading part. This role [. . .] belongs exclusively to the revolutionary minority.

(quoted in Keep, 1963: 14)

The way to do this was to form small, highly disciplined commandos of revolutionaries, who could engage in terrorist activity directed against the state. The existence of such commandos made the state constrain the space for political discourse in the latter half of the 1870s. In fact, a commando finally succeeded in assassinating Tsar Alexander II in 1881. The state reacted with such force that the Russian debate about Europe was transformed yet again.

Not only the populist, but also the Romantic nationalist position underwent important changes in the years leading up to 1881. As was mentioned at the outset of this chapter, some Romantic nationalists expected defeat in the Crimean War to force a break with Europe and a turn towards isolation. What happened was the diametrical opposite. The state traced the defeat back to insufficiencies in Russian economic and political organisation, and tried to rectify this with a bout of Westernising reforms. Nevertheless, the feeling of inadequacy ran too deep to be overcome by a 'quick fix'. As late as 1876, Foreign Minister Gorchakov allegedly remarked that Russia was 'a great, powerless country' and that, although it could masquerade as a Great Power, it had to be constantly aware of the make-believe of it all (Lieven, 1983: 23–4).

Where Gorchakov and the Russian state were concerned, then, the national humiliation of the Crimean defeat gave rise to a feeling of humility *vis-à-vis* Europe and European economic and political models. It is a well traversed point, however, that a national humiliation may also give rise to revanchism and increased nationalism. For the Russian Romantic nationalists, defeat at the hands of what they had held to be decrepit European dinosaur states was absolutely galling. Some had certainly acknowledged that Europe was ahead of Russia in technical and administrative efficiency. However, they had persisted in making light of this fact, maintaining that what really counted was spiritual strength (Pintner, 1986: 367). Such a reaction was hardly unique. Social psychologists have drawn attention to the way in which human collectives which perceive themselves to be inferior to an out-group will respond by trying to shift the ground of comparison (Hogg and Abrams, 1988). But the Crimean War had exposed this shifting of ground as a sham.

The Romantic nationalist reactions to the war did not, therefore, proceed down this vista. Instead, they emphasised the need to restore Russian national glory by means of revenge. Consequently, the move from Slavophilism towards pan-Slavism, which was initiated by those such as Konstantin Aksakov in the mid-1850s, gathered momentum throughout the period. Since the Romantic nationalists had been pushed to the margins of the debate when the state moved towards Westernisation, their moves were not very conspicuous. When, in 1869, Nikolay Danilevskiy's book *Rossiya i Evropa* appeared and undertook to shape pan-Slavism into a coherent whole, little notice was taken. It was only by the mid-1870s, when developments in the Balkans forced themselves on to the Russian agenda, that the Romantic nationalist position re-emerged as an important factor in the debate about Europe. At this point the book became a very hot item.

Danilevskiy was a natural scientist, and brought a positivist, classificatory language to his political task. Moreover, he shared with the positivists the urge to place social matters on a truly scientific base. According to Danilevskiy, previous writing of history had, without exception, been unscientific. Previous historians had failed to grasp that history is not a common human experience, but can only be studied scientifically at the *national* level. According to Danilevskiy, then, a study of history which postulates humanity – and not the nation – as its object cannot fail to be dilettantish.

By stating that humanity does not exist as an entity, Danilevskiy makes a very radical move. It is not only that humanity does not exist as a *civitas maxima*, that is, as a political entity. For Danilevskiy, it does not exist in *ethical* terms either. Previous Romantic nationalists had seen history as a relay race where Russia was about to receive the Olympic torch *on behalf of* humanity. While they had disagreed about the degree of contempt in which Russia should hold the previous runner, none of them had tried to exclude Europe from the ranks of humanity.

Danilevskiy does just that. He explicitly takes issue with the idea that the Slavs are destined to realise a common human idea. When Russia received the torch of history, he holds, it started to run for Russia and Russia alone, and there ceased to be anyone else in the race. In ethical terms, nothing but Russia and the Slavs exists. Against this backdrop, Danilevskiy proceeds to present what to him is the first natural system in historiography. Instead of one single 'humanity', there have existed ten strictly separate and different cultural-historical *types*. Nine of these types have already proven themselves to be non-historical. In other words, their time is already up. The tenth type, the Franco-German, is about to prove itself non-historical as Danilevskiy is writing, and a new Slav cultural-historical type is about to take its place. Since he defines Europe as being identical to the Franco-German cultural-historical type, it follows that Slavdom, under the leadership of Russia, is about to crowd out Europe (Danilevskiy, 1888: 59). The new world will be dominated by Slavdom and to a certain extent America, with Europe playing a steadily diminishing role.

It is the inherent tension between the terms 'type' and 'nation' which lends a distinctive flavour to Danilevskiy's work. The view that nation-states are actors in international politics not in and of themselves, but rather in their role as embodiments of a cultural-historical type, has important repercussions for Danilevskiy's perceptions of Europe. The Europeans have not considered Russia as part of the European family of nations, and in this, they have had history on their side. But Europe has not only passively overlooked Russia, it has also shown a strong and active hatred for it. Whence this Russophobia? Danilevskiy discards the possibility that it can be rooted in a feeling of threat; Russia is, after all, peace-loving, and not imperialistic like European states. Can it be a question of European dislike of Russian political practices? Certainly not; Europe's hatred for Russia has not abated when the latter has attempted liberal reforms, but has burnt with a steady flame. Instead, the reason for Europe's Russophobia must be sought in the incompatibility of the European and the Slav cultural-historical types, and in the fact that old Europe senses how it will be overtaken by young Russia. The Russian political tradition, tempered by stern but beneficial disciplinarians like the Varangians, the Tartars and their own landed gentry, will replace Europe's decadent feudal heritage.

Danilevskiy's assessment of Europe leads him to discard as indefensible the ongoing Westernising thrust of Russian policy. Since Russia and Europe are two different cultural-historical types, it is *impossible* to adapt European models to Russian conditions. Instead, he proposes two mutually contradictory courses for future relations. On the one hand, since Europe is in an advanced state of decay, the best thing for Russia would be to break off all relations except those of trade, while it waits for Europe to disappear. Nevertheless, the exigencies of the international system may not allow this course to be realised: Europe may take a last stand against history itself, and force Russia to finish it off:

> Throughout the book we have presented the thought that Europe is not only foreign to us, it is indeed hostile. Europe's interests cannot be ours, but not only that: in most cases they will be in direct opposition to one another. That does not yet mean that we could or should break off all our dealings with Europe and cordon ourselves off from it by means of a Chinese Wall. That is not only impossible, but would actually have been positively harmful. Dealings will have to be close, yet they must not be intimate, hearty, as if between kindred (*rodstvennyy*). Where political relations are concerned, the only rule must be an eye for an eye, and a tooth for a tooth – tit for tat. Yet even if it is impossible to cut ourselves off from European affairs, it is yet fully possible, useful and even obligatory to relate to them from our specific, Russian point of view. That must be our only criterion by which to judge how is this or that happening, this or that thought, this or that important personality going to influence on our specific Russo-Slav goals? Are they going to hurt them or to benefit them? Happenings, thoughts and personalities which are of no value we must treat with the utmost indifference, as if they took place or lived on the moon. [. . .]. What stands in our way, however, we must fight in all ways possible, whatever the consequences for Europe itself, for humanity, for freedom, for civilisation.
>
> (Danilevskiy, 1888: 480–1)

It is no coincidence that Europe is hostile to us, Danilevskiy repeats, and draws the conclusion that it can be harmless only when it is torn by internal strife. Therefore, it is in Russia's interest to stop participating in the management of international relations and instead to disrupt the 'political equipoise of Europe' – that is, the balance of power – in as large a degree as possible. Interestingly, Danilevskiy holds that *within* Europe, states have admitted that other states, too, had national interests. No such recognition has existed between Europe and Russia, however. This fact, he writes, was readily observable in the way Europe always denied the existence of Russian interests in Turkey, as seen in the events leading up to the Crimean War.

Perhaps Hedley Bull's distinction between an international system and an international society may shed light on Danilevskiy's position. Bull holds that a *system of states* exists when two or more states have sufficient contact between them, and have sufficient impact on one another's decisions, to cause them to behave – at least in some measure – as parts of a whole. However,

> A *society of states* (or international society) exists when a group of states, conscious of certain common interests and common values, form a society in the sense that they conceive themselves to be bound by a common set of rules in their relations with one another, and share in the working of common institutions.
>
> (Bull, 1977: 13)

The influence of German historicism on Danilevskiy is obvious, yet he follows the great majority of previous Romantic nationalists in not acknowledging his debt to European social philosophy of any kind. Danilevskiy sees a European international society to which Russia is no party. He acknowledges, however, that Russia is, for the time being, part of a European-dominated international system. It is this insight which causes him to play down the idea that Russia may keep itself aloof from Europe. Since isolation is not really a viable alternative, he holds, Russia should wait for the moment when Europe is maximally destabilised, and then give history a helping hand in obliterating it. None the less, it is interesting to note that not even Danilevskiy, who went further in dehumanising Europe than any Romantic nationalist before him, comes out one hundred per cent in favour of immediate and total war.[4]

To sum up this chapter, the first part of the period was characterised by the state's reaction to Europe's springtime of nations. Having wrought an immediate and severe contraction of political space, the state attempted to incorporate a Romantic nationalist concept of the nation into its position. Whereas the emphasis was still firmly on the state as the extension of the tsar's person, it was acknowledged that the tsar's power did not only emanate from God's grace, but also to some unspecified degree from his rapport with the people. What was seen as defeat at the hands of Europe in the Crimean War caused the state to re-evaluate. But while it widened public political space and implemented some Westernising reforms, it still refused to carve out a role in the political process for society as such.

The Romantic nationalist position – embodied by the Slavophiles – was strengthened by the events of 1848. Some Slavophiles reconciled themselves to the state to a larger extent than before. But the state's reaction to the defeat in the Crimean War pressed them back to the margins of the debate. The Slavophiles had tried to shift the ground of comparison between Russia and Europe from the technical to the spiritual arena. The humiliation of military defeat called into question the relevance of being spiritually superior. Thus, the Romantic nationalist reaction to the defeat was a turn away from spirituality towards a revanchist programme. Russia had a mission to fulfil, namely, the gathering of the Slav and Orthodox lands under its tutelage. And the inevitable confrontation with Europe which the implementation of this programme would entail would not necessarily deflect Russia from the path history had drawn up for it.

The Westernisers found themselves pushed to the margins of the debate during the state's crackdown in the first part of this period. But as the state traced the reasons for Russia's poor showing during the Crimean War back to the superiority of European political and economic models, the Westernisers were back at the heart of the debate. By then, the cracks which had developed in the Westernist position at the eve of the springtime of nations had already developed into a split. Whereas the liberal constitutionalists busied themselves in the new *zemstvo* movement, Gertsen and a number of other socialists remained in exile abroad. Whereas the liberals strove towards a law-governed state, Gertsen saw the organic nation and the social relations within it as crucial. He charged, furthermore, that the liberals would never succeed in bringing their programme to the attention of the people at large before they could offer a view of the nation as something more than an electorate.

The liberals and the socialists still shared an aversion to autocracy, but not much more. The difference between the liberal and the 'Russian socialist' views of Russia's relationship to Europe was thrown into sharp relief in an exchange of letters between Turgenev and Gertsen in the early 1860s. Gertsen held that Russia was a cousin of Europe, who had taken little part in the family chronicle, but whose 'rustic charms were fresher and more commendable than her cousins'' (Herzen, [1862] 1968: 1747). Turgenev begged to differ. 'Russia is not a maltreated and bonded Venus of Milo, she is a girl just like her older sisters – only a little broader in the beam', he held (Turgenev, [1862] 1963: 64–5; Moser, 1972: 56–88). Both Gertsen and Turgenev see the relationship in terms of family metaphors. When it comes to degree of kinship and to relative desirability, however, they part ways. To the liberals, Europe remained an ideal to be copied. To the 'Russian socialists', what Europe could teach Russia was first and foremost how important it was to avoid industrialisation.

During this period, the Russian socialist position was thoroughly radicalised, changed and renamed 'populist'. Whereas the Russian socialists were critical of many contemporary European practices, they always retained admiration for a number of European achievements. The populists did so in a lesser degree. The third, embryonically Marxist position which grew out of 1840s-style Westernism thoroughly disapproved of this attitude. Instead, it held the forces of history to be similar everywhere. Industrialised Europe, these socialists seemed to agree, showed Russia only the mirror image of its own future. The liberals, they continued, did not grasp that social relations were at the heart of historical development. The bourgeois society which existed in Europe and which the liberals wanted to copy in Russia, was bound to become no more than a transitional stage on the way to socialism.

5

FROM THE ASSASSINATION OF TSAR ALEXANDER II TO THE FIRST WORLD WAR

The assassination of Tsar Alexander placed Alexander III on the throne. As the new head of state, he immediately instigated a crackdown on public debate. The Censorship Statute of 1828 was tightened up in 1885, and yet again in 1890. During the 1880s, Romantic nationalists dominated the debate about Europe almost by default. During the 1890s, however, the heavy pan-Slavism which dominated the position was challenged by the more spiritual outlook of Solov'ev. In 1909, when the ranks of the Romantic nationalist position somewhat tentatively received an attachment of collapsed liberals, the spiritual faction of the position was strengthened, although the more xenophobic faction remained strong.

When Romantic nationalism had to let go of its dominant position at the end of the 1880s, it was because of the pressure from the arguing populists and Marxists. The populist commando which was behind the assassination of Alexander II in 1881 had seen it as a last-ditch stand against the introduction of capitalism in Russia, and had even given vent to the idea that public sentiment would react by propelling them to the centre of the political debate. If these particular populists left the debate with a bang, however, other populists were barely able to exhale a whimper as they saw themselves marginalised. Nevertheless, the populists came back to argue their case against Russia's copying of European-style industrialisation against the Marxists and all other comers.

The liberals and the embryonic Marxists were also marginalised from the debate of the 1880s. It speaks volumes about the state's attitude that, in 1884, not only Marx's works, but also Mill's and Adam Smith's *The Wealth of Nations* were banned from public libraries. The liberals kept their head down and their work in the *zemstvo* movement up. In 1894, as Alexander III died and Nicholas II acceded, they petitioned for a role on the national level, only to be rebuffed by the new tsar. European-style representative government was no more on his agenda than it had been on his father's, he confirmed.

By the 1890s, however, the Marxists had hogged the centre of the public debate. In a move which showed both the Marxist affinity to, but also their operative superiority to the liberals, it was a Marxist who took it upon himself to stand up to the tsar. In an open letter, he warned that the state, by failing to grant a political role to the public, was courting disaster. His words were borne out only ten years later, when, as Russia was losing a war against Japan, a public uprising did indeed take place. The uprising forced a new bout of reforms from the state. At that time, however, there had already occurred a realignment of the liberal and the Marxist positions, and the latter was itself facing a split.

The realignment of the Marxist and liberal positions took place at the beginning of the twentieth century, when the so-called 'legal Marxists' broke up from the Marxist position and made their way to the core of the liberal position, where they were instrumental in setting up the Kadet Party. Incidentally, in 1909 a number of the same people were to stage a half-hearted break with the liberal position and tentatively join the ranks of the Romantic nationalists.

The Marxist position broke into a Menshevik position and a Bolshevik position in 1903, and a third position represented by Parvus and Trotskiy hovered on the margin of their internal debates about Europe. The break between the Mensheviks and the Bolsheviks concerned how thoroughly Russia should copy European models and how squarely one should delineate a 'progressive Europe' from a 'stagnant Europe'.

One notes how, by studying Russian debate in its entirety, one comes upon the occasional opportunity to fill in a blank spot left by the lack of rapport between historians and historians of ideas. One case in point is the claim made by some students of the pan-Slavic Romantic nationalists in the 1880s, who seem to think they were in cahoots with the 'official nationality' of the state (von Schelting, 1948: 219, but see also Kennan, 1979: 184). This is not necessarily warranted. The state did not at this time act as it had done in 1848, when it tried to incorporate parts of the Romantic nationalist position into its own. In fact, the state's crackdown on political debate was not followed by any new initiatives at all. Leading official ideologists like Konstantin Pobedonostsev, Director General of the Holy Synod, saw themselves as caretakers of official nationality. The fluid foreign policy situation in arenas such as the Balkans and at the Congress of Berlin must also have been powerful incentives not to encourage the designs of the pan-Slavists.[1]

The pan-Slavists themselves were another matter. The check placed by the European great powers on Russian expansion in the Balkans did not deter them. To the contrary, they saw it as proof positive that Danilevskiy was right: old Europe was jealous of the new and rising Slav-Orthodox world under Russian tutelage. For example, Ivan Aksakov wrote in 1881 that there existed a double standard in the West, 'one for themselves, for the Germano-Roman tribes or for those who gravitate towards them spiritually, and another for us and the Slavs'. Humanity, civilisation and Christendom were slogans which Western powers reserved to themselves, and which they saw as irrelevant to the Eastern Orthodox world: 'As soon as it comes to us and the Slavs, all the West European powers show their solidarity towards one another' (quoted in Zen'kovskiy, 1955: 125). Aksakov followed Danilevskiy in foreseeing a coming clash between Russia and Europe:

> More than once in the future Europe will be divided into two camps: on one side Russia, with all Orthodox, Slavic tribes (not excluding Greece), on the other – the entire Protestant, Catholic, and even Mohammedan and Jewish Europe put together. Therefore Russia must care only about the strengthening of its own Orthodox-Slavic camp.
>
> (Riasanovsky, 1965: 85)

Danilevskiy's and Aksakov's moral assessment of and proposed relationship with Russia were not uncontested within the Romantic nationalist position, however. Although he failed to criticise Danilevskiy's placing of everyone non-Slav and non-Orthodox outside the community of mankind, and indeed harboured the greatest respect for his work, Fedor Dostoevskiy nevertheless departed from his views in crucial respects. Dostoevskiy sees Russia's relations with Europe in a Christian framework. For him, mankind is indeed an entity. Moreover, it is desperately in need of salvation. Since Russia is the salvation mankind needs, Russia's relation with Europe should be that of a shepherd who tries to gather lambs gone astray:

> The whole significance of Russia is contained in Orthodoxy, in the light from the East, which will flow to blind mankind in the West, which has lost Christ. All the misery of Europe, all, all, without any exception, came from the fact that with the Roman church they lost Christ and then decided that they could get along even without Christ. Well now, can you imagine, my dear friend, that even in such superior Russian people as, for example, the author of *Russia and Europe* [that is Danilevskiy] I have not encountered this idea about Russia, that is, about her exclusively Orthodox mission for mankind.
>
> (Dostoevskiy, 1986: 146–7)

Or again,

> Every people is only a people so long as it has its own God and excludes all other Gods on Earth irreconcilably; so long as it believes that by its Gods it will conquer and drive out of the world all other Gods. Such, from the beginning of time, has been the belief of all great nations, all, anyway, who have been specially remarkable, all who have been leaders of humanity, respectively.
>
> (quoted in Lednicki, 1966: 172)

Dostoevskiy did, however, also make moves where he was less categorical about the all-pervasive role of religion, and about the direction in which Russia's proselytising efforts should be directed. 'In Europe we were hangers-on and Slaves, whereas we shall go to Asia as masters', he wrote at a later date, and continued: 'In Europe we were Asiatics, whereas in Asia we, too, are European. Our civilizing mission in Asia will bribe our spirit and drive us thither'(Dostoevskiy, 1954: 1048). This move does not stress Russian spiritual superiority, but its profane backwardness: the Russians were 'Slaves' among the Europeans. Moreover, Dostoevskiy acknowledges that in the eyes of the Asians, Russians are Europeans, and that this assessment will prove to be irresistibly flattering to the Russians. He implies that Russians will take up the white man's burden *in order to* pass themselves off as Europeans.

There is an ambiguity about Europe here, which sets Dostoevskiy apart from the pan-Slavs but is reminiscent of the Slavophile attitude of the 1840s. On the one hand, he categorically marks ardent members of a Westernising persuasion as 'destroyers of Russia, enemies of Russia': 'a Russian who has become a genuine European, cannot help but become at the same time a national enemy of Russia' (Dostoevskiy, 1954: 357). Yet, on the other hand, in his famous address on Pushkin he holds a seemingly contradictory view, that 'the Russian's destiny is incontestably all-European and universal. To become a genuine and all-round Russian means perhaps to become a brother of all men, a *universal man*, if you please' (Dostoevskiy, 1954: 979).

Perhaps the crux to this seeming paradox is to be found in the aphorism he formed on George Sand's death: 'We, the Russians, have two Fatherlands – Russia (*nasha Rus'*) and Europe – even in cases when we call ourselves Slavophiles' (Dostoevskiy, 1954: 342). This move is reminiscent of Zhukovskiy's when he held that Russia was unique exactly because it managed to be two things simultaneously. It is both one of many European states, and in this sense, Europe is a Russian's Fatherland. At the same time, however, the Russian is the member of a nation with a holy mission: to save humanity. It is, perhaps, the Russian who forgets Russia's Messianic role *vis-à-vis* Europe and the rest of the world whom Dostoevskiy brands as a traitor. Europe may be greater in worldly power, and may treat Russia as the Roman empire treated Christ. But Russia, like a Christ of nations, endures its hardships in order to sacrifice itself for humanity. From Peter the Great onwards, Dostoevskiy concludes, this has been the *Leitmotiv* and true meaning of Russian foreign policy. 'For what else has Russia been doing in her policies, during these two centuries, than serving Europe much more than herself?' he asks rhetorically (Dostoevskiy, 1954: 979).

Another Romantic nationalist who was active in the debate in this period was Konstantin Leont'ev (Krag, 1932). Leont'ev shared with Dostoevskiy a Christian framework for assessing Russia's relations with Europe. Leont'ev was, however, first and foremost a disciplinarian, who held the core of the Christian message to be *timor Domini* – fear of God. Dostoevskiy, like the Slavophiles before him, stressed how tsar and people were of one collective mind. Leont'ev's understanding of the organic nation is different. To him, the idea which God has inscribed on each nation is of the essence, and the nation itself is merely a container for the idea. Russia was chosen to embody the Byzantine idea, where each estate's position is fixed irrevocably and each estate is thoroughly different from the others. His concept of the nation is thus closer to the one inherent in official nationality than that of any other Romantic nationalist. His stressing of the fixity of estates is also reminiscent of the state's position. Despite these idiosyncrasies, however, his view of the nation as a cultural carrier of a great idea seems to justify his present inclusion among the Romantic nationalists. Leont'ev is on the losing side of a long debate about the legal equality of states (Clark, 1989), and is indeed opposed to the entire principle of equality in all walks of life. The Russian Byzantine idea, he held, was the polar opposite of what he saw as the 'liberal-egalitarian process' of levelling which had swept Europe after the onslaught of the French Revolution. To him, equality between classes and equality between nations was all part of the same 'empty pretensions of Parisian demagogy, or as some little (*uezdnyy*) people's desire to be placed on an equal footing with all other nations in international law, come what may' (Leont'ev, 1912b: 186).

To Leont'ev, Europe was morally inferior to Russia exactly because it embodied the idea of homogeneity. Even so, Europe was a mortal danger to Russia, since Russia did not know how to guard itself against the thrust of its mediocrity. 'Everything goes in one direction', he complained, 'towards a European society of the mean and the rule of the human of the mean. This will be going on until all empires and states converge into a pan-European republican federation' (Leont'ev, 1912a: 157). The difference in European political thought between nationalism and cosmopolitanism, seemingly so important, he treats with disdain. The underlying current of events is pushing Europe further and further down into the quagmire of homogeneity and political unification (Leont'ev, 1912c: 389). His ideas about this are worth quoting at some length:

> The question is, if the European states [. . .] should really unite in a federal workers' republic, would we not have to consider this the end of the old European political order? At what price will such a union be bought? Would not this new Pan-European state in principle have to tear itself loose

from all local quirks, from all proud traditions, maybe . . .
who knows? . . . burn and annihilate the main capitals in
order to demolish the great centres which for so long split
the peoples of the West into hostile national camps? [. . .]
Such radical changes are not made by rosewater and sugar,
they are only available through iron, fire, blood and tears.
[. . .] One may say: They will never unite! I answer: He who
holds such views is a happy man [. . .] In order to break
down the last remnants of Europe's old political order we
need neither barbarians nor a foreign invasion. It is enough
that the insane religion of eudaemonism is further spread,
the religion whose faith is declared thus: 'Le bien-être
matériel et moral de l'humanité'.

(Leont'ev, 1912b: 250–2)

Like Danilevskiy, Leont'ev proposes two different ways in which
Russia may go about its relationship with Europe. The first
possibility is for Russia to save Europe from itself before it
drowns in its own egalitarian ideals. 'France is Athens, Prussia
is Sparta, and Russia is – Rome!', he exclaims at one point, and
thereby sums up how a disciplined, martial Russia may simply
overtake decadent European civilisation (Leont'ev, 1912d: 114).
Even a communist Russia would have something to offer
Europe, namely, discipline and the eradication of bland liberalism. The second possibility is to isolate Russia from European
influences not only in space, but also in time. Leont'ev made
this move in the form of an epigram which is perhaps the most
desperate protest against European modernisation that a Russian
Romantic nationalist ever produced: 'In order not to rot, Russia
must be frozen' (Leont'ev, 1913: 124). Whereas Danilevskiy
preferred confrontation, then, Leont'ev seems to come down on
the side of isolation.

It should be clear from the moves made by Danilevskiy,
Dostoevskiy and Leont'ev that, by the turn of the century, the
Romantic nationalist position was sprawling. Before the Balkan
War of 1877 and the assassination of the tsar three years later,
almost all Romantic nationalist moves had had a pan-Slav thrust.
Leont'ev, on the other hand, thought the South Slavs were so
contaminated by the European disease of egalitarianism that
Russia should keep them at arm's length. And Dostoevskiy,
although he eagerly accepted the need for Russia to grasp

Constantinople, couched his reasons for so doing in spiritual rather than in strategic terms. In this way, he gave it back some of the colouring it had had before the pan-Slavs began to dominate it, in the heyday of the Slavophiles.

At the century's end, Vladimir Solov'ev came up with some moves which nudged the Romantic nationalist position even further in this direction (Waage, 1988). Like Dostoevskiy, Solov'ev was convinced that Russia had the potential to cleanse the world, to initiate a new spiritual beginning. His thinking was, however, much more dialectical and his respect for Europe less ambiguous than was Dostoevskiy's. Like a number of Russian nineteenth-century thinkers – Belinskiy, Granovskiy, Kireevskiy, Khomyakov and Leont'ev, to name but a few – Solov'ev followed German thinkers like Hegel in analysing history as a play in three acts. At the outset of history, there exists a whole range of different possibilities. It is characteristic of phase one, however, that what development there is takes place according to the theocratic principle. This makes for a human community characterised by spiritual unity, as one can see them in the East. In the course of phase two, all the possibilities which were left dormant during phase one are realised. There is a cost, inasmuch as theocratic unity is lost and humanism takes its place. This, indeed, is what characterises the West. In a future third phase, however, the strengths of East and West are going to be resolved in a new whole. Humankind will once again become an organic whole, rooted in spirituality, but with the added experience of phase two meshed in. It is Russia's great mission to realise this third and final phase of world history.

From this vantage point, Solov'ev took issue with his fellow Romantic nationalists – and, incidentally, also with some former views of his own – for the way in which they misrepresented the history of Russia's relationship with Europe. Kievan Rus', he wrote, had had quite close contacts with Western Europe. It had, indeed, seen itself as part of 'European humanity' (*evropeyskoe chelovechestvo*). The Mongol invasions did, however, sever Russia's relations with Europe, and they remained broken throughout the Muscovy period. The damage done, Solov'ev holds, was twofold. First, the Mongols did not only hamper the development of Russia, but in many respects dragged it down to its own less advanced level. In many ways, he insists, the

Russians came to resemble their oppressors. Second, throughout their humiliation, the Russians retained their feeling of being a Christian and an historical nation (*natsiya*). Although this was of course beneficial, he muses, the blessing also had a sting in its tail. The Russians became overly conscious of their superiority compared to the Mongols. As a result, they became vain, supercilious and exclusive. The Russian was like a person who only mixes with the handicapped, Solov'ev writes. Although he is probably nothing out of the ordinary, he sees himself as standing head and shoulders above the rest (Solov'ev, 1905: 146). The Russian's inflated national pride became even worse as the Tartar yoke subsided, and grew to be unbearable after the fall of Constantinople. Before 1453, the Russians had looked up to the Greeks. After the fall, the Greek monks who came to Russia were treated as beggars, and for money they gave to Moscow the right to call itself the Third Rome.

Having carried out this out-and-out attack on some of the most central parts of the Romantic nationalist position, Solov'ev turns on the specific views of Danilevskiy. Danilevskiy, Solov'ev charges, explains Europe's hostility to Russia in terms of the envy of a dying culture upon beholding its successors. That is not the core of the matter. Rather, Europe's hostility is to a large extent of Russia's own making, provoked by things like Danilevskiy's own book. According to Solov'ev, Europe looks at Russia with hostility and fear because Europe understands that the Russian people represent a dark and elementary power, whose spiritual and cultural preconditions are frightfully small, but whose aspirations know no boundaries:

> In Europe nothing sounds louder than the clamour of our "nationalism", which wants to smash Turkey, smash Austria, rout Germany, conquer Constantinople, and, when the time is right, even India. But when asked what we intend to give to humanity in exchange for what we are going to destroy, which spiritual and cultural values we will contribute to world history, then we will have to keep silent or mutter some meaningless phrases.
>
> (Solov'ev, 1905: 137)

However, Rusia should rather try to grasp that its relations with Europe are fraternal. Instead of railing against Europe, it should confess its sins and put its own house in order. Bearing in mind history's intention, it should brace itself for the path towards spiritual perfection. This insight has still not permeated Russian minds, but in due course it will, Solov'ev concludes.

This is a very different face of Romantic nationalism than those represented by Danilevskiy, Dostoevskiy and Leont'ev. In place of a relationship with Europe characterised by confrontation, proselytising or isolationism, Solov'ev suggests a partnership in Christ. One should, however, not jump to the conclusion that Solov'ev's moves necessarily bring the Romantic nationalist position closer to official nationality. Alexander I and his successors advocated a Christian brotherhood of monarchs, of which their peoples, as the extensions of the royal sovereigns, would automatically and indirectly partake. Solov'ev, the mystical philosopher, on the other hand, advocated a partnership *between* the nations, *in* Christ.

One should not, however, overestimate the degree to which Danilevskiy's and Solov'ev's spiritual turn had done away with other variants of Romantic nationalism. Plenty of people still saw it as their main priority to hold up the industrialisation of Russia, which they held to be a sell-out to Europe. Two examples should suffice. In 1904, N. M. Sokolov published a book which reiterated the standard formulae of the old Romantic nationalism. Marx and Mauser, he wrote, were both proponents of a capitalism which could only bring South African concentration camps, class warfare and the like. 'We have noted, that the notion of the universality of European culture is the "ideological" veil for the very real aspiration of the European West to rule the world' (Read, 1979: 100–6). Therefore, when Russian intellectuals like Milyukov held that the Europeans knew a higher truth from which Russians should learn, he was simply being duped. The Russian land, however, would stand down the Europeanised city in the end. The framework Sokolov chose for discussing Europe, his moral judgement of it, as well as his proposed relationship with it, were all representative of the established Romantic nationalist position. Contemporary references like the one to the English practices during the Boer War aside, there was nothing here to indicate that Solov'ev's thinking had had an impact.

In the same vein, Sergey Sharapov criticised the state's investment in industry. The real riches of Russia remained its agriculture, which was being neglected. Worse still, the decline of agriculture meant that the organic way of life of the Russian village was being destroyed. Instead, the state's policy laid the land open for the Europeanising enemy: 'Our well-organized neighbors thirst for the cultural collapse of the Russian colossus. And at home every kind of economic chicanery by Jews and foreigners has reached a new height', Sharapov complained (von Laue, 1963: 286). The way to guard against morally inferior Europe was to isolate Russia by means of economic and cultural protective measures. In this way, economic encroachment and the tyranny of the gold standard could be avoided, he maintained.

The contrast between the moves of a Solov'ev and a Sharapov covers the span of the Romantic nationalist position at the turn of the century. Solov'ev sees the relationship with Europe within a spiritual framework, finds fault with its moral status, and proposes a relationship where it can be saved from itself by means of Russian spiritual guidance. He crucially refuses to see Europe as wholly Other, but stresses the extent to which the fates of Russia and Europe are intertwined, and how Europe's problems are in a very immediate sense Russia's, too. Later in this chapter it will be discussed how Solov'ev's moves inspired the so-called *vekhovtsy* to elaborate on the extent to which the Russian intelligentsia has to come to terms with its own self, split between a Russian present they only half acknowledge and a half-digested European vision of the future. Sharapov, on the contrary, sees Europe in a cultural framework where it is held to be wholly Other, and morally clearly inferior. He proposes a distanced relationship, and stresses the extent to which Europeans, as well as European influence on misguided Russians, must be held at bay so that Russia can be kept clean and undivided. This way of thinking also remained well represented for the rest of this period, and was institutionalised in fora such as the Black Hundreds.

Sharapov, like a number of Romantic nationalists before and indeed after him, saw the 'economic chicanery by Jews and foreigners' not only as a threat to their national, but also to their social identity. Industrialisation meant that a bourgeoisie would encroach on the landed gentry's social standing. The preservation of agriculture, however, meant that the social base of the landed gentry was secure, and more so the less the state interfered. It was this feature of Romantic nationalism more than

71

anything else which ruled out a partnership between the Romantic nationalists and the populists. Indeed, although a number of populists saw the Russian nation in organic terms and were well aware of their affinity with people like Aleksandr Gertsen, a tactical alliance with the Romantic nationalists was simply not seen as a possibility, however remote.

During the 1880s, the populists were both demoralised and marginalised from the debate. They despaired of the surge of industrialisation in the Russian lands. Indeed, the assassination of Alexander II by some of the verbally less articulate members of their rank had been partly precipitated by despair. To the more moderate populists, however, the assassination and its aftermath were hardly a consolation. By 1883, their leader Mikhaylovskiy wistfully described himself as 'a voice in the wilderness' (Kindersley, 1962: 8). Nevertheless, as the 1880s subsided and public debate picked up yet again, moderated populism was able to bounce back (Shanin, 1984: 12–13). During the 1890s, their exchanges with what had now become a fully fledged Marxist position took centre stage in the Russian debate about Europe. In terms of new moves, however, it was the Marxists who did nearly all the running.

For example, it was Struve who began to highlight the differences between the two positions by comparing their differences to those debated in the 1840s (Pipes, 1964: 441–58; but see also Walicki, 1969: 5). The point of the exercise was, of course, to enrol the common totemic ancestors of the left in the Marxist ranks. These moves must have met with some success, since in 1894, Mikhaylovskiy also decided to stake his claim. The occasion was plain enough. In a book on the economic development of Russia, Struve had stressed that capitalism was not only an evil, but also a creative force in the development of Russia:

> The whole of contemporary material and spiritual culture is closely tied to capitalism: It emerged either together with capitalism, or on its soil [. . .] No, we must admit our uncultured state (*nekul'turnost'*) and go to school with capitalism.
>
> (Struve, 1894: 288)

Mikhaylovskiy immediately sharpened his pen in order to fend off this umpteenth attempt at corrupting Russia by means of European models. He decided, moreover, to take a feather from his opponent's cap and stage his move in the style pioneered by

Struve himself. Struve's Marxism, Mikhaylovskiy charged, was reminiscent of Belinskiy's Hegelianism inasmuch as it revolved around an opposition between subjectivity and historical necessity (Walicki, 1988: 436–40). The point to note about Belinskiy, Mikhaylovskiy insisted, was that he abandoned his belief that Russia should copy all the stages of Europe's development. He put such determinism behind him, and substituted for it a belief in Russia's ability to fend for itself. So should Struve: instead of insisting on the necessity of industrialisation, he should turn his mind to the uniqueness of the Russian case.

To Plekhanov, another Marxist, the use Mikhaylovskiy made of Belinskiy was all but inadmissible. He, too, recognised the duality of Belinskiy's thought. When Belinskiy railed against historical necessities, however, it was not in a mood of voluntarism, but of sheer utopianism. And so, Plekhanov moved to clinch the Marxist argument against the adversary on the left: The populists, he concludes, are the inheritors of Belinskiy's utopianism, whereas the Marxists are the carriers of the final stage of Russian Westernism. To cap it all off, he sums up his argument with a quote from Belinskiy: 'The inner process of civil development will begin in Russia only after the Russian gentry has become transformed into a bourgeoisie' (Walicki, 1969: 163).[2]

It would not necessarily be wrong to suggest that the main role of the populist position in this period was the one of playing whipping-boy to the Marxists. It would, nevertheless, be a Cyclopean assessment. The skirmishes between populists and Marxists notwithstanding, a number of studies comment on the continuity of thought and also personnel between the populist movement and Russian social democracy, which institutionalised itself in 1898 (Berdiaev, 1960; Keep, 1963; Offord, 1986; Venturi, 1960; also Shanin, 1984: 216–17).

The history of social democracy in the remainder of this period is the history of two splits, both of which were inextricably linked with the debate about Europe. In 1900, the 'legal' Marxist branch staged an exodus in the direction of the liberal position. The main issue at stake was the delineation of 'false' or temporary Europe from the true or final Europe. At this time, moreover, a crack was also beginning to emerge between the groups which, after 1903, were to be known as Bolsheviks and Mensheviks. A key question in that break was one which had been hotly debated by Marxists and populists throughout this period. Should Russian revolutionaries try to stage a coup before capitalism became firmly entrenched, or should they resign themselves to the necessity of copying European capitalism in order to reach socialism? There was a crucial difference between the Marxist–Slavophile debate and the Menshevik–Bolshevik debate, however, and it hinged on one, single move. Revolutionary populists like Tkachev had wanted to stage a coup in order to keep industrialisation *out of* Russia. The Bolsheviks, on the other hand, wanted to seize power so that they could surge ahead with industrialisation. The revolutionary populists and the Bolsheviks were both voluntarists in that they thought it was possible to will a transfer of power. The populists, however, had wanted to use that power to steer Russia clear of decadent Europe and its perverted course of development. The Bolsheviks wanted to save Russia from the clutches of false, bourgeois Europe and to plunge it directly into the final stage of historical development – that true Europe of which Russia was a part – socialism.

As already noted, the assassination of Alexander II had, at least temporarily, settled the debate between voluntarism and historical necessity. The move that the *obshchina* could be willed to play the role of a launching pad for a specifically Russian non-industrial socialism only recurred in the occasional stage-whisper in the wings of the debate. For Plekhanov, the assassination settled the matter once and for all. 'I see no essential difference between Russian history and that of the West', he reproached a populist in 1882 (Kindersley, 1962: 25). He was, however, not blind to the irony that socialists, because of their sense of historical necessity, should find themselves advocating the building not of socialism, but of capitalism. 'The peculiarity of our history in recent years consisted in the fact that even the Europeanization of our bourgeoisie was being accomplished under the banner of Marxism', he was to write at a later stage (Walicki, 1969: 170).

It is easy to see the vulnerability of the moves made by people such as Plekhanov. In times of upheaval, moves which appeal to historical necessity are easy to challenge by an appeal to the power of the human will. Why should not history be given a helping hand? On the other hand, if the role of a Marxist should be to assist the bourgeoisie in the development of capitalism, then why should one not try to do that from the most efficient vantage point, that is from inside the state system? As the 1890s wore on, a number of Marxists asked themselves these questions. The underground pondered the former question, whereas the 'legal' Marxists toyed with the latter. The consequences were to transform the Marxist position.

One of the incidents of the irony alluded to by Plekhanov, that in Russia it was the Marxists who were to demonstrate to the liberals how their European models went about their business, occurred in 1894–5. As Nicholas II acceded to the throne, the *zemstvo* liberals moved to petition him for a greater role in public affairs. The tsar's response was swift and unequivocal:

> I am aware that of late, in some *zemstvo* assemblies there have been heard voices of persons who have been carried away by senseless dreams of the participation of *zemstvo* representatives in the affairs of internal administration. Let it be known to all that I, while devoting my energies to the good of the people, shall maintain the principle of autocracy just as firmly and unflinchingly as did my unforgettable father.
>
> (Kindersley, 1962: 180)

This move was intended as a reiteration of the state's position that it would not let itself be diluted by the political models of the false Europe of its time. The liberal *zemstvo* men took note, and made no substantial countermove. It was left to Struve, the leader of the legal Marxists, to put the case for European-style representative government. Struve, while acknowledging the class character of any state as inescapable, was not wholly dismissive of the Russian state of his day. Like any other state, it was first and foremost 'an organisation of order', whose great service it was to mediate between different groups within the polity (Kindersley, 1962: 181; see Elster, 1985: 398–458 for a similar reading of Marx). By jeopardising the development of the state along European lines, however, the tsar would not be able to ward it off, but was simply asking for a public upheaval. This was the thrust of the open letter with which Struve countered the tsar's speech, where he charged that if the autocracy identified itself 'with the omnipotence of officialdom, it is digging its own grave, and sooner or later, but in any case in the near future, it will fall under the onrush of the living forces of the public' (Kindersley, 1962: 181).

If Struve was highly critical of the autocracy, neither was he much impressed with the liberals, who had proved to be unable to speak up for their own position. When he drafted the programme for the founding congress of the Russian Social Democratic Workers' Party in 1898, experiences such as the one of three years before were still dictating his moves. 'The further east one goes in Europe', he wrote, 'the weaker, meaner and more cowardly in the political sense becomes the bourgeoisie, and the greater the cultural and political tasks which fall to the lot of the proletariat' (Carr, 1950: 4).[3]

Only two years later, however, Struve, and most of the other legal Marxists, made a move which discontinued their association with the Marxist position and placed them in the liberal constitutionalist camp. Throughout the 1890s, the legal Marxists had held that the copying of European capitalism was simply a necessary prelude on the way to socialism. Contemporary, 'false' Europe had to be emulated not as an end in itself, but as a means for both Russia *and* false Europe to reach the true Europe of socialism. The move made in 1900, however, was simply to ditch the idea of the coming of a 'true' socialist Europe and to start treating contemporary Europe as the true Europe, worthy of emulation for its own sake. Consequently, Struve and most of the legal Marxists broke up from the Marxist position, and drew close to the liberal *zemstvo* movement, whose work he had done in 1895. Taking the *zemstvo* movement as their base, Struve and his associates also set about constructing a liberal political party, the Constitutional Democrats (the KDs or Kadets).

To Marxists such as Lenin, the defection of the legal Marxists strengthened the case against revisionism. In a book from 1902, *What is to be Done?*, Lenin set out the case for transforming the Russian Social Democratic Workers' Party into a fighting organisation of professional revolutionaries. The move was not entirely new; as mentioned above, a similar concept was presented by Tkachev already in 1869. The way Lenin presented it and the combination of reasons he gave were, however, new. Moreover, they were all to do with the debate about Europe. Lenin's book was a polemic against a little group of Marxists which went by the name of 'the Economists'. The Economists argued that judged by Western standards, Russian workers were still politically immature. They could, therefore, not be expected to rally around a programme which placed a political revolution on top of the agenda. Such a programme, moreover, was hardly likely to get off the ground given the political conditions in Russia. Therefore, they argued, Russian social democracy should choose an incremental strategy, whereby the workers could, little by little, improve their conditions.[4]

Lenin went along with a number of the Economists' assumptions. Certainly, he argued, the Russian workers are not able to constitute themselves as a fighting force all by themselves. They need the leadership of intellectuals. To Lenin, however, this was not a condition specific to Russian workers as such, but was equally valid in Europe. In Germany, which had the strongest social democratic movement in the world, Bernsteinian revisionism was very popular at the time. This only proved that there was always and everywhere a danger that 'trade unionism' would threaten to waylay the revolutionary cause. Schapiro (1967b) goes so far as to maintain that it had not occurred to Lenin before reading Bernstein's *Die Voraussetzungen des Sozialismus und die Aufgaben der Sozialdemokratie* in 1899 that the revolution in Europe may never come. Like all other Russian Marxists, Schapiro goes on, Lenin had always expected the revolution to occur first in the most advanced countries of Europe and then to spill over to Russia. Now he suddenly realised that, due to the rising revisionist sentiment of the social democrat leaders, the revolution might not get started. It was only then he set his mind to work at the problem of how to initiate a revolution in Russia and came up with the idea of the party of a new type, Schapiro maintains. This may be so. Yet, Schapiro does not present any textual evidence for this Damascene interpretation of what went on inside Lenin's brain, and so his interpretation seems underdetermined (see also Harding, 1977: 296).

Certainly, Lenin agreed, in Russia, where it was even forbidden to put the word socialism into print, conditions were harder. However, he went on, and this is where he really has it in for the Economists, it did not follow from any of this that Russian Marxists should necessarily have to constrain themselves to building capitalism and improving the lot of the worker incrementally. Rather, it meant that the case for a party of a new type was even stronger in Russia than in Europe. Since Lenin's party of a new type, once it was realised, proved itself fifteen years later to be the Russian organisation most able to seize and retain power, it was indeed momentous. It is, however, also of immediate interest to our concern because its critics at once assailed it as a breach with what for them remained the very core of the Marxist position. If this party model were to be adopted, they argued, it meant that Russia would stop copying the models of the most advanced section of true Europe, namely, the European social democratic movement. A number of scholars have seen Lenin's concept of the party of a new type as a specifically Russian answer to a specifically Russian problem. The idea of the party of a new type was the fruit of a specifically Russian discourse which took part in a specifically Russian socioeconomic setting. Yet something more seems to be at stake here. Keep (1963: 94) argues that the focus on Russian conditions is 'something of a red herring', not because it is wrong, but because Lenin went on to propose this mode of organisation universally. In our context, the crucial point is Lenin's insistence that he knows better than the European comrades themselves which mode of organisation better fits 'advanced' European conditions.

During its second conference in 1903, the Russian Social Democratic Workers' Party split over what was ostensibly an organisational issue. Lenin and his Bolsheviks immediately set about constructing a party of a new type. The Mensheviks continued much as before. Lenin's 'party of a new type' was a new concept in the sense that it was different from the European-style party the Mensheviks wanted. It was also new inasmuch as it presupposed a theory of representation which was, as it were, highly abstract. The most severe critic of the idea of representation behind the 'party of a new type', however, was Lev Davidovich Trotskiy. He held that were Lenin's model for the organisation of the party to win through, an inexorably centralising logic would start to work within it, whereby the party would be replaced by the organisation of the party, the organisation by the central committee, and the central committee by a dictator.

Drawing attention to the Manichaean quality of Lenin's thinking, Trotskiy pointed to the experience of the French Revolution to bolster his move against Lenin. Quoting Robespierre to the effect that 'Je ne connais que deux partis, celui des bons et celui des mauvais citoyens', he adds that 'that political aphorism is printed on the heart of Maximilian Lenin' (Trotskiy, 1904: 96). As a member of the so-called 'minority', Trotskiy goes on, he would like to take issue with the idea of 'party discipline' and the idea of substituting discipline and the terror of theory for open debate: 'It is necessary once and for all to turn away from "accelerated" methods of substitutism (*zamestitel'stvo*)' (Trotskiy, 1904: 106). And it is at this point that Trotskiy constructs his dichotomy between the 'Asiatic' Bolsheviks and the 'European' Mensheviks which was to become a dominant theme in Marxist debate in the years to come. Outside the capitals, Trotskiy noted, the Bolshevik following consisted mainly of country bumpkins from east of the Urals. This was no coincidence:

> It is really only in the dense forests of the Urals or in the thickets of the Siberian taiga one may meet specimens of that race – noble, yet threatened with extinction – of 'hard-line Iskra-ists' of the first order, *les Jacobins comme les rayons du soleil*, Jacobins clean as the sunlight. Of course, the corrupting spirit of criticism and doubt also reaches them. But they bravely fight against it, and try to throw it west of the Urals so that they can save their social-democratic Asia.
>
> (Trotskiy, 1904: 69)

'For European socialism', on the other hand, 'the Jacobin tendency is a closed phase', Trotskiy concludes (1904: 104). The same theme surfaced in Plekhanov's criticism of Lenin's 'party of a new type'; it was undemocratic, and therefore un-European. For example, it would make it possible for the central committee to decide who should be elected to what should ostensibly remain the party's highest organ, namely, the congress. 'Then, in reality, there would be in the party neither a majority nor a minority, because we would then have realized the ideal of the Persian Shah' (Baron, 1963: 360). The Shah's Persia is used here as a sign of everything, including Bolshevism, that is not European, and therefore inferior.

At this time, the Russian state had already initiated a war against Japan. It was going badly. The prospect of defeat inspired Aleksander Gel'fand, a Russian social democrat living in Germany and known by his *nom de plume* Parvus, to make a stunning move. In a book published in 1904, he characterised Russia as 'an absolutism in the Asian manner, propped up by a European type army', a state which had consistently tried to isolate itself from Europe. 'But no kinds of ditches or barrages could cordon off Russia from Western Europe', Parvus (1904: 96–7) writes. To the contrary, capitalism itself forced the capitalists into conflict, and these conflicts would inevitably lead to world wars, which would be the harbingers of revolution: The capitalists 'begin to push each other out of markets, and their conflicts, when other means are lacking, lead inevitably to world wars'(Parvus, 1904: 88–9). Following this, Parvus goes on to state that,

> The world process of capitalist development brings about a political upheaval (*perevorot*) in Russia which cannot but affect political development in all capitalist countries. The Russian revolution will shake the capitalist world to its political foundations, and the Russian proletariat may play (*mozhet sygrat'*) the role of the vanguard of the social revolution.
>
> (Parvus, 1904: 133)

What is new here is not the idea that capitalist countries would fall as dominoes once the revolution did away with one of them, but the prediction that the world revolution would not necessarily break in Western Europe, but perhaps in Russia. The idea that capitalism would give where it was the least developed, that is, in Russia, rather than in the most advanced capitalist countries in Europe came to be known as the theory of the weakest link.

> Helphand's thesis on the development of capitalism into a universal system, on the decline of the importance of nation states, and on the parallel extension of both the bourgeois and the proletarian interests outside the framework of these states, all this Trotsky took over *in toto*.
>
> (Zeman and Scharlan, 1965: 66)

Indeed, within a year, it was to form the stepping-stone for Trotskiy.

That year, however, was to change the Russian debate about Europe yet again. The war against Japan was lost, and there was considerable unrest in the capital. In January 1905, Father Gapon gathered a number of uprooted peasant-workers for a march to the tsar's winter palace. Gapon and the peasants acted on an understanding of the state which was not too far removed from that of the Romantic nationalists. To them, the tsar remained the people's 'little father', which is to say that the people could be viewed first and foremost as an extension of the tsar's household, and not a self-organised entity. Like the Romantic nationalists, they held the view that the state bureaucracy was little more than a self-serving nuisance which interfered with the flow of information between the tsar and his people. It was in this spirit that they wanted to present their petition for better living conditions directly to the tsar, above the heads of the state machinery. As they gathered outside the winter palace, however, the tsar's guard opened fire, and a number of people were killed. Father Gapon's reaction was immediate. He threw himself to the ground and exclaimed that the Russian people no longer had a tsar.

This was indeed a farreaching move. If people like father Gapon held the tsar to be an impostor who did not care about his people, then a likely next step was for them to surge into political space to try and rectify this unwanted state of affairs. This was indeed what happened. The external defeat to Japan and the 'bloody Sunday' of January 1905 sparked an uprising of the kind Struve had warned against ten years before. Some, notably Trotskiy, went so far as to declare the situation revolutionary. To him, Parvus's view that Russia's defeat by Japan would bring about a revolution seemed to be vindicated.

There was certainly rapid political change. Different workplaces set up their own *sovety* or councils. No other than Trotskiy was instrumental in forging the Soviets in the capital together under the umbrella of the Petersburg Soviet, of which he became the chair. The *zemstvo* movement rallied yet again for a role in public political life. Most Mensheviks shared the confidence of their leader that they would be up to the task. 'We have the right to expect', Martov wrote, 'that sober political calculation will prompt our bourgeois democracy to act in the same way in which, in the past century, bourgeois democracy acted in western Europe, under the inspiration of revolutionary romanticism' (Deutscher, 1954: 119).

And indeed, whereas ten years before the tsar had written off the whole idea of *zemstvo* representation in public affairs, he now edged closer to the liberal position by allowing the setting up of a somewhat representative organ with limited powers, the Duma. The state's position was immediately characterised by a contemporary German commentator as one of 'fake constitutionalism' (Weber, 1906: 165–401). This was certainly a break with the tradition of Russian autocracy, and a breakthrough for the liberals. Among the snags, however, was the cultural lag inherent in the state's copying of Western political models. At this time, in Western Europe the campaign for the principle of one man one vote had already gathered considerable force.[5] In Russia, however, the liberals had to accept that the Duma would be elected, not by the citizenry at large but by estate. Actually, in what should have been its finest moment since 1864, when the *zemstva* were set up in the first place, the liberal position cracked over the extent to which one should cooperate with the state. At the November 1905 congress of the *zemstvo* movement, the pro-compromisers founded the Octobrist Party, whereas the more reticent majority remained in the Kadet Party. The crack was further widened when the state staged a coup in 1907, and did away with some of the powers of the Duma.

Out of the two different liberal attitudes to the existing Russian state and to what was politically viable, there emerged two different approaches to Europe. The Octobrists were more prone to make amends for conditions which they saw as specifically Russian. The Kadets, however, continued to campaign for the copying of the European political and economic models of the time. As had been the case throughout the nineteenth century, the liberal constitutionist position continued to have sympathisers within the state. In 1906, Foreign Minister Izvol'skiy wrote to the leading liberal constitutionalist Pavel Milyukov that 'basic political reform will bring us closer to Europe, and ease the foreign minister's task abroad' (Riha, 1969: 123). It remained a potent move in favour of reform to trumpet the advantages of having a political system compatible with the main European models of the day.

The new rapport between the state and the liberals after 1905 marginalised the Romantic nationalists from the debate, much as had happened after the Crimean War. And, similar to what happened in 1856–63, in the years from 1905 to 1909 the Romantic nationalist position underwent a transformation. The whole position was lifted away from pan-Slavism, towards the spiritual outlook of Solov'ev. The vital moves were made in a collection of essays on the Russian intelligentsia published in 1909 under the title *Vekhi* (*Landmarks*). A number of the authors belonged to the same circle which – under the name of 'legal Marxists' – had dominated the debate about Europe in the 1890s, and which, it now turned out, had drifted through the liberal camp on their way to Romantic nationalism. Their main target was the uncompromising, atheist and internationalist outlook which they took to constitute the Russian intelligentsia. To Berdyaev, Romantic nationalists such as Solov'ev and Trubetskoy were 'better Europeans' than the social democrats, because they were 'bearers of the universal philosophical spirit and, at the same time, national philosophers laying the foundations for a philosophy of concrete idealism' (Berdyaev, 1967: 19).

This is a by now familiar Romantic nationalist move; the best Russian is, of necessity, the best European, because the spirit can only manifest itself within the community of the nation, and Europe is nothing else than the sum total of its constituent nations. Universalism, it is held, can manifest itself only in an indirect, and therefore particularist, manner. In this fashion, the framework for assessing Europe, the moral judgement of it as well as the relationship which is proposed between Europe and Russia are all reminiscent of Solov'ev's Romantic nationalism: the ideal remains a partnership between European nations in Christ (Zernov, 1963; Read, 1979).

The contributors to *Vekhi* were even prepared to make amends for Europe's secularism, because it was a fruit of organic national developments (and, one may speculate, could therefore also in time be healed by those living organisms). However, no such excuses exist for the Russian intelligentsia. Sergey Bulgakov wrote that Russians borrowed their atheism from the West and accepted it as the last word in European civilisation: 'From the many-branched tree of Western civilisation, with its roots deep in history, we only admired one branch, not wanting to know about the others' (Bulgakov, 1967: 32).[6] This attitude will not do; Russia must find a middle course between what another contributor labels 'the naive, rather starry-eyed Slavophile faith' and 'the rosy utopia of the old Westernism' (Berdyaev, 1967: 22). The point of departure must be the Russian national idea:

> The national idea is not only ethnographic and historical but primarily religious-cultural. It is founded on the religious-cultural Messianism into which any conscious national feeling necessarily flows. This is how it was with

the greatest bearer of the religious-Messianic idea, ancient Israel, and so it remains for any great historical nation (*istoricheskiy narod*). The striving for national autonomy, for the preservation and defence of nationhood (*natsional'nost'*), is the negative expression of an idea whose value lies only in its implied positive content. This is precisely how the national idea was understood by the most prominent exponents of our national self-consciousness – Dostoevskiy, the slavophiles, Vladimir Solov'ev. They linked it with the universal mission of the Russian church or Russian culture. Such an understanding of the national idea does not by any means have to lead to nationalistic exclusiveness. On the contrary, only this understanding can place the idea of a brotherhood of peoples on a positive footing, and not the nation-less, atomised 'citizens' or 'proletarians of all countries' who spurn their homeland (*rodina*).

(Bulgakov, 1967: 61)

Russia has been the 'sentinel of Western civilisation against both savage peoples and the sands of Asia'. An internal Russian development has, however, started to threaten both its organic wholeness and its ties to Europe. The Russian intelligentsia, by renouncing Christ and casting the proletariat in the role meant for the whole nation, has split Russia 'into two seemingly irreconcilable halves'. Only by once again turning to Christ, Bulgakov concludes, can Russia make itself whole again and go on being the vessel of its historic mission. Here, he links up with the main theme of the volume as a whole, which was a call for a new *rapprochement* between state and society in the name of a new spirituality.

The *Vekhi* group was not only able to eschew other variants of Romantic nationalism to make this *the* Romantic nationalist position for the rest of the period, by dint of already being at the heart of the debate about Russia and Europe as individuals, they were also able to bring the Romantic nationalist position back into the thick of the debate.

If the liberals were disturbed by the partial defection of the *Vekhi* group, the Marxists simply saw it as a further sign of the increasing decadence on the right (Lenin, 1961b: 167–75). Their main concern, however, was to diagnose where on the highway of history the events of 1905 left Russia. The

Mensheviks saw it as only one in a series of small steps whereby the burgeoning Russian bourgeoisie would wrest cultural hegemony from the landed gentry. Lenin, however, had pronounced capitalism to be firmly established in Russia already in his first major theoretical work (Lenin, 1958: 1–609, esp. ch.1). Now he moved to pronounce 1905 the end rather than the beginning of bourgeois supremacy in Russia's political life. He wanted the proletariat to carry out the democratic revolution by uniting with the mass of the peasantry, so that it could forcibly crush the opposition of the autocracy and paralyse the instability of the bourgeoisie:

> *The proletariat must complete the socialist revolution (perevorot) by uniting to itself the mass of semi-proletarian elements in the population, in order to break by force the opposition of the bourgeoisie and to paralyse the instability of the peasantry and of the petty bourgeoisie.*
>
> (Lenin, 1960b: 90)

Although Russia did not need to hanker after Europe's example in this respect, that should not be taken to mean that Russia did not remain dependent on Europe's example. The revolutionary struggle in Russia would take its inspiration from progressive Europe. 'The European workers will show us "how it is done", and then we together with them will make the social revolution', Lenin wrote at the end of 1905 (Lenin, 1960b: 157).

Whereas the Mensheviks and the Bolsheviks saw in the events of 1905 only a confirmation of their previous views of Russia's relationship with Europe, it provoked a full-scale new theory of that relationship from Trotskiy. In jail for his leadership of the Petersburg Soviet during the uprising, he wrote a long concluding chapter for a book which was to be called *Our Revolution* (Trotskiy, 1906: 224–86). The starting point of the analysis he took from Parvus. As mentioned above, Parvus held that Russia's development was certainly derivative of its peripheral role in the world capitalist system. A crisis in that system was, however, imminent. It would set off a world revolution, the first act of which would come in Russia. Trotskiy took that move and kitted it out in what is perhaps the first ever fully fledged theory of what was later to be baptised dependent development within the Marxist tradition. Development economics, dependency theory and world system theory share an important – and shamingly unacknowledged – precursor in Trotskiy.

Trotskiy's point of departure is that Russia's historical development did not take place in a vacuum, but rather in constant interaction with surrounding political entities. Although he concedes that climatic considerations placed Russia at a disadvantage because it served to shorten the crop-growing season and thus limit population growth, and that Russia was encircled by hostile forces such as the Tartars, these are to him secondary considerations. The main trait of Russia's development is to be found in the economic base: its 'primitivity and slowness' compared to Europe. It was the military pressure not of the Tartars, but of Lithuania, Poland and Sweden which was decisive. Their military prowess sprang from a more developed economic base.

Up to this point in his comparison of Russia and Europe, Trotskiy has explicitly followed Milyukov. He agrees with the latter, moreover, that 'As a result of the pressure from Western Europe, the state swallowed a disproportionally large share of the surplus products' (Trotskiy, 1906: 236). Their paths separate, however, over the question of the state's autonomous role in Russian development, and to what extent the Russian state is qualitatively different from those of Western Europe. To Trotskiy, the state – in Russia, in Western Europe or anywhere else – remains a tool in the hands of the ruling forces (Troskiy, 1906: 244). As the following long quote should indicate, however, that holds only for a very final analysis:

> Thus the Russian state, erected on the basis of Russian economic conditions, was being pushed forward by the friendly, and even more by the hostile, pressure of the neighbouring state organisations, which had grown up on a higher economic basis. From a certain moment – especially from the end of the seventeenth century – the state strove with all its power to accelerate the country's natural economic development. New branches of handicraft, machinery, factories, big industry, capital, were, so to say, artificially grafted onto the natural trunk. Capitalism seemed to be the offspring of the state.[7]
>
> (Trotskiy, 1906: 228)

Where the difference between the Russian and the West European type of state is concerned, Trotskiy of course concedes that non-socialist societies may operate on different hierarchical principles. However, these differences remain reflections of the economic base, and are therefore not of the essence (Trotskiy, 1906: 226–7). Thus, he agrees with Milyukov that 'at the time when, in the West, the estates created the state, our state power created estates in its own interest (Milyukov)', but is quick to qualify the entire comparison with the comment that estates cannot be fabricated.

The Russian state had to copy European economic development in order to meet the military challenge which sprang from that development. In the process, however, Russian development itself acquired an artificial tinge. For example, the middle class which the state had urged into existence remained extremely weak. Capitalism, Trotskiy writes, entails the town's increasing domination of the land. In Europe, the towns were able to mop up the surplus and use it to create and monopolise a number of social functions which were carried out by and defined the middle classes. Russian towns were, on the other hand, 'similar to the towns of Asian despotisms' in that they remained hollow centres of state administration, unable to dominate the surrounding countryside and thus unable to sustain more than a very tentative bourgeoisie. This, Trotskiy argues, along by now well-established lines, meant that the working class would be compelled to transform the Russian bourgeois revolution into a socialist one. Whereas in France in 1789 'the whole nation' had been behind the bourgeoisie, in Russia the proletariat would embody the nation's will (Trotskiy, 1906: 235, *passim*).

History, Trotskiy held, had put the Russian proletariat in a tricky situation. On the one hand, it had permanently to do what in Europe had once fallen to the bourgeoisie. The absence of strong class opposition and the experience which the Russian proletariat had gained in 1905 and before, soon made it 'a certainty' that the revolution would break out in Europe. On the other hand, Western Europe remained politically and economically more developed than Russia. If the Western European proletariat were not to seize power and thereby remove the ancient military threat to any Russian state, then the world revolution kindled in Russia was doomed: 'Without the direct state support of the European proletariat, the working class of Russia will not be able to remain in power and transform its temporary rule into a lasting socialist dictatorship' (Trotskiy, 1906: 278).

Trotskiy did not, however, see this as much of a problem in practical terms, since history itself would solve it one way or another: 'If the Russian proletariat, having temporarily gained power, does not carry the revolution of its own initiative on to the ground of Europe, then the feudal-bourgeois reaction will *force* it to do so' (Trotskiy, 1906: 280). The end result of this revolutionary process would overcome the differences in development between Russia and Europe by leading to the establishment of what he calls a 'United States of Europe'.

Against this background, Trotskiy performs what is perhaps his most original move. Russia, he writes, is backward compared to Europe not because it is lagging behind it in all respects, but rather because its development is *unbalanced*. Russia was simply not able to copy Europe's development step by step. It had not and could not develop in stages similar to the ones Europe had already gone through, but rather in leaps and bounds. It was this development in fits and starts which had bequeathed on it such an amorphous social structure. It is worth quoting his image of Russia at some length:

> A population of 150 million, 4.4 million square kilometers of land in Europe, 17.5 million in Asia. Within this vast space every epoch of human culture is to be found: from the primeval barbarism of the northern forests, where people eat raw fish and worship blocks of wood, to the modern social relations of the capitalist city, where socialist workers consciously recognize themselves as participants in world politics and keep a watchful eye on events in the Balkans and on debates in the German Reichstag. The most concentrated industry in Europe based on the most backward agriculture in Europe. The most colossal state apparatus in the world making use of every achievement of modern technological progress in order to retard the historical progress of its own country.
>
> (Trotskiy, 1971: 53)[8]

To Trotskiy, then, it was simply *impossible* to abstract Russian developments from European ones; the two were both part of a capitalist world system, whose logic had to be grasped as a whole. But if he refused to reify the differences between Russia and Europe, he was perhaps the one within the Marxist position who most fervently insisted on the difference between progressive Europe on the one hand and the rest of the world, including stagnant Europe, on the other. The way he singles out the town as the agent of all progress and the countryside as the passive recipient of change echoes the difference made by Aksakov between the town and the Land, but inverts the normative judgement passed on the two. Trotskiy does not, however, stop here, but goes on to invest certain parts of the world with an exclusive historical mission. Whereas progressive Europe at any point in time equals 'civilisation', the rest of the world is, in its various incarnations, written off as 'barbarian'. There is 'the barbarism of absolutism and serfdom', the historical barbarism of Russian intellectuals and peasants in lacking a stage of 'bourgeois individualist traditions', the barbarism of the capitalist world in general, as well as of capitalist foreign policy in particular. Lastly, to forestall any remaining doubt about the progressive and civilised status of revolutionary Russia, Trotskiy approvingly quotes Kautsky to the effect that it is no longer possible to see Poland as 'the Eastern-most detachment of revolutionary Europe, cutting it off from Muscovite barbarism' (1906: 254, 262, 282, 281).

Trotskiy's moves were not widely read at the time, and Marxist debate largely continued to discuss the question of how means of production and relations of production differed between the two as if they were compatible entities moving through time with one unequivocally ahead of the other. Other themes, such as the revolutionary potential of different class forces, the preferred tactical alliances between proletarian and non-proletarian forces and the extent to which specific political movements, in Russia and Europe, 'embodied' different class forces were mulled over. In these exchanges, the tradition initiated by Trotskiy in 1904 of always baiting the Bolsheviks for paying too much heed to developments in Russia to the detriment of developments in Europe, continued. E.H. Carr has collected some juicy examples which are worth reproducing here:

A Menshevik journal which appeared spasmodically in Petersburg after the 1905 revolution dubbed the Bolsheviks 'Slavophilizing Marxists'. Plekhanov, as well as the Mensheviks, denounced Lenin's attitude towards the peasantry as non-Marxist and a revival of *narodnik* heresies. In 1912 the Menshevik Axelrod was preaching the need 'to

Europeanize, *i.e.* radically to change, the character of Russian social-democracy, [. . .] and to organize it on the same principles on which the party structure of European social-democracy rests'; and Lenin angrily retorted that 'the notorious "Europeanization" about which Dan and Martov and Trotsky and Levitsky and all the liquidators talk in season and out of season' was 'one of the chief points of their opportunism'. [. . .] Axelrod was like 'a naked savage who puts on a top-hat and imagines himself for that reason European'.

(Carr, 1958: 17–18)

The matter rested there. Trotskiy, convinced of Russia's dependence on European developments – past, present and future – remained adamantly opposed to Russian exceptionalism and Messianism, both in its revolutionary and reactionary guises. He was caustic in an article from 1912 about the 'Russian idea', where he charged that Russians were poor with the accumulated poverty of over a thousand years and that 'our social thought has so far failed to cut its way even with the thin edge into the development of universal human thought'. In the past, Trotskiy continued, the Decembrists had tried to speak for a yet unborn middle class. The populists tried to give voice to the inarticulate peasantry, and now the Marxists tried to speak on behalf of a newly born working class. However, the events of 1905 had intimated the end of this 'substitutism' by pointing to a political reality where the class spoke for itself (Deutscher, 1954: 187–90). 'Substitutism' was the very word Trotskiy used to criticise Lenin's 'party of a new type', and his analysis of Russian–European relations throughout the ages was, among other things, the background for that criticism.

On the eve of the First World War, then, Russian social democrats were at one in separating 'true Europe' from 'false Europe', and in equating the latter with liberal, bourgeois Europe in the same way it had been done in the first party programme of 1898. For example, in 1913 Lenin started an article entitled 'Backward Europe and Advanced Asia' by writing that

The comparison seems like a paradox. Who does not know that Europe is advanced and Asia backward? But the words of the title contain a bitter truth. In civilised and advanced Europe, with its highly developed machine industry, its

90

rich, multiform culture and its constitutions, a point in history has been reached when the commanding bourgeoisie, fearing the growth and increasing strength of the proletariat, comes out in support of everything backward, moribund and mediaeval. The bourgeoisie is living out its last days [. . .] The Europe of our day is advanced not *thanks* to, but *in spite* of, the bourgeoisie [. . .] In 'advanced' Europe, the *sole advanced* class is the proletariat.

(Lenin, 1961b: 166)

To sum up this chapter, the state's reaction to the assassination of Alexander II in 1881 was to narrow political space considerably. The populists, within whose ranks the assassination plot had been hatched, became disillusioned about the extent to which it was possible to stop Russia's copying of Europe and keep industrialisation away from the Russian lands. People like Plekhanov, who, partially under the influence of the events of 1881, were to constitute a self-proclaimed Marxist position before long, saw the answer to the state's repression in an incremental strategy by which socialists assisted the Russian bourgeoisie in copying the economic and political models of bourgeois Europe. The liberals continued to see this as an end in itself. In the 1880s, however, all three positions were marginalised from public debate. By default, the 1880s were dominated by the moves of the Romantic nationalists. Their position was, however, no longer unequivocally pan-Slav, but branched out into a plethora of proposals for how Russia should go about its relations with Europe. Solov'ev's spiritual outlook, with its emphasis on a Russo-European partnership where the Russians were to play a guiding role, inspired people like the *vekhovtsy*, and through them came to dominate the Romantic nationalist position in the last few years of the period. The more xenophobic elements of the position were, however, still very much present, both through their verbal participation and through their key role in the many pogroms of the early 1900s.

The populists, although able to stage a comeback in the 1890s, did not make any innovative moves during the period which has been discussed in this chapter. Their main function in the debate was to serve first as sparring partner and then as whipping-boy for the Marxists. One should, however, be careful about interpreting the populist position's scepticism about the detrimental effects of industrialisation on Europe, and potentially on Russia, as a wholesale refutation of Europe. The Social Revolutionary Party set up by populists in 1902 did after all have a programme which referred to the 'forward countries of the civilised world', meaning the West, and their leading theorist, Viktor Chernov, acknowledged and nursed an active interest in European developments. Nevertheless, since the populists first and foremost held Europe to be the embodiment of a possible Russian future which they did not want, their moral assessment of it was on this basis negative, and the proposed relationship with it one characterised by distance.

The Marxist position became institutionalised in 1898, but within two years, the most active Westernising branch defected to the liberal camp. They quickly established themselves as a vital part of the infrastructure of the liberal position. This was mainly because the state, in reacting to the tumults of 1905, decided to move sufficiently close to the liberal constitutionalist position to establish a national assembly. Like those other rudimentary conduits for popular participation, the *zemstva*, the Duma broadened public space, and made the liberals and their activities more visible.

Already before the liberals embarked on what was to be their finest hour, the Marxist position had suffered a split. It came in 1903 and hinged on whether the Social Democratic Workers' Party should be organised along the lines already realised by European social democracy or whether it should be turned into a tightly disciplined party of a new type.

The Mensheviks, who took up the former position, saw the Russian bourgeoisie as a genuinely revolutionary class. In order to topple tsarist autocracy, the proletariat should therefore make a tactical class alliance with it. The preferred *modus operandi* for the prolatariat in this task, as well as in the incremental struggle to wrest from the autocracy and the bourgeoisie small victories in terms of higher wages, a shorter workday and so on, was to organise and activate a broadly based workers' movement. Russian Marxists, they held, should copy what had happened in Western Europe in the latter half of the nineteenth century and try to gather as many progressive forces as possible within a mass party. In organisational as well as in political work, European social democracy was an indispensable source of inspiration and support. Indeed, for the Mensheviks, European social democracy *was* progressive Europe. As summed up by E.H. Carr, the Mensheviks came to stand for a series of ideas familiar in the practice of Western European socialists – a legal opposition, progress through reform rather than revolution, compromise and cooperation with other parliamentary parties, economic agitation through trade unions. Thus, Menshevism was firmly rooted in Western thought and Western tradition, whereas Bolshevism was not (Carr, 1950: 40; also Deutscher, 1954: 180).

Both among the Mensheviks themselves and among their Bolshevik opponents, the epithet 'European' was used to denote the Menshevik position. Plekhanov, the 'father of Russian Marxism' whom the Mensheviks claimed as their totemic ancestor, had pronounced himself ready to stand 'under the banner of an intelligently conceived Westernism' already at the time when he entered the Russian debate (Keep, 1963: 302). Moreover, the Bolsheviks were on a number of occasions branded as 'Slavophile Marxists' because of their habit of emphasising the advanced cultural and political level of the Russian worker against Menshevik sceptics. The Bolsheviks saw the Russian state as being in the hands of an inner enemy, made up by feudal and to a limited extent bourgeois class forces, which acted in collusion with the bourgeoisie in Europe against the interests of the Russian people. To them, Europe as such was not morally good or bad, but different classes in it were either historically progressive or stagnant. The European bourgeoisies and their tools, the European state apparatuses, were negative forces, while the European working classes and the social democratic workers' movement were historically progressive and therefore positive forces. For the Bolsheviks, the Other was not only stagnant Europe, but included the stagnant part of the social structure *within Russia*. Similarly, progressive Europe included the Russian proletariat. As most Russian nineteenth-century participants in the debate, they saw the issue of Russo-European relations in terms of the philosophy of history. The Other was not merely morally bad, it was an historical abomination. The proposed relationship with the Other was basically one of class struggle. There was, nevertheless, room for tactical alliances with classes which were not decidedly opposed to progress. History moved from feudalism to capitalism to socialism by way of revolutions. Progressive forces in Russia and Europe would make common cause in order to do away with stagnant forces. For the Bolsheviks, the question of Russia and Europe was, therefore, the Manichaean one of delineating the good from the bad. As the Great War broke, it soon became abundantly clear that for the Bolsheviks, contrary to what was the case for the Mensheviks and the great majority of European social democrats, those lines did not coincide with national borders.

6

FROM THE FIRST WORLD WAR TO DE-STALINISATION

The Russian debate about Europe in the period from the First to the Second World War was, like almost all other Russian debates and developments in this period, a rather messy affair. Its dynamism was not generated by the sheer number of positions and the lively interaction between them, as had been the case in the preceding period. To the contrary, the debate contained an ever-decreasing number of positions. Neither was the messiness due to great divisions where different frameworks and moral judgements were concerned. When, at the time of the Russo-Polish War, only the Bolshevik and the Romantic nationalist positions were left in the debate, these issues were all but laid to rest. Instead, the messiness of the debate stemmed from the plethora of views of how to delineate 'Russia' and 'Europe', in-group and out-group. The First World War set the nationalist cat among the social democratic pigeons, inasmuch as the definition of their supra-national in-group – 'true Europe' – came under immediate pressure. The question of the relative importance of national and class identities created immediate confusion as to who the social democratic 'we' actually referred to.

The social democrats were not the only ones to grapple with this problem during this period. When the tsarist regime fell in March 1917, the problem of delineating the in-group also confronted all those who saw Russia as an autocratic project. This problem was then extended to all non-Bolshevik groups once the 'liberal moment' in Russian history came to an end with the Bolshevik coup in November 1917. The non-Bolsheviks had to face up to a reassessment of what Russia and Europe meant to them once the Russian state apparatus had fallen into Bolshevik hands.

However, this reassessment only had a limited impact on the debate, since the state, once captured by the Bolsheviks, immediately redefined public political space. If the state's *ability* fully to control this space was, at least up to the early 1930s, not total, then its *claim* to doing so certainly was. As already mentioned, by the early 1920s the Romantic nationalist position was already the only non-Bolshevik position which was able to find a tenuous foothold at the margin of the debate. As that foothold slipped, only the state's position was left. From that moment onwards, the Russian debate about Europe was reduced to a debate about the position of the state. The Bolsheviks fought it out between themselves as to whether Russia's relationship to Europe should be one of economic integration or isolation, and how 'true Europe' should be delineated from 'false Europe'. Thus, by the 1930s, the Russian debate about Europe was reduced to only one question: How far was it possible for Stalin's state to contract public political space and the in-group of persons who represented 'true Europe'?

At the outbreak of the First World War, the dynamism of the debate was still at a peak. As social democrats throughout Europe stood up for their national leaderships, the carpet was drawn from under the feet of the Menshevik as well as the Bolshevik positions. They were thrown into such a disarray, and were discussing matters along so many different and criss-crossing faultlines, that it may be more appropriate to speak of a social democratic position united in a number of internecine feuds than to stick to the delineation of two separate positions. This confusion was not due directly to the outbreak of war between capitalist European states, the possibility or even the likelihood of which had been casually referred to on a number of occasions within both positions. Capitalism was, after all, held to epitomise 'false Europe', the passing away of which might prove to have unpleasant side effects, but which was nevertheless to be welcomed. Rather, the problem raised went straight to the heart of the delineating of self and Other in the Russian social democratic debate about Europe. A number of Mensheviks and Bolsheviks refused, at the crucial moment, to place the interest of what had up until then been seen as 'true Europe' – that is, the European working movement, including the Russian one – above the interests of 'Russia', however defined. Although there was little overt rallying behind the Russian state from these quarters, their attitudes towards the war effort were so varied that for this reason alone it makes little sense to speak of a Menshevik position and a Bolshevik position on Europe at this particular time. The issue of delineating 'true' Europe from 'false' Europe was corroborated by the existence of similar and concurrent debates about how to react to the war within all the other divisions of European social democracy. In an even greater degree than in Russia, the majorities within these parties rallied around the respective states on whose territories they were active, thus preferring state and nationalism to class and internationalism.

A clear example of the turning of former 'in-groupers' into an enemy is afforded by a private comment of Plekhanov's to a visiting Bolshevik. 'If I were not old and sick', Plekhanov stated, 'I would join the army. To bayonet our German comrades would give me great pleasure' (quoted in Harding, 1981: 12). In this instance, the 'German comrades' are made into Others simply *because* they are 'German'. Another violent reaction against former 'comrades' – that is, people previously held to be the foremost representatives of 'true Europe' – came from Lenin, who dubbed the leaders of the other European social democratic parties 'social chauvinists', 'renegades', 'Kautskyite shits', and so on. Plekhanov and Lenin are at one in redefining humans from in-group to out-group. But whereas Plekhanov does away with the entire *idea* of the European working movement as his 'true European' in-group, Lenin merely pares it down by excluding the present leadership and keeping the masses.

Lenin's new delineation of 'true Europe', which excluded the existing West European social democratic leaderships, had immediate repercussions for the proposed relationship between the Russian and the West European parts of it. If those supporting his slogan of a 'European civil war' were not compromised by class cooperation, it followed that this group was also the natural leader of 'true Europe' in its entirety. It alone was able to read the unfolding of historical forces correctly and draw the appropriate consequences. One of these was to treat the Second International as defunct, and to advocate the setting up of a new International.

None the less, there remained the problem of Russia's comparatively less developed economic base. Lenin still held that '*Only* the advanced countries of the West and North America are ripe for socialism' (Lenin, 1960b: 111). The issue of stages aside, the division drawn here between 'the West' and 'North America' should be noticed as a usual, and *not* an exceptional, usage at this time.

Lenin, however, still did not miss an opportunity to under-line the interdependence of Russia with Western Europe. For example, he held that the bourgeois revolution in Russia was of a piece with the socialist revolution in the West, and, vitally, that if the Russian proletariat could only succeed in concluding the bourgeois revolution in Russia, then that could in and of itself ignite the proletarian revolution 'in the West' (Lenin, 1962f: 27). For Lenin, then, the inclination towards leadership of the entire European social democracy went together with a gravitation towards Trotskiy's general view of how Russia should bridge the gap in economic development separating it from Western Europe by initiating a bourgeois-democratic revolution and then gradually changing it into a socialist one.

Trotskiy, for his part, reacted to the First World War by reit-erating his basic analysis, established nine years before. In November 1914, he wrote that

> In the present historical conditions, the proletariat is not interested in defending an anachronistic national 'Father-land', which has become the main impediment to economic advance, but in the creation of a new, more powerful and stable Fatherland, the republican United States of Europe, as the foundation for the United States of the World. To the imperialist blind alley of capitalism the proletariat can oppose only the socialist organisation of world economy as the practical programme of the day.
>
> (quoted in Deutscher, 1954: 215)

Here was a clear suggestion as to how Russia should relate to a Europe which did not single out a revolution as an absolute breaking point in the sense that one set of relations was neces-sary before the revolution, and another afterwards. All European socialists so inclined could begin to work towards a United States of Europe immediately, since cooperation between capitalist states would strengthen the proletariat more than it would the capitalists. By working for closer international ties of all kinds, Trotskiy maintained, one was also stirring revolutionary ferment.

Bukharin, on the other hand, was not so sure. In *Imperialism and the World Economy*, an abridged version of which first appeared in September 1915, and also elsewhere, he stressed the strength rather than the weakness of the capitalist state, which was being centralised, militarised and perhaps incomparably powerful (Cohen, 1974: 29–30). Bukharin stresses how the *state as entrepreneur* will alert the workers to its class character. Yet he also held that this militaristic state capitalism also had the effect of dampening capitalist competition within the domestic arena, and channelling it to the international one. Whereas capitalist competition was becoming less severe within each particular capitalist state, the world economy remained 'characterized by its highly anarchic structure' (Bukharin, 1972: 53). The conflicts which would inevitably arise between different militaristic state capitalisms would inevitably escalate to war-fighting. In the event, the patriotism which state capitalism had to some extent succeeded in 'penetrating into the souls of the workers' would evaporate, and proletarian revolutions would occur throughout the highly advanced capitalist countries.

Although Bukharin reaches a conclusion which points in the direction of revolution, he does so by sketching a possible future scenario which blurs the line between false, stagnant Europe and 'true', progressive Europe. His suggestion that capitalism has been able somewhat to stabilise itself on the domestic level by availing itself of the state, not only as a check on intracapitalist competition but, crucially, also as a mechanism for instilling false consciousness or 'patriotism' into the working classes, has far-ranging consequences. First, the capitalist state is seen as less of an epiphenomenon than it had before. Second, nationalism is acknowledged as an effective coopting device for the bourgeoisie. Where Trotskiy holds that the idea of a 'Fatherland' has no appeal to the European proletariat, Bukharin acknowledges it as a potent force. In much of the extant Western literature about Bolshevik thinking on nationalism, the assumption is made that Bukharin is opposed to the slogan of national self-determination because he sees nationalism as a negligible force. In fact, the opposite is true. It is exactly *because* Bukharin stresses nationalism as a potent force, not only in less-developed countries but even in advanced capitalist countries where it is no longer economically progressive, that he discards the tactical use of it, *anywhere*, as playing with fire. And third, Bukharin seems to suggest that revolution in advanced capitalist countries can only come about in conditions of severe turmoil on the international level. Since war is an inevitable outgrowth of militaristic state capitalism, this obstacle to revolution may not be too severe (Bukharin is, after all, writing in the midst of the Great War). Nevertheless, Bukharin's argument, that monopoly capitalism inevitably leads to imperialism which in turn leads to war, remains an abstract one. To Bukharin, capitalist Europe is not decisively dead, but retains something of its historical dynamism. Therefore, he does not share Trotskiy's conclusion that it would be conducive to the cause immediately to start working towards a United States of Europe. For him, this would entail playing into the hands of the capitalists. Therefore, he does not support a relationship of cooperation between Russia and other capitalist European states, but limits his support for the building of a United States of Europe to the period when the revolution had already happened.

Lenin wrote a laudatory preface to Bukharin's *Imperialism and the World Economy*, and used it as a launching pad for his own views. Two of them stand out. First, Lenin does not see the European proletariat as permeated by social chauvinism. This is a disease of the social democratic leadership only: 'the national movement is a thing of the *past*' among 'the advanced countries of Western Europe' (cf., Service, 1991: 126, 362 note 172). In 'Eastern Europe', however, it is a thing of the '*present*'. Second, for Lenin this difference in development is but one example of a general, concrete law of historic development, the law of the uneven growth of capitalism within different states. Where Bukharin sees contemporary false Western Europe as a system of more or less undifferentiated militaristic state capitalisms, Lenin pinpoints the *time dimension*. At any given point in time, capitalist states will be more or less advanced and more or less stable relative to one another. In this way, moreover, Lenin adds a crucially important factor to explain the likely occurrence of war between capitalist states. As the relative strength of their economic bases shift, so do their military capabilities. The need to shift the established balance of power between them – the reflection of the relative strength of their economic bases at the time of the previous war, crucially fortified with colonial acquisitions – in order to reflect the ever-changing balance of their economic bases, *must* be resolved by war. Thus, Lenin roots Bukharin's abstract formula of monopoly capitalism leading inevitably to imperialism leading inevitably to war in 'objective' factors, in the proposed law of the uneven development of capitalism. Since the capitalist countries faced different and differently changing economic and social circumstances, there would *always* be a rationale and indeed an inevitable necessity for them to go to war against each other or against third parties. 'Uneven economic and political development is an absolute (*bezuslovnyy*) law of capitalism' (Lenin, 1961d: 354). The incentives for cooperation, on the other hand, would be only relative. Therefore, cooperation between capitalist states objectively had to be of a temporary kind. Such temporary cooperation would, furthermore, be of an objectively reactionary nature, ostensibly because the only incentives strong enough to bring it about would be division of colonies or suppression of the working classes. Lenin did not deny the internationalisation of capital. Instead, he stressed the historical concomitance of capitalism and the nation-state, and maintained that the flow of capital to the colonies was more important than the intercapitalist flows, and that the urge towards military expansion resulting from the law of unequal capitalist development was more important than any political result of the internationalisation of capital (Lenin, 1962d: 299–426). In line with this, he commented that a United States of Europe was possible, 'but to what end? Only for the purpose of jointly suppressing socialism in Europe, of jointly protecting colonial booty *against* Japan and America' (Lenin, 1961d: 354).

To sum up, the First World War scuppered the Menshevik and Bolshevik positions on Europe by bringing up the basic question of delineating self and Other. For some, the idea of 'true Europe' shrunk to cover only Russian social democrats and their Russian allies, and the framework within which they saw the rest of Europe became one of armed confrontation and survival. For others, the framework remained one of economic and political progress, with a 'true', progressive Europe facing a stagnant, false Europe. There were differences over the extent to which the Western European masses could be counted on to remain part of 'true Europe'. Lenin never doubted that they could, and created a separate category which he dubbed the 'workers' aristocracy' to accomodate those who nevertheless seemed not to pass the litmus test. Bukharin feared that the masses could be coopted by 'false', capitalist Europe (and Radek thought that this might already have happened to some extent). Morally, they were at one in condemning false Europe as an inevitably militarist, yet historically *passé* phenomenon.

Where the relationship between Russia and Europe was concerned, only Trotskiy did not place a watertight compartment between pre-revolutionary and post-revolutionary relations. He wanted to work towards implementing a United States of Europe immediately. Lenin's view of trying to turn the ongoing relationship of war into a 'European civil war' of revolution, where the front was to be one of class rather than one of states, clashed with a number of passively defeatist and actively patriotic views. The only issue on which there was anything approaching consensus was that of post-revolutionary relations between Russia and Europe. The main point of contention here was the question of to what extent the principle of national self-determination should characterise the initial stages of these relations. To Trotskiy, the question was immaterial, since he held the nation-state to be an outmoded unit of production. Bukharin, starting from the opposite premise of nationalism's potential strength, wanted to deny any role to the principle altogether. The two were at one in advocating an immediate implementation of the United States of Europe. Lenin held that national self-determination had a role to play in a transitory phase, but concurred that the United States of Europe was the goal to be striven for.

FROM THE NOVEMBER COUP TO THE RUSSO-POLISH WAR

Few of the above ideas would have been worth recording here if it had not been for the fact that, before the First World War came to an end, they had acquired a state apparatus to prop them up. In February 1917, it appeared that the autocracy's mismanagement of the political debate was such that it could mobilise no support whatsoever once it came under a mild direct threat. The change in government personnel and policy transformed public political space. As a result, the balance between the different positions in the Russian debate about Europe changed utterly. The constitutionalist position took centre stage for little over half a year, only to be eschewed by the Marxist debate after the coup in November. Different assessments of the potential for 'true Europe' to do away with 'false Europe' on a pan-European scale played a role in the Bolshevik debate on the eve of the coup, with Zinov'ev and Kamenev voting against what they saw as premature action. Stalin, on the other hand, stated that 'There are only two lines: one sets the course for the victory of the revolution and relies on Europe, the second does not believe in the revolution and counts only on being an opposition' (Stalin, 1950b: 381). Stalin held that,

> The possibility that Russia will be the country which will point the way to socialism is not excluded ... the basis for our revolution is broader than in Western Europe [...] It would be unworthy pedantry to demand that Russia should 'wait' with socialist transformation as long as Europe does not 'begin'. The country to begin is the one with the greatest possibilities.
>
> (Stalin, 1950a: 186, 174)

The Bolsheviks put all their eggs in the basket of progressive Europe, and went through with the coup.

The delineation of public space imposed by the Bolshevik state, which from 1919 onwards saw increasing efficiency, was more restrictive than anything seen during the nineteenth century. 'There cannot be two powers in the state', Lenin had declared in the April thesis which laid down the Bolshevik line. Since state and people were said to have a fully coinciding commonality of interests, it followed that there could not be more than one power, or one public opinion, anywhere within public political space. A resolution passed by the Eighth Party Congress in 1919 spelled this out with admirable clarity:

> The Communist Party makes it its task to win decisive influence and complete leadership in all organizations of the workers: in trade unions, cooperatives, village communes, etc. The Communist Party strives especially to establish its programme and its complete leadership in the contemporary state organizations, which are the Soviets. [...] The Russian Communist Party must win for itself undivided political mastery in the Soviets and practical control over all their work.
>
> (quoted in Carr, 1950: 219)

Since the formula 'the organizations of the workers' here effectively covers *any* organisation allowed to exist by the state under the principles of 'revolutionary legitimacy', the *claim* to equate power and knowledge is indeed total.

This way of delineating public political space had direct repercussions for the Russian debate about Europe. If 'there cannot be' more than one power in the state, and that power has to be the party, and the party-permeated state is the only 'real' state in the sense that it is the only historically progressive state, then any power and knowledge outside it must necessarily be atavistic. Thus, Stalin maintained in October 1920 that

> The so-called independence of so-called independent Georgia, Armenia, Poland, Finland, etc., is only a deceptive appearance masking the complete dependence of these – pardon the word – states on this or that group of imperialists.
>
> (Stalin, 1950d: 353)

This attempt to restrict the debate does not in and of itself tell us what discursive practice will be like. But neither does it allow for anything other than a Manichaean practice where 'false Europe', that entity consisting of internal and external enemies, is concerned. The proposed relationships with 'false Europe' – tsarist technical personnel, Russian middle peasants, German petit bourgeois, Polish officers, and so on – can vary. Yet the moral assessment of them as wholly Other than Bolshevik Russia and the 'true Europe' of which it stands at the head – morally inferior, held to be hostile of intent because of the historically non-productive role ascribed to them – is given as one of the very limits of discussion. It is therefore 'no coincidence' that, whereas in the tsarist period the debate focused on the *relationship* with Europe, in Bolshevik discourse this question always had to share centre stage with the *delineation* of 'true Europe'. We now proceed to examine these two questions, starting with the relationship to 'false Europe'.

The state which the coup-makers took over was allied to some European states, and at war with others. The German enemy stood on its territory. Before long, the former allies would intervene militarily in the civil war on the side of stagnant Europe's Russian chapter. Two questions presented themselves where the relationship with 'false Europe' was concerned. The first was whether the Bolsheviks should align their proclaimed workers' state with certain capitalist countries – that is, whether tactical alliances disregarding the class content of states were warranted. The second question was to what extent the class war of the workers' state and progressive Europe against stagnant Europe should be pursued, and in what manner. These two questions were often discussed together, and two basic views existed.

The first view stressed the importance of fighting the remnants of stagnant Europe *within* the workers' state – the inner enemy – first, and only then allying with the rest of progressive Europe to do away with stagnant Europe at large. Stalin, who only months before had exhorted his fellow Bolsheviks to 'rely on Europe', at the Seventh Party Congress in January 1918 maintained that 'there is no revolutionary movement in the West, no facts, only a potential, and we cannot count only on a potential' (Stalin, 1950c: 27). Ryazanov argued squarely that the party 'was bound to be confronted with a dilemma at the moment when it seized power, and would have to decide the question whether to rely on the [Russian] peasant masses or on the proletariat of western Europe' (Carr, 1953: 52). Lenin, however, argued that it was simply a matter of order of priority which enemy should be confronted first, the outer or the inner. On the eve of the coup, he stated that

> Because of the revolution, Russia in a few months was able to catch up (*dognat'*) the advanced countries where *political* organisation is concerned. But this is [too] little. War is inexorable and puts the question with unsparing sharpness: either perish, or catch up and overtake (*peregnat'*) the advanced countries *economically* as well.
>
> (Lenin, 1962b: 198)

The unspoken assumption here is that Parvus and Trotskiy's view of the combined development of Russia, that is, the view that Russia's development did not copy that of Europe stage by stage, but unevenly, and always in the closest dialectical sequence with it, could be applied to the situation immediately at hand. Lenin does not stress how Russia and Europe can be brought up to par by means of an immediate political victory for progressive Europe in the West, too. Rather, he stresses how Russia must now concentrate on balancing economic developments within Russia and Western Europe. For Lenin, however, the economic dimension remains a decisive one in terms of socialism's final victory. In November 1917, he asserts that 'We shall march firmly and unswervingly to the victory of socialism which will be sealed by the leading workers of the most civilized countries and give to the peoples solid peace and deliverance from all oppression and all exploitation' (quoted in Carr, 1950: 107). Russia, despite its 'catching up' politically, remains less 'civilised' than economically advanced progressive Europe.

Having excluded the European social democrat leadership from progressive Europe for their 'social chauvinist' position at the outbreak of the First World War, Lenin did not, for the time being, proceed to pare it down even further. This becomes abundantly clear in an episode from the Executive Committee rendered by E.H. Carr:

> When an anarchist deputy in a debate in the VTsIK [the All-Russian Central Executive Committee] in 1918 pointed out that, whereas the Russian proletariat was not 'state-minded', the western proletariat 'feels itself as the bearer of a fragment of power and as a part of this same state which it is at present defending', Lenin retorted with unusual asperity that this view of the western worker was 'so stupid that I do not know how it could be more so'.
>
> (Carr, 1953: 180)

For Lenin, then, the progressive character of the European working class remained a basic premise. In a fashion characteristic of Bolshevik thinking about ends and means, Lenin also specified that progressive Europe was not defined by its actions, but by its goals. 'While the revolution in Germany still lingers', he wrote at this time,

> it is our task to teach ourselves the state capitalism of the Germans, to imitate it *with all our strength* not to spare *dictatorial* methods in order to hasten the copying of Westernism by barbarous Russia (*Rus'*) even more than did Peter, not shrinking from barbarous methods of struggle against barbarism.
>
> (Lenin, 1962c: 302)

In the interim before progressive Europe has done away with stagnant Europe, clashes with that external enemy were certain to occur, and recur. This point Lenin made repeatedly, as to the Eighth Party Congress in March 1919:

We are living not merely in a state, but in a *system of states* (*v sisteme gosudarstva*); and it is inconceivable that the Soviet republic should continue to exist for a long period side by side with imperialist states. Ultimately one or the other must conquer. Until this end occurs, a number of terrible clashes between the Socialist republic and bourgeois states is inevitable.

(Lenin, 1963a: 139)

Nevertheless, developing workable relations with capitalist Europe was at the same time clearly a priority. Hence, Lenin and others more than once referred to early agreements with Britain (on prisoners) and Estonia (a peace treaty) as the first 'windows on Europe' which the Bolsheviks were able to open (Carr, 1953: 157). This metaphor, well known in Russian tsarist discourse as the rationale behind Peter the Great's construction of St Petersburg as a 'window on Europe', now emerged in acknowledgement of the need to establish some kind of rapport with stagnant Europe, however doomed it was historically.

The second view on the question of to what extent and in what manner the class war of the workers' state and progressive Europe against stagnant Europe should be pursued, was represented primarily by Bukharin. He favoured a relationship with stagnant Europe characterised by 'a holy war against militarism and imperialism' (quoted in Cohen, 1974: 66). Stephen Cohen has suggested that this may have been a result of Bukharin's moral judgement of capitalist Europe as a threat, not only to the Bolsheviks as such but to the Bolsheviks' charge, namely, world civilisation itself, or 'mankind's culture'. 'Humpbacks', as Bukharin remarked at another occasion, 'are only cured by death' (quoted in Cohen, 1974: 99). The problem with the ossified capitalism of Europe, however, was that it would not curl up and keel over by itself, but could, as Bukharin had asserted already three years before, most easily be broken in an international war. Therefore, the Bolshevik state should not enter tactical alliances with capitalist states, but should, on the contrary, seize the opportunity presented by the turmoil of war to ally with progressive Europe in an apocalyptic struggle against stagnant Europe in order to save European and world civilisation.

Bukharin was far from being the only one to call for a 'holy war' with capitalist Europe at this time. Already, in December 1917, Trotskiy had exclaimed that 'we, the party of the Bolsheviks and, I hope, the Left SR's, will summon all to a holy war against the militarists of all countries' (quoted in Carr, 1953: 33). Still, as Trotskiy and others gradually left this position, it ceased to be viable. It reappeared in the debate during the Russo-Polish War of 1920, when the Red Army stood at the Vistula and it was debated whether to press on westwards. After that, this position of a war of movement against stagnant Europe was eschewed to the margin of the debate by those favouring a war of position.

Western historiography on the initial period of Bolshevik power is forever pondering the existence of these two widely different models for the relationship with Europe within the state (for example, Melograni, 1989). For our purposes, however, the important thing to notice is that the Bolshevik debate was conducted *between* these two positions; at no time during this period did one or the other position disappear from the debate. The same literature often highlights the restrictions imposed on the debate when the party put a lid on organised opposition, and insists that since the spring of 1921, external opposition to the Bolsheviks came to a halt. E.H. Carr, for example, concedes that 'sharp differences of opinion continued to exist. But they were now concentrated within the party. The party had drawn into itself the whole political life of the country. Its internal affairs were henceforth the political history of the nation' (Carr, 1950: 177).

At least where the debate about Europe is concerned, Carr's view is certainly an overstatement. A number of discursive moves from inside and outside of 'the workers' state' continued to be made, and to crop up in the domestic discourse. Indeed, the Bolsheviks' rearranging of the debate in and of itself generated more new moves from other positions than had the First World War. In fact, the Great War had remarkably little effect on the non-social-democratic positions. Whereas social democrats had to reconsider the question of who constituted their in-group afresh, the other positions all held 'Russia', variously defined, to be their in-group, and so did not have to re-delineate it as a consequence of the war.

There seems to be only one additional reaction to the First World War worthy of mention, and it came from within the

Romantic nationalist position. Nikolay Berdyaev, a member of the *Vekhi* group discussed in the previous chapter, proclaimed the war to be the midwife of a new global culture. Berdyaev built explicitly on Dostoevskiy's and Solov'ev's idea of Russia as a world unto itself, standing as it did between East and West, yet being for this very reason also the most 'all-human' *(vsechelovecheskiy)* of all the world's peoples. This position, Berdyaev maintained, made Russia uniquely able to counter two provincialisms which had crippled it in the past. One is the provincial debate between Westernisers and Slavophiles, which will disappear together with the hard and fast distinction between East and West. The other is *Europe's* provincialism. To Berdyaev, Europe is not a cultural ideal at all, but is itself provincial. Under the new circumstances, the political mind everywhere has to grasp the whole plurality of different cultures, and this will necessarily imply the end of Europe's cultural monopoly both as a subject, and as an object of the attention of other cultures (Zen'kovskiy, 1955: 155 *passim*).

This is a highly interesting position for the student of international relations. Berdyaev sees Europe's cultural hegemony over international society as unwarranted, and demands and expects its demise. Morally, Europe's right to lay down the law in international relations is called into question. Instead, Berdyaev advocates that Russia's relationship to Europe should be a culturally pluralistic one, where Europe recognises Russia's cultural specificities and enters into a partnership with it on the basis of respect for that specificity. While the view that the Russian people is the most 'all-human' of all peoples led Dostoevskiy to advocate proselytising and Solov'ev to press for a Christian partnership, Berdyaev elaborates on Solov'ev's stand and spells out the pluralist implications of it.

Whereas the First World War had thrown the social democrats into utter disarray, leaving the other positions remarkably stable, the revolutionising activity of the Bolsheviks in the wake of the November coup forced rethinking from within the other positions (Burbank, 1986). Just as the war had forced the social democrats to re-evaluate the delineation of 'true Europe', the regime change in Russia and the havoc it wrought for the configuration of state, government and nation forced all non-Bolsheviks to reconsider just *which* Russia was their in-group. As the First World War subsided, Mensheviks tried once again to lay claim to the socialist high ground. Aksel'rod charged the Bolsheviks with having 'betrayed socialism by abandoning Western ideals like political freedom, democracy, constitutionalism and parliamentary institutions for a "special Russian path"' (quoted in Burbank, 1986: 46–51). To Martov, Bolshevik activity was a premature attempt 'to plant a European ideal on Asiatic soil' (quoted from a private letter in Burbank, 1986: 21), a project which could lead to nothing but a distortion of socialism. Liberal constitutionalists like Milyukov joined in, and even former social revolutionaries like Chernov now started to talk about the Russian backwardness which perhaps necessitated such developments as those set in train by the Bolsheviks (Burbank, 1986: esp. 67–85). These musings remained the voices of isolated men, however, and the positions from which they sprang were not able to reconstitute themselves within Russia for another fifty years.

The only non-Bolshevik position which managed to remain in the debate as such was Romantic nationalism. Berdyaev and his associates from *Vekhi* had a second volume printed in 1919.[1] Whereas in the period before 1917 Berdyaev followed Solov'ev's lead in seeing Russia as part of a 'European civilisation' from which it could learn, Berdyaev the exile eulogised Russia and treated Europe as a spiritually dead entity for which only one cure remained: 'Fascism is the only creative phenomenon in the political life of contemporary Europe' (Berdyaev, 1924: 28). Politics literally boiled down to a question of *blood*: 'The question of national self-determination is not an abstract juridical question, but above all a biological, and in the last instance a mystico-biological question' (Berdyaev, 1923: 74). Indeed, Berdyaev was not discriminating in his faith in the healing power of organic nationalism, whatever institutional fashion it chose to avail itself of.

However, it was not Berdyaev and associates who carried the can of Romantic nationalism inside Russia, but a number of literary tendencies such as Scythianism and 'Fellow Traveller-ism', propped up by two political coteries: *smenovekhovtsy* and the Eurasianists (*evraziysty*).

The *smenovekhovtsy* named themselves after one of their journals (*Smena vekh*, change of landmarks), the name of which was a take-off on the *Vekhi* group formed by Berdyaev and associates.[2] Their leader, Nikolay Vasil'evich Ustryalov, saw the state and the nation as synonymous, and repeatedly stressed the importance of size, and consequently of territorial expansion, for the well-being of the state. 'The foreign policy of Russia', he had written already in 1916, 'must be the policy of imperialism. Imperialism is the legitimate way of all great states. Russia must behave aggressively' (Agursky, 1987: 185). Yet, as he stressed after the revolution, Russia was not alone in this:

> Only a 'physically' powerful state can possess a great culture. The natures of 'small powers' have the possibility to be elegant, honourable, even 'heroic', but they are organically incapable of being great. This requires a grand style, a grand sweep, a grand scale of thought and action – 'the brush of a Michelangelo'. A German, a Russian, an English 'messianism' is possible. But, let us say, a Serb, Rumanian or Portuguese messianism grates on the ear like a false note.
>
> (quoted in Carr, 1950: 372 note)

Nevertheless, Ustryalov followed Danilevskiy, Berdyaev and earlier Romantic nationalists in seeing Russia as the youthful and therefore superior challenger to Europe, whose 'idea' was burning out. He came to see the Bolsheviks as an organic outgrowth of Great Russia, and, moreover, as the force which would be able to infuse it with a nourishing programme of expansion. Indeed, he conceptualised contemporary Russian politics as a struggle between neo-Westernisers and neo-Slavophiles, with his own group thrown in with the latter and victory-bound side. As another *smenovekhovets* expressed it, the Russian intelligentsia was penetrated by the mystique of the state, and this could propel it towards the sublime goal of making the Russian state into 'the way of God on earth' (Carr, 1958: 57). Isai Lezhnev, characterised by Ustryalov as belonging to the opposite wing of the same trend as he did, wrote an article in 1924 where he forecast that the twentieth century would be a cataclysmic struggle between a 'coalition of those countries and races with low fertility and highly advanced culture and another coalition of those countries and races with high fertility and a relatively low level of culture' (Agursky, 1987: 314). In this struggle, Europe would not emerge victorious, but Russia would be the mediating and synthesising focal point out of which the new world would dawn.

This forecast dovetails with the thrust of the other coterie making up the Romantic nationalist position in the debate, the *evraziysty* or Eurasianists. In a closely argued book published in 1920, *Europe and Humanity*, Prince Nikolay Sergeevich Trubetskoy delivered a blistering attack against the very idea that Russia and other non-European countries should look to Europe for political and economic models. Before the revolution, Trubetskoy wrote, it had been almost 'organically inadmissible' for most people, educated as they were in the European manner, to grasp the idea that Russia's involvement with Europe was an historical mistake (Trubetskoy, 1920: III-IV). Europe does not equal civilisation; this is merely a 'formula of chauvinistic cosmopolitanism' (Trubetskoy, 1920: 2). Rather, Europe is 'the product of the history of a specific ethnic group', and 'the so-called European "cosmopolitanism"' should 'openly be called *common Romano-Germanic chauvinism*' (Trubetskoy, 1920: 5, 6). Russia has not grasped this, but has looked to Europe as a 'higher culture' and a model for its own development. But since there exists no rational yardstick by which to compare cultures, such an attitude is unwarranted. It is, moreover, impossible to implement, and any attempt to do so is fraught with negative consequences which the Russian intelligentsia has not thought through.

If a people opts for a Europeanising course, Trubetskoy argues, then it has to gear its entire development towards European models, and to shear off all the discoveries which do not square with this concept. Its originality sacrificed, it is condemned to the Sisyphean role of the epigone. Cultural dependence and degeneration are the inevitable outcomes. The Europeanised people

> must relate not to its own psychology, but to a foreign, Romano-German psychology. Without batting an eyelid, it must adopt all that constitutes and is considered valuable by the Romano-Germans themselves, even if it contradicts its national psychology.
>
> (Trubetskoy, 1920: 61-2)

Since it cannot do all these things in one step, the Europeanised people will be torn to pieces by generational and social tensions. National unity will suffer. And to what end? No matter *how* hard it tries, some of its specific traits will remain, and it will, 'from the European point of view, always look "backward" (*otstalyy*)' (Trubetskoy, 1920: 64). The result is that 'only the government and the ruling political circles' will retain a national outlook, while the rest of the people will be demoralised and self-loathing (Trubetskoy, 1920: 65).

This state of affairs will be aggravated by the sporadic events of the backward people mustering its forces and making a dash to catch up (*pryshka nagnat'*), trying to take in its stride developments which the Romano-Germans may have undergone over a prolonged period of time.

> The result of such 'evolution' by fits and starts (*skachyshchiy*) is indeed horrific. Every leap is inevitably followed by a period of seeming (from the European point of view) stagnation (*zastoy*), during which the results of the leap must be made to dovetail with the backward elements of the culture.
>
> (Trubetskoy, 1920: 68–9)

The inevitable result is a cycle of 'progress' and 'stagnation'. 'And so', Trubetskoy concludes, 'the upshoot of Europeanisation is so heavy and horrible that it cannot be considered a good, but [, on the contrary,] a bad thing' (Trubetskoy, 1920: 69–70).

Trubetskoy, one of the fathers of Prague Structuralism, stresses that his is a *structural* analysis, where European intentions play no role. Yet Europe happens to be militaristic and capitalist (Trubetskoy, 1920: 70). For the non-European world, therefore, the choice is really one of either being colonised or adopting Europe's military technology in order to fight Europe lock, stock and barrel, which would necessarily also entail accepting its technology in its entirety. 'This entails that in one way or the other, Europeanisation seems unavoidable' (Trubetskoy 1920: 71–2). After all, even Peter the Great only wanted to borrow from Europe so that Russia could eventually turn her back on it. The only reason for hope is that militarism and capitalism are not eternal phenomena. Socialism seeks to put an end to them. Yet this is a paradox, since the socialists more than anybody else stand for internationalism and armed cosmopolitanism, and are therefore inevitably condemned to perpetuate Europeanisation as a phenomenon. The only real solution seems impossible to implement, Trubetskoy writes, yet he nevertheless offers it: 'Slavs, Chinese, Indians, Arabs, Negros and other tribes' constituting humanity, 'not the humanity about which the Romano-

Germans love to talk, but the real humanity', must fight the Europeans (Trubetskoy, 1920: 76). Their first task must be to win back their own, Europeanised intelligentsias. This is the drama of world history, Trubetskoy exclaims in the last sentence of the book: 'there is truly only one conflict: the Romano-Germans versus all the rest of the world, *Europe and* [that is, versus] *Humanity*' (Trubetskoy, 1920: 82).

In a book published by the Eurasianists two years later, in 1922, Trubetskoy suggested that this strategy was no longer impossible to implement, but, on the contrary, that its time had come (*Na putyakh: Utverzhdenie evraziytsev, kniga 2*, 1922). In another volume of Eurasianist writings, moreover, P.N. Savinskiy argued that

> the centre of world culture had moved along a declining temperature gradient at a rate of five degrees centigrade approximately every thousand years: from ancient Mesopotamia and Egypt with an average yearly temperature of 20 °C; to Greece and Rome at 15 °C; to Gaul (10 °C); to northern Europe (5 °C). No historical evidence could be decisive, he admitted, but this trend boded well for Canada and Russia in the third millennium A.D.
>
> (quoted in Burbank, 1986: 216–17)

Themes from earlier Romantic nationalists such as the Slavophiles, Leont'ev and Danilevskiy are readily recognisable in the writings of Trubetskoy and the other Eurasianists: the idea of history as a relay race where Russia is about to accept the baton, the idea that Russia should seek allies in Asia in its fight against Europe and the characterisation of European culture as a specific Romano-German type from which Russia should keep its distance. The idea that Europe has usurped the role of representative of 'humanity' echoes Sokolov, and also Berdyaev's critique of what he saw as European provincialism. Yet, coupled with the analysis of the derivative and unbalanced nature of 'Europeanisation' as a general phenomenon, where Trubetskoy echoes themes from the writings of Milyukov and Trotskiy on the development of Russia, these ideas add up to a powerful diagnosis of Russo-European relations.

Furthermore, by developing his analysis of global social change within a structuralist framework, where the position of any one element is dependent on the position of all the others,

Trubetskoy presents an argument which is echoed in the literature on structural dependence between 'the core' and 'the periphery' which emerged in international relations literature after the Second World War. Even the central idea of under-development as a phenomenon which is *inherent* in these relations, and not external to them – 'the development of under-development' – is clearly present in Trubetskoy's argument (see Frank, 1969: 3–17). Trubetskoy's moral assessment of Europe as an aggressive, *passé* and wholly alien culture, and his stress on the need for a relationship of struggle, and if necessary armed struggle, were, however, hardly new to the Romantic nationalist position.

The Romantic nationalist position as a whole was, then, at one in undertaking a radical re-delineation of the Russian in-group. Romantic nationalists all saw the revolution as the culmination of the conflict between the land and the town – between the Europeanised elite and the people – with which Romantic nationalists had struggled throughout the nineteenth century. Jane Burbank, in her aforementioned study of the intelligentsia's reaction to the revolution, sees the thrust of nationalist thinking in their point that 'the people had acted on their hatred not only of the government, but of the "city", the "bourgeois", the Jew, everything not their own' (Burbank, 1986: 235–6). The intellectual Romantic nationalists, reared as they were in a European tradition, acknowledged that in the eyes of simple, non-Europeanised Russians, they belonged with the European out-group. Yet this state of affairs threatened to falsify their view of Russia as an organic nation by introducing a lack of cohesion between head and body. Rather than trying to fill this white spot with new meaning, they chose to leave it unexplored. But this also entailed that the Russian people itself was largely left unexamined, making its appearance in Romantic nationalist texts only as an ill-defined blur.

The tension within the Romantic nationalist position between those who want a head-on clash with Europe and those who stress that nations are at one in striving to realise their historical idea, is pronounced. The relationships between Russia and Europe proposed by Danilevskiy and Solov'ev respectively, are perpetuated by Trubetskoy and Berdyaev, with Ustryalov's stress on territorial expansion placing him closer to the former than to the latter.

As the 1920s wore on and public political space became more and more circumscribed, the Romantic nationalist position was forced to the margins of the debate. The return of a number of Romantic nationalist exiles to Soviet Russia during this period did not impact this trend in the slightest. For the rest of the interwar period, and indeed up to the mid-1960s, the Bolshevik position was the only one present in the debate. At the same time, the diversity of the Bolshevik position declined more and more, to the point where, at the end of the 1930s, it was wholly identical with the state's position. That is the drama of the rest of the chapter.

FROM THE RUSSO-POLISH TO THE SECOND WORLD WAR

Defeat in the Russo-Polish War as well as domestic developments, such as the Kronstadt rebellion and the introduction of the New Economic Policy, combined to constrict and concretise the political field for Russian Bolsheviks. In his closing speech at the Tenth Party Conference in May 1921, Lenin held that 'The current international situation is such that some sort of a temporary, unstable equilibrium (*ravnovesie*), but equilibrium for all that, has been established' (Lenin, 1963b: 340). This statement opened the possibility that the existence of two social systems might drag out further than earlier anticipated. The Soviet debate would, from this time onwards, recurrently contain statements to the effect that the force of capitalism was not yet spent. This debate about the state of the capitalist world and the correlation of forces provided a backdrop for the debate about Europe for the rest of the Soviet period (Light, 1988: esp. 249–93; Lider, 1986).

The dynamics of this debate were found in two successive developments which played themselves out in a steadily contracting public political space. They took place against the backdrop of the Russo-Polish War, which did much to temper enthusiasm for military action. Petr Wandycz (1969: 286) goes as far as to see it as epoch-making: 'The settlement of 1921 stopped the Soviet westward advance, stabilized the situation in Eastern Europe – and indeed in Europe – and excluded Russia from international politics for at least sixteen years. This was a breakdown of the Bolshevik revolutionary programme.'

The first of the two developments was entangled with the power struggle between Trotskiy and Stalin and posed two different views of relations with 'false Europe' in stark opposition to each other. Trotskiy, who, during the years of war communism had advocated Russian economic isolation, now came to see Russia as politically strong enough to re-enter economic relations with the rest of Europe. Resuscitating the slogan of a 'United States of Europe', Trotskiy's 'integrationist' view stressed how economic interaction with Western Europe would strengthen Russia's economic base, and also how it would further the economic development of Europe as a whole, thereby helping the coming of socialism. Against the integrationists stood the isolationists, such as Stalin, who emphasised the building of 'socialism in one country' and saw it as economically feasible for Russia to do this without being part of a single and steadily integrating world economy. The second development in the Russian debate about Europe in this period concerned the further delineation of 'true Europe', and was bound up with the feasibility of forcibly industrialising Russia by means of a 'revolution from above'. Stalin's interventions into the debate steadily decreased the size of 'true Europe', placing ever new persons and groups outside the perimeters of the Bolshevik in-group. At the same time, he steadily increased the unity of 'false Europe' by stressing how different out-groups were working in tandem: 'Enemies of the people', 'wreakers' and 'double-dealers' were also invariably spies of some West European country.

This clash over relations with 'false Europe' was not a question of different frameworks being used or different moral assessments made. 'False Europe' continued to be seen by Bolsheviks in terms of the antagonism of two different economic systems: the modernising socialist and the moribund capitalist. The moral assessment of the system characterising false Europe as reactionary and inferior was, moreover, not in doubt. Rather, the question was whether the triumph of 'true Europe' could best be furthered by means of a relationship of economic integration or economic isolation. The view that the relationship between 'true Europe' and 'false Europe' should be one of holy war was not wholly absent from the debate. For example, the manifesto of the Workers' Group presented at the Twelfth Party Congress in 1923 left no doubt, stressing that 'the party of the proletariat must with all its strength and energy preach civil war in all leading capitalist countries' (quoted in Carr, 1954: 269). Nevertheless, this view, which had been one of the two main views in the late 1910s, was now clearly at the margin of the debate.

The integrationist view was represented by Trotskiy. Russia was the mainstay of progressive Europe, the rest of which would in due course come to sustain it. 'The revolution', he wrote in 1923, 'means the final break of the people with Asianism, with the 17th century, with holy Russia, with ikons and cockroaches, not a return to the pre-Petrine period, but on the contrary an assimilation of the whole people of civilization' (quoted in Carr, 1958: 144). Russia was turning away from the 'Asianism' of tsarist autocracy and Muscovy traditions, towards the most advanced 'civilization' ever, that of progressive Europe. In an article in *Pravda*, Trotskiy tied this analysis to his slogan of the United States of Europe. The peoples of Europe, he wrote, 'should work together as closely as possible to save our continent from economic demoralisation and enslavement by American capital' (Trotskiy, 1924: 369; see also Goodman, 1960: 153–9). 'Europe is not a geographical term, but an economic one', he continues. By uniting, it can hatch in its midst the beginning of a world federation, a process which is easier to initiate on a European than on a world scale, since Europe is immeasurably 'more concrete' than the world economy. And the faster this process of unification can be implemented, the faster comes the revolution, Trotskiy concludes.

Whereas Lenin in 1915 had seen a united capitalist Europe only as one of three vying centres of the capitalist world economy, Trotskiy depicts it here as a force for the defence of European culture *vis-à-vis* young, brash and virile America. When Trotskiy stresses that the whole Russian people will assimilate culture, moreover, he refers not to the proletariat, which is already part of 'progressive Europe', or to the Russian bourgeoisie, which is the local remnant of 'stagnant Europe', but to the peasantry. Significantly, the Russian peasantry is seen as an entity which is neither self nor Other, but which is hovering somewhere between progressiveness and stagnation. This highly significant issue was highlighted more clearly by Gorkiy, who, in 1924, argued that the fundamental obstacle on the path of Russia's progress towards Europeanisation and culture was 'the overwhelming predominance of the illiterate countryside over the town, the zoological individualism of the peasantry, and its almost total lack of social feelings.' For Gorkiy it is not the peasants, but the Russian intelligentsia, by which he meant 'the educated people and the workers', which could bring Russian history forward (Carr, 1958: 122–3).

The problem of delineating progressive Europe from stagnant Europe where the European workers' movement was concerned, therefore had a domestic parallel, which was also discussed in terms of 'Europeanisation'. Now, the crucial point in Trotskiy's integrationist view was that 'false Europe' still had a part to play in the 'Europeanisation of Russia'. Since not only Europe, but the entire world, was economically of a piece, and since Soviet Russia was now so well established that it could hold its own in economic interaction with the rest of the world, relations with 'false Europe' should be characterised by as much economic intercourse as possible (White, 1985).

'The operative question for Trotsky', Richard Day argues in his book on the economic debates of the 1920s, 'was not *whether* Russia could build socialism in advance of the international revolution, but *how* to devise an optimal planning strategy, taking into account both the existing and the future international division of labour' (Day, 1973: 4). From the moment when Trotskiy thought Russia could afford to treat the question of foreign trade as an economic rather than a political one, he was an 'integrationist', opposed to Stalin's 'isolationism'. The isolationists, Day continues, 'tended to look upon Soviet Russia as an exile from the world economy; the integrationists, in contrast, believed that, despite the country's unique political order, in one manner or another Russia must resume her previous position in international affairs' (Day, 1973: 5). A closed economy (*zamknutoe khozyaystvo*) could only lead to stagnation. Moreover, trade with the capitalists would also deliver a new lever into their hands: 'capitalism is not experiencing any kind of industrial recovery and cannot manage without us. All Europe is crying out about this ... they are forced to come to an agreement with us', the Narkom of Finance, Sokol'nikov, argued. He warned against fortifying the economic protectionist line between Russia and Europe into a 'Chinese Wall' (Day, 1973: 74). Trotskiy elaborated on this by arguing that the more diversified Soviet foreign policy became, the harder it would be for its possible enemies to fight it. Whatever obstacles they could place in its way, be it war or blockade, would still be less of a problem to live with than the belated development and weakness which would be the result of a policy of so-called self-sufficiency (Trotsky, 1926: 128).

The isolationists inveighed against integrationists such as Trotskiy that they 'lacked faith' in the Russian peasant and his progressive nature. This was the main charge in an article by Stalin published in December 1924, where he introduced the phrase 'socialism in one country' (Stalin, 1947b: 362 *passim*). The phrase itself was culled from a 1915 article by Lenin, and Stalin presented the policy as the antithesis of the 'Menshevik' theory of permanent revolution, part of which was made up by what we have chosen to call 'integrationism'.

The struggle within the party between integrationists and isolationists was settled in a Central Committee resolution of January 1925, which was passed as a dressing down of Trotskiy. It postulated a 'Trotskyism', and defined it as the 'falsification of communism in the spirit of approximation to "European" patterns of pseudo-Marxism, i.e. in the last resort, in the spirit of "European" social democracy' (quoted in Carr, 1958: 146). Trotskiy, the old Menshevik, was grouped with his former comrade-in-arms, and thus associated with the Other or 'false Europe'.[3] The showdown between the integrationists and isolationists was thereby made into something more than a mere power struggle for the state's position in the debate about Europe. The loser did not only lose the argument, but also his association with the in-group, with 'true Europe'.

Having already excluded the leadership of European social democracy as well as non-Bolshevik Russian social democrats from 'true Europe', and also the left SRs and other allies from the months after the November coup, the time had now come when Bolshevik leaders were assigned to the same category.

The exorcisation of Trotskiy set a pattern which was repeated when Bukharin and Stalin set their position firmly apart from that of Zinov'ev and Kamenev at the Fourteenth Party Congress in December 1925. It was later used with similar success by Stalin against Bukharin himself. When, during the purges, the fallen leaders were said to have spied for capitalist countries and led Russian representatives of 'false Europe' in their attempted 'wrecking' of Soviet power, the charge was, in Bolshevik parlance, no more than a widening of the accusation from 'objective' to 'subjective' association with 'false Europe'. The Other was seen as monolithic, not only in the abstract, as it always had been, but also in concrete terms. One notes, moreover, that the exorcised leaders always stressed their membership in 'true Europe' and the 'Asianism' of their opponent, just as the Mensheviks had done in their attacks on the Bolsheviks in the period before 1917. Bukharin, for example, attacked Stalin's programme of super-industrialisation as a policy 'in line with old Russia', and referred to it at a number of occasions as being 'Asiatic'. Stalin himself he privately referred to as a 'Genghis Khan' (Cohen, 1974: 291).

The ever tighter delineation of the in-group went together with an ever stronger emphasis on the leadership of the Soviet Union within what was left of the in-group. In his report to the Fourteenth Party Congress in 1925, Stalin gave particular attention to the 'pilgrimages of workers to our country' which had 'inaugurated a new phase in the development of the worker movement in the west', and held that if 'the working class of Europe, or at least the revolutionary section of the European working class, regards our state [. . .] as their own child whose fate is of supreme importance to them, then war against our country becomes impossible' (Stalin, 1950e: 284–5). This was nothing new; the family metaphor of progressive Europe, with Russia assigned the role of a child, was a familiar theme in Bolshevik discourse. Yet only two years later, in August 1927, Stalin would say that

> There is one question which acts as a watershed between all possible groups, tendencies and parties, and is the test of their revolutionary or counter-revolutionary character. This question is now the question of the defence of the USSR ... An *internationalist* is one who without reservations, unconditionally, openly, honestly, is ready to defend and protect the USSR, because the USSR is the base of the revolutionary movement.
>
> (Stalin, 1949a: 50–1)

The strength assigned to the two parts of 'progressive Europe' – Russia and parts of the workers' movement in Europe – hardly fits the child/parent metaphor which had still been employed only two years before. Unconditional support for Russia has become an 'unconditional' defining trait of progressive Europe. The metaphor of Russia as the child of the workers' movement

121

in the most advanced countries in Europe has given way to the metaphor of a Russian *paterfamilias* who threatens to disown children who do not show absolute loyalty.

Where relations with 'false Europe' were concerned, at the Fifteenth Party Congress in December 1927, Stalin said of state-to-state relations with stagnant Europe that *'the period of "peaceful co-existence" is receding into the past'* (Stalin, 1949b: 288). New emphasis was put on the speedy breakdown of capitalism. Yet this theme went hand in hand with an insistence on 'vigilance' and the activities of inner and external enemies. In 1928, Stalin substantiated his point by maintaining that a mining disaster was due to sabotage by Russian engineers acting in cahoots with foreign spies. The two themes of the imminent breakdown of 'false Europe' and the intensified activities of its lackeys within the Soviet Union (the 'internal Other') were linked in the following way: as the Soviet Union moved closer to communism, the resistance of the class enemy, now growing desperate, intensified. As a result, the move towards communism meant *an intensification of* the class struggle.

Although Stalin had at this time taken new measures to limit public political space even further, like having his sometime comrades manhandled in the streets and exiled from the country, views opposing his analyses could still be seen in print. A March 1928 issue of the principal party journal contained an article which argued that, 'Tactically, it is harmful because it results in a wrong perspective and a wrong orientation' to foresee the speedy breakdown of western capitalism (Gol'denberg, 1929: 35). In September 1928, moreover, *Pravda* carried an article by Bukharin called 'Notes of an Economist', where he warned that a super-industrialist programme would 'put the USSR in the historical line of *old Russia*' with its 'backward, semi-serfdom agriculture, pauper-peasant . . . and merciless exploitation of the muzhik' (quoted in Cohen, 1974: 173). These two moves were made by representatives of what was now referred to by Stalin and almost all other participants in the discourse as 'the right deviation *(uklon)*'. E.H. Carr (1979: 120) has drawn attention to the discursive significance of this term: it was previously unknown in Marxist political discourse, but belonged rather, he writes, to the language of 'doctrinal heresy', that is, to a theological discourse.

If Bukharin's moves tried to brand Stalin as an Oriental despot who had reverted to tsarist, non-European ways of transforming the country, Stalin's referred to the European context in order to emphasise the need for industrialisation. Time and again, he would underline the need for the peasants to 'pay some kind of tribute' so that the Soviet Union could 'catch up and overtake' Europe economically. This move had been employed already in 1917, and was now pressed into service again. Stalin re-employed another move. In earlier years, Trotskiy and others had doubted whether the peasants were historically progressive, and Stalin had been among those who had charged them with showing a 'lack of faith' in the Russian peasant. At this point, Stalin easily combined the two moves: he held that part of the peasants, the kulaks and the 'subkulaks', was a stagnant element which should be liquidated. At the same time, however, he saddled those who doubted the possibility of enforced indus-trialisation with a 'lack of faith'.

When Stalin's super-industrialist, isolationist programme was implemented, beginning in December 1929, the images of old Russia which accompanied it were not only contrasted with Russian contemporaneity. Old Russia was first contrasted with its conquering neighbours, and its economic backwardness was singled out as the root cause for its defeats. It followed that Russia had to catch up and overtake the main contemporary enemies. In a famous speech, Stalin put the argument in the following way:

> The history of Old Russia contains among other things a number of losses due to backwardness. She was beaten by Mongol khans. By Turkish beys. By Swedish feudal lords. By Polish and Lithuanian pans. By English and French capitalists. By Japanese barons. Everybody beat her, because of her backwardness [. . .] We are 50 to 100 years behind the advanced countries. We must catch up with them in ten years. Either we manage, or else we will be shattered.
>
> (Stalin, 1951: 38–9)

This quote also has a decidedly statist bias, inasmuch as what is ostensibly being compared – the level of differentiation of social organisation in Russia and elsewhere – is treated not as an object of immediate interest, but interesting only to the extent that it is alleviated by the military shell of the state. For the discussion of Europe, this change of emphasis is pivotal, since it signals the further fading away of the dichotomy of 'true Europe'/'false Europe' and a corresponding strengthening of the dichotomy of Soviet Russia/Europe. This change of emphasis concerning the communist movement was present already in Stalin's 1927 definition of an internationalist, and was now being generalised. It is often noticed that 1934 was a growth year for the use of Russian national rhetoric, which was now being firmly established as a central part of Stalin's and the state's position. To give but one example, when a 1936 *Pravda* editorial criticised the mathematician N. Luzin for servility towards the West, inasmuch as he had taken steps to publish abroad, it did so in the following terms: *'The Soviet Union is not Mexico, not some Uruguay, but a great socialist power'* (quoted in Tucker, 1990: 571).

To wheel out yet another long quote, a similar subtext can be read out of the new all-Soviet history book on the party, where the reader is told that the Bolsheviks tried

> to create a *new* Party, to create a party of a *new type*, different from the usual Social-Democratic parties of the West, one that was free of opportunist elements and capable of leading the proletariat in a struggle for power. In fighting the Bolsheviks, the Mensheviks of all shades, from Axelrod and Martynov to Martov and Trotsky, invariably used weapons borrowed from the arsenal of the West-European Social-Democrats. They wanted in Russia a party similar, let us say, to the German or French Social-Democratic Party. They fought the Bolsheviks just because they sensed something new in them, something unusual and different from the Social-Democrats of the West.
>
> *(History of the Communist Party of the Soviet Union (Bolsheviks). Short Course*, 1948: 171–2)

Here is the old theme of the 'Westernising' Mensheviks from the social democratic debates of the 1900s and 1910s, pegged down by the victorious Bolshevik state, complete with a negative normative bias.

The two developments of extreme delimitation of public political space and the way previously separate categories were collapsed one into the other seem to have been mutually reinforcing. As the 1930s wore on, categories like 'true Europe', 'internationalists', 'old Russia', 'new Russia', 'great Russian nation', 'Soviet society', 'Soviet state', 'old Bolsheviks', 'Party', 'Central Committee', 'leader' and 'Stalin' were used more and more interchangeably. Similarly, the enemy grew more and more monolithic; there were no more 'false Europe', 'European social democracy', 'left opposition', 'right opposition', 'foreigners', 'foreign spies', 'Soviet spies', etc., but simply one huge, multi-tentacled enemy. *Pravda* editorials carried indiscriminate catch-all titles like 'Trotskiy–Zinov'ev–Kamenev–Gestapo' (Haslam, 1984: 129).

In short, not only did the debate about Europe come to a standstill, since there was little or no movement either outside or within the state's position, but the state's position itself became absolutised to an extent not easily matched. This gave rise to an extremely interesting phenomenon. At first thought, one should think that the divide between self and Other, sharpened throughout the Soviet period to the point where, during the purges, it had become razor-like, should have the effect of separating the two groups of the Soviet Union and its enemies in a wholly clear-cut way. Indeed, this is what *Pravda* kept telling its readers when it argued that

> by exterminating without any mercy these spies, provocateurs, wreckers, and diversionists, the Soviet land will move even more rapidly along the Stalinist route, socialist culture will flourish even more richly, the life of the Soviet people will become even more joyous.
>
> (quoted in Cohen, 1974: 380)

Yet, what actually happened was *not* an absolute division of in-group and out-group, but an *internalisation* of the self–Other divide. Since actions and views could 'objectively', that is, unintentionally, benefit the enemy, any one Soviet citizen was in constant danger of running the enemy's errand. The word *dvurushnik* – 'double-dealer' – was widely used to denominate people who ostensibly belonged to the in-group, but who were also dabbling in dubious business.

The great purge trials, where the forging of this entity culminated, furnish us with an eminently tangible example of discourse doctored by the state. Take the case of General Tukhachevskiy, who at first denied guilt. However, following a series of rather active measures, he confessed at last. How brutal these measures were, Tucker writes, becomes clear in the light of the finding that some greyish brown spots on pages of the protocols of his interrogation are bloodstains whose unusual shape indicates that they came from a body in motion, in other words that Tukhachevsky was reeling from blows to his head or body at the moment of 'confessing'.

(Tucker, 1990: 435)

One should, perhaps, stop to ask whether discourse analysis, concentrating as it does on how texts struggle, clash, deconstruct and displace one another, is the right tool to analyse a political sequence where it seems to be the literal body politic rather than the word which is on the rack. Yet this would be a mistaken distinction. The state's intention in mauling Tukhachevskiy was, after all, to get him to sign a text, which was to be placed in the context of a show trial, the intent of which was to add to the construction of an Other. At this particular point in space and time, power and knowledge had indeed become one.

The coming of the Second World War to the Soviet Union in June 1941 forced an immediate and twofold response in the state's position. First, the paring down of the in-group came to an immediate halt. The stress formerly put on the existence of an inner enemy gave way to references to the indivisible socialist Fatherland. When Stalin appeared on the air for the first time after the German invasion, on 3 July, it was to address his Soviet 'brothers and sisters', that is, the members of that quasi-familiar community which is the modern nation state (Ulam, 1974: 316). In line with this, public political space was extended to allow institutions deemed to have a mobilising potential, such as the Russian Orthodox Church, to participate, albeit in a tightly circumscribed way. Second, references to 'Western Europe' in large measure gave way to more differentiated references by wartime status (that is, enemy/allied), or by country. Whereas before 22 June the war had been defined as an unjust inter-capitalist war, it was now redefined as a just war against fascism (Light, 1988: 221).

As the Second World War came to an end with the defeat of Nazi Germany, public political space shrank once more. Nevertheless, a somehow expanded role was found for the Russian Orthodox Church as compared with the interwar period. The church under the newly elected Patriarch Sergii did not, however, aspire to stake out a position for itself different from the state's. The state's position on Europe reverted to what it had been on the eve of the Second World War, but with an added emphasis on the historical mission of the Russian people past, present and future. In answer to suggestions made by Evgeniy (Jenö) Varga that capitalism in Europe and Northern America was fairly well entrenched and that a war with these states was avoidable, Stalin insisted that a capitalist collapse, prefaced by inter-capitalist wars, was imminent (Lynch, 1987: 20–5, 151–2 note 32). Where relations with Western Europe were concerned, the occurrence of a wartime alliance did not leave any mark on the public debate. On the contrary, Stalin and Zhdanov reaffirmed the image of the world as consisting of two incompatible social systems – two camps – which had underlaid the Russian debate about Europe before the war. In doing so, they were helped by the socialist camp's ongoing acquisition of a number of new members. Socialism no longer existed only in one country, but was being imposed in a number of new states as a number of 'people's democracies' were established to the west (and also to the south) of the Soviet Union. In his opening speech to the founding meeting of Cominform in September 1947, Zhdanov juxtaposed two camps, 'the camp of imperialism and anti-democratic forces, whose chief aim is the establishment of a world-wide American imperialist hegemony and the crushing of democracies: and the anti-imperialist, democratic camp, whose chief aim is elimination of imperialism' (quoted in Kubálková and Cruickshank, 1980: 151).

The meeting was a secret one, yet the speech entered the public debate when it was published the following year. The consolidation of the 'socialist camp' went together with a campaign against 'cosmopolitanism' which was also one of the period's important backdrops to the debate about Europe. Once again, the image of Russia/the Soviet Union/'true Europe' as the young, dynamic force of the future was offset against the image of an old, conflict-ridden 'false Europe' writhing on its deathbed. For example, an unsigned leading article in the main Soviet history journal, explicitly taking its cue from Stalin's exhortations to fight imperialism and Zhdanov's to fight bourgeois ideas, complained about a lack of vigilance and class perspective among Soviet historians. This had kept them from adequately demasking 'bourgeois cosmopolitanism' and its campaign to 'weaken national conscience, culture and tradition' in the 'Marshallised countries of Europe and Asia', by means of 'producing a historically false "European" or "American" community (*obshchnost'*)'. To the contrary, certain historians had shown servility towards bourgeois science:

> Kowtowing before bourgeois science often takes the form of objectivism, a refusal to take the Party, class point of view. [. . .] History, like philosophy, is a scientific weapon in the hands of a proletariat which fights for its liberation from capitalism.
>
> (*Voprosy istorii*, 5, 1949: 11–12)

To this end, historians should focus on the universal moral and practical superiority of everything Russian. A 'resolute stop' should be put to the anti-scientific practice of studying modern and contemporary history isolated from the history of Russia and the history of the USSR. The vital task of historians should be 'to demonstrate the formidable influence Russian culture, literature and science have had on the culture and science of all other peoples [. . .] in Europe, Asia and America' (*Voprosy istorii*, 5, 1949: 11–12).

The idea that false, bourgeois cosmopolitan Europe is 'Marshallised', and the juxtaposition of Europeanism and Americanism – that is, Atlanticism – has joined the former ideas about a morally inferior Europe whose very decadence nevertheless may be alluring to the Russian who is not sufficiently vigilant.

The 'Marshallisation' of Europe and the rise of Atlanticism as dominant themes of the Russian debate, growing as they do out of the effect of the Second World War on the distribution of power in the international system, pose the problem of how to understand the expression 'the West' in the Russian political debate. As noted above, at the time of the November coup people like Lenin compared Russia to 'the West and North America', thus indicating that the United States was a relevant category for comparison, yet distinct from 'the West', which could still be taken to mean Western Europe. Throughout the period under discussion in this chapter, however, the United States became an ever more important category for comparison. For example, one slogan in use during the First Five Year Plan exhorted the masses to 'catch up with and overtake the United

States' (*dognat' i peregnat' Ameriku*) (Allen, 1988: 271). As mentioned above, when this phrase was used earlier, for example by Lenin in 1917, it was related to Western Europe, the West, or simply 'the advanced countries'. Rapid American industrialisation and the eruption of imperial ambition in 1898 had also given that country a foothold in the Russian political debate. By the end of the Second World War, the American prevalence in international relations generally, and European affairs specifically, was such that the image of 'the West' in the Russian debate about Europe was seriously affected. The Zhdanov statement above brings out how the United States was seen as the dominant force within 'the imperialist camp'. It would, therefore, be unwarranted to equal the term 'the West' with 'Western Europe' in the 1949 quotation given above. Indeed, as will be demonstrated below, the extent of the American hegemony in Western Europe was a central theme of the entire Russian debate about Europe in the period after Stalin's death in 1953.[4]

Summing up this chapter, the First World War opened the way for the February overthrow of the tsarist state and the Bolshevik coup of November 1917. The Bolshevik position, built around the dichotomy 'false Europe'/'true Europe', became the state's position. Other positions were forced out of the debate. By the early 1920s, only the Romantic nationalist position was left, in the two-headed form in which it had existed for the last fifty years. On the one hand, the emphasis was on the organic Russian nation's ties with other European organic nations, a relationship of ambiguity. On the other, there were those like the Eurasianists who stressed the organic Russian nation's need to take on Europe in a long drawn-out fight, where Russia availed itself of Europe's own instruments. The extent to which the latter variant fed into the Bolshevik position, as well as the eventual chronology of this process, has been the topic of acrimonious debate (Agursky, 1987). What is certain is that the drama of the Bolshevik position in the 1920s lay elsewhere, in the debate between integrationists and isolationists. The stakes in this clash were high, since loss entailed not only marginalisation, but eradication from the debate.

With the isolationist position emerging victorious, the 1930s saw a further delimitation of political space and a reinforced emphasis on the Soviet Russian party-state as the in-group to be counterpoised to its enemies, who were collapsed into one single grouping. During the Second World War, public political space expanded somewhat, yet the Russian debate about Europe was suspended to make way for debates about wartime allies and fascism. In the early post-war years, public political space reverted to its interwar shape, as did the state's position on Europe, with nationalist sentiment serving to underline the moral superiority of Russia over Europe even further. Europe's position as the supreme Other to the Russian self, however, was seriously challenged by the imposing role of the United States in the international system.

7

FROM DE-STALINISATION TO *PERESTROYKA*

If the previous period was notable for the contraction of public political space, where the Russian debate about Europe was stripped of positions alternative to the state's and public discussion of what that position should be was all but eradicated, then the period under discussion in this chapter saw a tentative expansion of public political space. The public debate about the state's position was resuscitated in the form of professional debates between foreign affairs specialists, the *mezhdunarodniki*. These debates did not call into question the basic framework within which Europe was seen, and the debate about moral judgement was limited to a question of how much less advanced capitalist Europe was as compared to the socialist bloc. The focus was rather on how to interpret the relations between Western European states themselves, and also those between Western Europe on the one hand and the United States (and to some limited extent also Japan) on the other, as well as on what kind of relationship Russia should have with Western Europe. The tone was set by Khrushchev's speech at the Twentieth Party Congress in 1956, where he announced that Soviet foreign policy was based on peaceful coexistence between states belonging to different social systems. This is, incidentally, an example of how a theme which is not new may invade the centre of the debate simply by being reiterated enough times and in a forceful enough fashion. For foreshadowings of the theme of peaceful coexistence during the first half of the 1950s, cf. Light (1988: 216–17).

Following the ousting of Khrushchev in 1964, the fully public Russian debate about Europe continued along the same lines, with remarkably little variation of themes and views. Throughout the period, the focal points of this part of the Russian debate about

Europe remained the nature of EC integration and the extent of Western Europe's independence from the United States. There was, however, also a steep increase in the number of writings disseminated at the margins of the public debate, the *samizdat* or privately manifolded literature. While the foreign affairs specialists concentrated on the position of the state, it was left to *samizdat* writers to resuscitate the old Romantic nationalist position, and to attempt the resuscitation of other positions as well. While the images thus presented were seldom original, but were more often explicitly lifted from or latched on to the views of Russian tsarist and/or *emigré* authors, they nevertheless had an original impact, since the Russian debate into which they were reinserted was rather different from what it had been at the time when these images were first presented. The subterranean publication of a collection of essays under the title *Iz-pod glyb* (*From Under the Rubble*) in 1974 captures the significance of what was happening. The title of the collection was doubly significant. First, by alluding to Soviet life as the 'rubble' from under which the collection could emerge, it placed itself in direct opposition to the state. Second, by self-consciously alluding to the follow-up volume to *Vekhi*, *Iz glubiny* (*From the Deep*), which was the last book-length Romantic nationalist publication to emerge within Soviet Russia, a claim was made to take up the cudgels for this position and thus burst the state's monopoly on the debate. Third, Alexander Solzhenitsyn further sharpened the critique of the state's political practice by naming the first article of the collection 'As Breathing and Consciousness Return', thus placing the years between the Bolshevik suppression of *Iz glubiny* in 1918 and the emergence of his own article within a spiritually void parenthesis.

FROM DE-STALINISATION TO THE OUSTING OF KHRUSHCHEV

The death of Stalin set in motion a train of events which was to result in the expansion of public political space. The resurgence of debate coincided with a resuscitation of political contacts. For example, in setting out to research *détente*, van Oudenaren found that

> it became clear that little of what we associated with the détente of the 1970s was really new. Efforts to trace regular

summits, political consultations, bilateral economic institutions, and contacts between Soviet and West European nongovernmental organizations to their origins invariably led not to the 1970s or even the 1960s, but to the two or three years after Stalin's death.

(van Oudenaren, 1991: vii)

This manifested itself, among other things, in the way in which new research institutes and publishing channels were established, and the greater leeway given to specialist debate. For example, in 1956, after nine years of Stalinist neglect of the foreign affairs intellectuals (*mezhdunarodniki*) and their institutes, the Minister of Foreign Trade, Anastas Mikoyan, told the Twentieth Party Congress that the Soviet Union needed to expand public political space:

We are lagging seriously behind in the study of the contemporary stage of capitalism; we do not study facts and figures deeply; we often restrict ourselves for agitation purposes to individual facts about the symptoms of an approaching crisis or about the impoverishment of the working people, rather than making a comprehensive, profound assessment of the phenomena of life in foreign countries.

(quoted in Malcolm, 1984: 4)

This exhortation does not stress the importance of debate as such, but rather the instrumental value of debate as a way of finding the 'correct line' at any one historical point in time. Debate is seen in terms of an input into the political process with a certain potential to meet the decision-maker's need for comprehensive background analyses. The reason for broadening public political space, then, was little to do with factors such as public pressure or intellectual curiosity, but sprang directly from the state's need for information processing. Consequently, it is hardly surprising that only professional public debate was allowed, or that the debate had as its point of departure – and seemingly also as its point of arrival! – the position and need of the state.[1]

The Soviet foreign policy specialists – the *mezhdunarodniki* – went about their discussion of Europe by focusing specifically on two questions: the nature of West European integration, and especially the nature of the EC, and the role played by the US in Europe. Where the latter was concerned, the discussion focused on the question of how independent West European capitalist states were to follow their own policies.

The interest in West European integration was caused by the number of such institutions which were established in the late 1940s and early 1950s, with or without US participation. When, in 1957, the European Economic Community and Euratom were founded, the Soviet state published a note in which the new institutions were described as serving the US and German interest in German rearmament and as representing further steps towards a bloc division in Europe. All-European economic coop-eration was presented as an alternative to going through with the signing of the Treaty of Rome ('Soviet Proposals', 1957). And the very first issue of a new Soviet journal, *Mirovaya Ekonomika i Mezhdunarodnye Otnosheniya* (*MEiMO*), contained a set of seventeen theses on the EEC and Euratom, issued by the newly re-established Institute for World Economy and International Relations (IMEMO AN SSSR, 1957: 83–96).

According to the seventeen theses, the Common Market can be seen as one of a series of economic, political-ideological and especially military-political institutions to 'integrate' the aggres-sive bloc of Western capitalist states. (The terms integrate and integration were persistently put between quotation marks by Soviet writers up to 1968.) The integration initiatives 'often happened on the initiative of, and in all cases with the most active support from, the ruling circles of the US, head of the imperialist camp' (IMEMO AN SSSR, 1957: 83). All the countries participating in the EEC are characterised, according to the theses, by the process of monopolies fusing with the state. Thus, the EEC and Euratom are agreements between *monopolies*, 'the most powerful banks and industrial cartels, concerns and trusts' (IMEMO AN SSSR, 1957: 83). These monopolies have strong ties to their American opposite numbers and the theses state that the governments signed the agreements without any regard to the masses. Indeed, it was asserted that the agreements contra-dict the objective interests of the workers, the farmers, and the middle strata of the population, that is, most if not all non-monopoly interests. The tendency for the monopolies of different countries to make agreements with each other may be traced back to state-monopolist capitalism having reached an especially high level of development, but also to the fact that the correlation of forces on the world arena had sharply changed in favour of socialism and against capitalism (IMEMO AN SSSR, 1957: 83).

The theses go on to assert that the EEC and Euratom are products of capitalism's mustering of forces against socialism. The initiators 'openly admit' that the paramount goal of the unification of Europe 'is "the creation of a strong Europe as a counterweight to Soviet Russia", and also "the annihilation of the internal communist threat"' (IMEMO AN SSSR, 1957: 84). The theses also state that influential political circles in Western Europe and the US see the Common Market as the European military-economic base of NATO and the Western European Union (WEU).

According to the theses, many public figures hold that forging European unification can make Europe a third force in world politics. Nevertheless, since the participants intend to remain inside NATO and thus under American hegemony, and also want to strengthen economic ties with American imperialism, this is hardly a realistic programme. The authors point to Lenin's criticism of ultracapitalism to disclaim the bourgeois and right-socialist view of the EEC as potentially a step towards a new, conflictless capitalism and a chance to push Europe to the left. They assert that, under capitalism, genuine (*podlinnyy*) cooperation between the peoples and the creation of genuine economic complexes are not possible. Yet, as already pointed out by Lenin, temporary agreements between monopolists, such as the ECSC, are nevertheless possible.

The framework within which the theses view Europe is the same that the Bolshevik position has availed itself of all along. The idea that there is a 'true Europe' of workers and progressives, and a 'false Europe' of capitalists is once again brought to the fore. Yet there is a new twist: the ambiguity of relations between American and European monopolies is explicitly mentioned, and the contradiction between seeing the Common Market as part of a bloc of capitalists versus seeing it as a countering move by European capitalists in the face of overwhelming American competition is resolved in favour of the former. The latter idea is hardly new, but closely resembles the 1923 writings of Trotskiy mentioned in the preceding chapter. The moral judgement passed on 'false Europe' remains negative, yet 'false Europe' is not presented as anywhere near so wholly monolithic and evil as was the case in the Stalin years. Where relations with Europe are concerned, there is a marked change: the possibility of all-European integration is formulated as a possibility, even as an ideal, however unattainable for the time being.

The theses sum up the themes in circulation in the Russian debate about Europe at the time (Chelnokov, 1957: 95; Törnudd, 1963: 137–46). Yet, in 1958, Knyazhinskiy published a book called *The Failure of the Plans for 'European Unification'* (1958). The book starts off with a discussion of the new supranational capitalist institutions in Europe, and explicitly aims to show the continuities of views and intentions between the initiators of the EEC and the pro-Europeans in the interwar period and indeed before the First World War. The stress is on Count Coudenhove-Kalergi's Pan-European Movement. Briand's attempt to form a Pan-European Union of the European members of the League of Nations is seen as the classical failure of capitalist cooperation in the interwar period. The pro-Europeans, and therefore also their monopolist backers, are said to have been important in bringing the attempt about. The gist of the book's argument, however, is that the pacifist rhetoric of the pro-Europeans hid a conspiracy against the Soviet Union:

> The contemporary 'Pan-European' ideologists try to falsify history by maintaining that the spread of the idea of 'European unification' in the 1920s had been called for by the European peoples in order to guarantee peace and security by forming a 'European federation' [... On the contrary,] the acute imperialist plans for the 'unification of Europe' were directed against the Soviet Union, the main obstruction in the imperialists' path towards enslaving the peoples of Europe and unleashing a new war.
>
> (Knyazhinskiy, 1958: 55)

The only reason why contemporary West European integration can be said to differ from the version set out in the Briand plan, is that 'The general crisis had not yet reached the stage where the European bourgeoisie started to look for a way to salvage the capitalist order by means of a stronger imperialism' (Knyazhinskiy, 1958: 77).

Knyazhinskiy's emphasis on the military implications of West European integration, and especially the proneness to war ascribed to its planners, give the book a different thrust from the IMEMO theses of the year before. Debate, albeit veiled, was definitively back as a feature of public deliberations about the Soviet Union's relationship to Europe. The book is also important as the first substantial Russian discussion of European federalist writings. If one of the main functions of academic Russian debate about Europe is indeed to 'Westernise' the Russian debate at large by bringing in new perspectives, then this book is a case in point (Malcolm, 1989b; Hough, 1986).

In 1959, IMEMO arranged a congress on the Common Market and its economic and political role under contemporary imperialism, where the debate centred on whether the EEC was primarily of an 'economic' or 'political' nature. The opening address was a spirited attack on the 'Economists', whose position was summed up in three main points (Popov et al., 1959: 108–16). First, the forces of production need more space than they can get within the present national framework; second, the need to re-enmesh German capital with the capital of the West European states; third, the European monopolists' perceived need to withstand US pressure. This 'Economist' position was then knocked down for its lack of emphasis on the role of the EEC as the base of the imperialist struggle against socialism. The French Foreign Minister Pinot was quoted to the effect that plans for the EEC were of the nature of a political pact to withstand Soviet influence in Europe rather than an economic union. Popov seems to imply that since part of this territory is in the Soviet Union, the use of the phrase gives away the users' revanchist territorial ambitions.

The Economists rose to the challenge by quoting Lenin's dictum that "politics is the concentrated expression of economics', and attacking the opposition for 'speaking about politics as if it were wholly foreign to economics' (Popov et al., 1959: 110). The Economists emphasised that foundation of the Common Market was part of the spreading of state monopolist capitalism on a world scale, and a logical step along the same path as the foundation of the ECSC. The tendency for the advanced capitalist home markets to be too small in relation to the level of development of the forces of production had been aggravated in the post-war years. 'Therefore big capital tries to monopolise its home market, and so compels the state to organise importation of goods from other countries' (Popov et al., 1959: 111). Of course, like all contemporary capitalist moves, the Common Market was also part and parcel of the struggle against socialism. Yet in the political sense, it was first and foremost an attempt by France and Germany to unite in order to overcome their historical enmity and stave off the inevitable fall of capitalism. The formation of the EEC was a fundamental threat to the British capitalists, who dreaded a political situation where Western Europe would be divided into members and non-members of that organisation (cf., Solodkin in Faminskiy et al., 1959). This would indeed imply a major challenge to capitalism. The British tried to avoid this by suggesting a free trade area.

Another participant at the congress emphasises how, not having been able to set up a European Defence Community or a European Political Community in 1954, the European reaction pooled their forces and formed the Common Market. By building supranational organisations, the monopolists tried to liquidate the bourgeois-democratic national rule. They attacked the social gains which had after all been made in Western Europe (Suslin et al., 1959: 104–18).

The congress did not reach any conclusion on the nature of the EEC, other than the contention that it was 'impossible to separate political from economic factors, and let alone contrast them, when analysing such a novel, complex and imposing phenomenon as the European Economic Community' (Kuznetsov et al., 1959: 81). The conditions for capitalist development were very different from what they had been in the interwar period. The general crisis of capitalism – that is, the problems created by the progress of socialism and decolonisation – was further advanced. In economic terms, Western Europe was ripe for socialism long ago. It was only with the help of American imperialism and the support of the social democracy that the monopolist bourgeoisie was able to cling to power. Only socialism could solve Western Europe's problems. It was, however, helpfully spelled out that this did not mean that all attempts to implement economic 'integration' of Western Europe were doomed to fail, since 'social laws do not manifest themselves spontaneously, but through the conscious activities of human beings' (Kuznetsov et al., 1959: 82). Yet there are limits to the impact spontaneity may have. Capitalist contradictions remained too deep to allow for the formation of a United States of Europe. 'Only after the victory of socialism is a union of all

European peoples and governments on a really equal footing possible' (Kuznetsov et al., 1959: 83). This conclusion, echoing as it does Lenin's position on the slogan of the United States of Europe, is offered as a least-common denominator of the debate and also as a demarcation of its general boundaries.

By 1962, when IMEMO issued a new set of theses, the 'political nature' of the EEC received most attention. It was stated that by means of international state monopolist unions the imperialists showed their class solidarity and tried to counter the sores and defamations of capitalism at the expense of the working class. They needed this as an answer to the increased strength of world socialism, but their attempts would be in vain. 'As shown in the Programme of the CPSU, the basic contradiction of the modern world – the contradiction between socialism and imperialism – does not do away with the contradictions rending the capitalist world' (IMEMO AN SSSR, 1962: 4). The unequal growth of capitalism, it was claimed in the new theses, had spawned a new reactionary form of capitalist cooperation, the EEC. In turn, the EEC brought about a new form of competition on the world market. 'During the third stage of the general crisis of capitalism the conflict between the level of development of the forces of production and the relations of production have deepened even further' (IMEMO AN SSSR, 1962: 4). The third stage of the general crisis of capitalism, a general ideological development that seemed to owe much to the occurrence of the EEC, followed the first stage, ushered in by the October revolution, and the second stage, which dated from the foundation of a socialist system in the wake of the Second World War. This time too it was the increased strength of the socialist camp that initiated the new stage, ostensibly in the mid-1950s. The EEC was viewed in the theses as the economic base for the North Atlantic front in Europe and thus a weapon in the Cold War.

Great Britain's application for membership was seen as the result of a struggle that Great Britain had lost. 'Of course Britain is economically strong enough to keep up the struggle and remain outside the "Common Market". However, the line taken by the ruling circles in this question is first and foremost determined by political motives, i.e. fear about the weakening of NATO' (IMEMO AN SSSR, 1962: 8). All this was seen as being of crucial importance, first and foremost, because, for the first time in the post-war years, the possibility for the formation of a West European 'power centre' equal or close to the US in population, material resources, industrial output and foreign trade, had begun to materialise (IMEMO AN SSSR, 1962: 9).[2]

The theses noted that FRG, France and also Italy had started to demand a larger role in planning NATO's 'global' policy. Under these conditions, integration was accompanied by the intensification of relations between the West European states and USA:

> The US concurrently sees West European "integration" as a political necessity and a threat. They try to neutralise the economic threat by getting closer to the "Common Market" and resolve the threat by including the EEC in a set of wider, "Atlantic", state monopolist agreements.
>
> (IMEMO AN SSSR, 1962: 9–10)

Yet Atlanticism of course would not solve any of the real problems facing Europe. All-European cooperation was needed to solve the problems that the capitalists could not solve among themselves within organisations like the EEC and Euratom. Yet, since it did not include the socialist countries, the West European 'integration' of the imperialists was in fact directed against such cooperation (IMEMO AN SSSR, 1962: 9–10).

The 1962 IMEMO theses about the Common Market make up a full inventory of the Russian debate about Europe at the beginning of the 1960s. There is a change of emphasis inasmuch as the possibility of a European 'power centre', independent of the US, is seen as a distinct possibility. Yet the ambivalence about the Common Market being more than an epiphenomenon is still permeating the debate. This can also be seen in the summing up of the state's position offered by General Secretary Khrushchev in the same year, where he characterised the EEC as a reality, but where the emphasis was on the culturally superior socialist cooperation (Khrushchev, 1962; Binns, 1978: 250–1; Adomeit, 1979: esp. 3; Marsh, 1978: 27). The tension between stressing the significance of West European capitalist integration, and of stressing the limits laid down against it by history, remained paramount (Forte, 1968: 384; Schulz, 1975: 80). The disagreement over the question of Europe's relative independence of the US became part of the power struggle which resulted in the ousting of Khrushchev, with his detractors attacking the very idea as ludicrous.[3] In rounding off this first section of the chapter, it should perhaps be stressed that the theme of Europe's possible independence of American hegemony did not rule out the theme of how the US and the Soviet Union shared an interest in dominating Europe and the world: it was a theme of Khrushchev's that 'history' had imposed upon the Russian and American peoples 'great responsibility for the destiny of the world' (Adomeit, 1986: 512). The state's position incorporated both these themes simultaneously, and did not address any possible contradiction between the two.

FROM THE OUSTING OF KHRUSHCHEV TO *PERESTROYKA*

With the fall of Khrushchev, the de-Stalinisation process which he had set in motion came to a halt. Public political space was not expanded any further for the rest of the period in question. As a consequence, the foreign policy specialist debate about the state's position on Europe continued within the same parameters, with the same foci and the same disagreements which had emerged during de-Stalinisation. The exception was a general debate about whether the existence of nuclear weapons was not a global problem whose solution could not be found on the level of states, but only on an 'all-human' level.

Characteristically, this debate first emerged not in *mezhdunarodnik* debate, but in the semi-public writings of Andrey Sakharov. It is indeed a general point that the most interesting developments during the second half of the period were not to do with the debate over the state's position, but with what happened at the margins of the public debate. Taking their cue from the expansion of public political space characteristic of de-Stalinisation, there appeared a literature written by people who attempted to expand public political space *themselves*, by the very act of disseminating their writings in manifolded form, outside the available state channels of publication. By September 1965, Khrushchev's successors decided clearly to demarcate the limits of public political space by arresting the two authors Yuliy Daniel and Andrey Sinyavskiy, and seizing some of Solzhenitsyn's writings (Spechler, 1982: xvi, 219–30). In so doing, however, they also gave a boost to *samizdat*, which was greatly expanded by the influx of writers alienated by the crackdown. (But cf. Meerson-Aksenov, 1977 who stresses the fate of

Pasternak as a more important factor.) The clearing up of the grey zone at the limits of public political space, moreover, entailed forcing the writers to a greater extent than before to opt either for public channels of dissemination or *samizdat*, and once writers had crossed out of public political space, the state often proceeded to ostracise them, thus giving them little incentive to cross back. As a result of all this, the *samizdat* body of literature grew rapidly. The upshot was that *samizdat* writings went on to burst the state's monopoly on the Russian debate about Europe, to resuscitate the Romantic nationalist position and clear the ground for the resuscitation of other positions as well.

For example, in 1968, Andrey Sakharov wrote his notes on progress, coexistence and intellectual freedom, starting from the presupposition that the possibility of thermonuclear war makes the Clausewitzian idea of war as a continuation of politics by other means outdated (Sakharov, 1968: 36). Together with other threats of destruction to mankind, it calls for new patterns of peaceful cooperation and competition. Cooperation is possible with all ideologies which do not 'reject all possibility of rapprochement, discussion, and compromise' as do, 'for example, ideologies of Fascism, racism, militaristic, and Maoist demagogy' (Sakharov, 1968: 28). He notes the 'many common features' of fascism and Stalinism (Sakharov, 1968: 52). Defining his own views as 'profoundly socialist' and acknowledging but not embracing charges of 'Westernism', he sees hope in the role played by 'leftist Leninist Communists (and leftist Westerners)' in the socialist countries, which may lead to a multiparty system. At the same time, 'the leftist reformist wing of the bourgeoisie' will move the United States towards socialism and thus further a convergence between the two systems (Sakharov, 1968: 54, 8, 82).

Sakharov's piece gave pride of place to the problem of the arms race, and so it did not focus specifically on Europe or even on 'the West', but on the United States. Yet the implications for the Russian debate about Europe were clear, and became even clearer in the answer Sakharov's piece sparked from Aleksandr Isaevich Solzhenitsyn. Appearing first as a *samizdat* essay in 1969, already the title of the piece – 'As Breathing and Consciousness Return', alluding as it did to the upsurge of semi-official political activity generally and *samizdat* publications specifically – signalled the writer's intention of bursting the limits on political public space imposed by the state (Solzhenitsyn, 1975b). Solzhenitsyn attacked Sakharov for not including Soviet communism on his list of unmitigated evils, on a par with 'fascist, racist, militarist or Maoist ideologies' (Solzhenitsyn, 1975b: 9). Sakharov, moreover, is taken on for not being nationally minded. Since Solzhenitsyn's clarity in denouncing his opponents is exemplary, extensive quotes seem in order:

> Underrating as he does the vitality of the national spirit, Sakharov also overlooks the possible existence of vital national forces in Russia. This shows through quite comically in the passage where he enumerates the 'progressive forces of our country' – and finds what? 'The left Leninist-Communists' and the 'Left Westernizers.' Is this all? We should be spiritually poor indeed, we should be doomed, if Russia today consisted merely of such forces as these.
>
> (Solzhenitsyn, 1975b: 16)

Rather, Russia's salvation lies in exposing and doing away with the West's false ideas about freedom:

> The West has supped more than its fill of every kind of freedom, including intellectual freedom. And has this saved it? We see it today crawling on hands and knees, its will paralyzed, uneasy about the future, spiritually racked and dejected. Unlimited external freedom in itself is quite inadequate to save us. Intellectual freedom is a very desirable gift, but, like any sort of freedom, a gift of conditional, not intrinsic, worth, only a means by which we can attain another and higher goal.
>
> (Solzhenitsyn, 1975b: 18)

Where Sakharov's suggestion for introducing the multiparty system is concerned, Solzhenitsyn wants nothing to do with it, but wants to 'rise above Western conceptions to a loftier viewpoint'. The multiparty system is an idol 'to which the whole world bows down'. The word party comes from part, so cannot represent the whole. '[A] society in which political parties are active never rises in the moral scale [. . .] can we not, we wonder, rise above the two-party or multiparty parliamentary system? Are there no *extraparty* or strictly *nonparty* paths of national development?', Solzhenitsyn asks (1975b: 19). Almost all Soviet

people 'whose opinions do not conform to the official stereo-
type' have been taken in by this false idea:

> This almost perfect unanimity is an example of our tradi-
> tional passive imitation of the West: Russia can only
> recapitulate, it is too great a strain to seek other paths. As
> Sergei Bulgakov aptly remarked: 'Westernism is spiritual
> surrender to superior cultural strength'.[4]
>
> (Solzhenitsyn, 1975b: 20)

And so, Solzhenitsyn concludes along lines familiar from
Karamzin's ruminations of the early 1800s:

> unlimited freedom of discussion can wreak a country's
> resistance to some looming danger and lead to capitulation
> in wars not yet lost [. . .] authoritarian regimes as such are
> not frightening – only those which are answerable to no
> one and nothing. The autocrats of earlier, religious ages,
> though their power was ostensibly unlimited, felt them-
> selves responsible before God and their own conscience
> [. . .] If Russia for centuries was used to living under auto-
> cratic regimes and suffered total collapse under the demo-
> cratic system which lasted eight months in 1917, perhaps
> – I am only asking, not making an assertion – perhaps we
> should recognize that the evolution of our country from
> one form of authoritarianism to another would be the most
> natural, the smoothest, the least painful path of develop-
> ment for it to follow?
>
> (Solzhenitsyn, 1975b: 20–4)

If this article takes on the West and Russian Westernisers, then
another contribution printed in *From Under the Rubble* draws the
line against what Solzhenitsyn refers to as 'National Bolsheviks'.
'The nation', writes Solzhenitsyn, 'is mystically welded together
in a community of guilt, and its inescapable destiny is common
repentance' (Solzhenitsyn, 1975c: 113). Yet, not any nationalism
is worthy of support. A harsh, cold current of opinion

> has become discernible of late. Stripped to essentials, but
> not distorted, it goes like this: the Russian people is the
> noblest in the world; its ancient and its modern history
> are alike unblemished; tsarism and Bolshevism are equally
> irreproachable; the nation neither erred nor sinned either

before 1917 or after; we have suffered no loss of moral stature and therefore have no need of self-improvement; there are no nationality problems in relations with the border republics – Lenin's and Stalin's solution was ideal; communism is in fact unthinkable without patriotism; the prospects of Russia-USSR are brilliant; blood alone determines whether one is Russian or non-Russian. As far as things spiritual, all trends are admissible. Orthodoxy is not the least bit more Russian than Marxism, atheism, the scientific outlook, or, shall we say, Hinduism. God need not be written with a capital letter, but [*Gosudarstvo*, that is, the state] must be. Their general name for all this is 'the Russian idea'. (A more precise name for this trend would be 'National Bolshevism.')

(Solzhenitsyn, 1975c: 119–20)

Yet Russia is not the only one in need of repentence: 'We shall not say that Russia has brought little evil into the world. But did the so-called Great French Revolution, did France, that is, bring less? Is there any way of calculating? What of the Third Reich? Or Marxism as such?'(Solzhenitsyn, 1975c: 122). 'Have we memory and courage enough', he continues,

to recall the first fifteen years after the revolution, when 'proletarian messianism took on a blatantly' *Russophobe* character? [. . .] Did not the revolution throughout its early years have some of the characteristics of a foreign invasion? When in a foraging party, or the punitive detachment which came to destroy a rural district, there would be Finns and there would be Austrians, but hardly anyone who spoke Russian? When the organs of the Cheka teemed with Latvians, Poles, Jews, Hungarians, Chinese? [. . .] We are not the only ones, there are many others. Indeed, almost everyone when the time comes gives way, gives up, some times under less pressure than we succumbed to, and at times even eagerly. (The brief period of our history from February to October 1917 has turned out to be a compressed résumé of the later and present history of the West.)

(Solzhenitsyn, 1975c: 125–8)

Against this background, Solzhenitsyn reaches a clear conclusion about his preferred relationship between Russia and Europe:

'This is what the Russian people must do: spend most of its time alone with itself, without neighbors and guests. It must concentrate on its *inner* tasks: on healing its soul, educating its children, putting its own house in order' (Solzhenitsyn, 1975c: 140-2; also 1980a: 107). Russia should look to its unspoilt Northeast – 'Pinega, Mezem, Pechora' – where 'free people with a free understanding of our national mission can resurrect these great spaces, awaken them, heal them'. The path to truth and resurrection lies, then, in isolation from Europe and the world.

That Solzhenitsyn sees this 'truth' as being of a piece, becomes clear in his Nobel lecture. Humanity, being one, needs one scale of values. 'Given six, four, or even two scales of values, there cannot be a unified world, a united humanity' (Solzhenitsyn, 1980b: 17). '[A]ll *internal affairs* have ceased to exist on our crowded earth! The salvation of mankind lies only in making everything the concern of all' (Solzhenitsyn, 1980c: 32). Yet, humanity remains an abstract notion. Nations are the real communities:

> the disappearance of nations would impoverish us not less than if all men should become alike, with one personality and one face. Nations are the wealth of mankind, its generalized personalities; the least among them has its own unique coloration and harbors within itself a unique facet of God's design.
>
> (Solzhenitsyn, 1980c: 20)

Nations, he holds elsewhere, are characterised by a native language and a common sense of history, and are blessed by God: 'by descending upon the apostles with many tongues the Holy Ghost confirmed the diversity of the nations of mankind, as they have existed since that time' (Solzhenitsyn, 1975d: 263). Nations, moreover, should be the main actors in international politics, yet organisations like the UN do not live up to this ideal: 'It is not a United Nations Organization but a United Governments Organization, where governments freely elected are equated with regimes imposed by force or with those that have gained control by an armed seizure of power' (Solzhenitsyn, 1980c: 27).

This point calls to mind Belinskiy's formulation, that nations are the individuals of humanity. Yet, there remains in Solzhenitsyn's suggestions a tension between the views that nations are organic and therefore in a sense self-contained (witness his insistence on isolation as a 'cure' for Russia), that Russia is morally superior to West European nations, and that everybody is responsible for everything, everywhere. Solzhenitsyn and associates self-consciously lift the Romantic nationalist project back into the debate. If hardly anything of what they say about Europe and Russia's relationship to Europe is new in the sense that it has never been said before, they are nevertheless very important for the Russian debate about Europe inasmuch as they are justified in their claim to having rescusitated the Romantic nationalist position and thereby blocked out the limits of political space. In so doing, they also broke the state's monopoly on positions.

In this task, Solzhenitsyn and associates were assisted by the publication of a fully fledged *samizdat* journal, *Veche* (Popular assembly). If Solzhenitsyn and associates signalled their affinity to the *vekhovtsy* by naming their main publication after that group's second book, then *Veche* did the same by choosing a name phonetically close to their first book, *Vekhi*. *Veche* printed a number of articles on earlier Romantic nationalists such as the Slavophiles, Danilevskiy and the *vekhovtsy*, thus signalling their aim of reestablishing this position in the debate. The articles often underlined the contemporary significance of the views of these authors, and reproduced not only Romantic nationalist material, but also quotes which could in one sense or the other be represented as patriotic. For example, the longest article ever published by the journal was entitled 'The Teaching of the Slavophiles – The Highest Flight of National Self-Consciousness in Russia in the Period before Lenin'. As indicated already in the title, the author attempts to enrol Lenin – and also other icons of the Soviet state – in a broad nationalist tradition, pointing out that Khomyakov, Gertsen, Belinskiy, 'Danilevskiy, Dostoevskiy, the members of Narodnaya Volya and Lenin' all came up with 'theories about the special historical path and call of Russia' (Antonov, 1971: 28).

There were also other Romantic nationalist *samizdat* writings in circulation around 1970, which stated the same themes of Russia's moral superiority *vis-à-vis* Europe and Europe's otherness in starker terms. For example, a manifesto called 'The Word of the Nation' stated that the spirit of evil, 'having disguised its horns under a Beatles haircut', is trying to conduct its demoralising, disintegrative and degrading activity within the Christian

Church by preaching the ideology of the Jewish diaspora, that is, egalitarianism and cosmopolitanism (Yanov, 1987: 253; see also Duncan, 1989: 462).

The Beatles, making an unlikely appearance as a *pars pro toto* for the West, suggests the insidious quality of Western influence, which threatens to overwhelm those who do not show the necessary vigilance. The relationship suggested with the West and its Russian allies, which are not only held to be morally inferior but actually to embody evil incarnate, is one of *Kulturkampf*. It is the structural similarities between views such as these and views embodied by the Russian state which warrant Solzhenitsyn's attack on certain fellow Romantic nationalists as 'National Bolsheviks'. One notes, however, that Solzhenitsyn and associates, although they most often call for a relationship with the West based on isolation, also call for a *Kulturkampf* with the West, albeit in less absolute terms. Since Romantic nationalism takes as its common point of departure the organic character of the nation, these differences of views take place within rather than between positions, and thus have the character of a family quarrel.[5]

In 1980, the nationalist position was enriched by yet another suggestion for how to relate to Europe. In an article which was published in an official journal and later turned into a book, academician Dmitriy Likhachev used Russia's differences from Europe as a point of departure for delineating the national character. Likhachev's organic view of the nation becomes immediately clear in the way he stresses how the national character literally grows out of the soil: 'Like a big tree, Russia has a large root system, and a large crown which infiltrates with the crowns of different trees' (Likhachev, 1980: 10). In trying to delineate the typically Russian, moreover, he explicitly defends and builds on Dostoevskiy's views in the following manner:

If I now go on to talk about how and why the Russian artist is especially sensitive to changes in the seasons, in the hour of the day and in the atmospheric conditions, then the great French painter C. Monet comes to mind immediately: How the London Bridge in fog or the cathedral in Rouen [. . .] Yet these 'Russian' traits of Monet's in no way change my observations, they just go to show that Russian traits are in some measure all-human traits.

(Likhachev, 1980: 21)

Still, Likhachev resolutely denies being a nationalist: 'There exists a wholly mistaken notion that by underlining national specificities and trying to pinpoint the national character, we try to separate the nations from one another and so indulge in chauvinistic instincts', he complains, and separates healthy patriotism – 'the most noble of feelings' – from sick nationalism (Likhachev, 1980: 35, 37). Patriotism is indeed a necessity, since 'We are all citizens of our people (*grazhdane svoego naroda*), citizens of our great Union and citizens of the earth. Do not take that in a pompous way. I say that of all my heart, and what comes from the heart cannot be an empty phrase' (Likhachev, 1980: 38).[6]

The muddling of the concepts of state and nation in the phrase 'citizens of our people' and the appeal to childlike, 'natural' immediacy between heart and words are typical of the Romantic nationalist. Yet Likhachev's refusal to see Europe as wholly other – his insistence that 'today, we perceive Europe as our own' – further substantiates his metaphor of the nations of Europe and the world as being trees of perhaps different types, but making up a common panoply above mankind (Likhachev, 1980: 33). Thus, his proposed relationship with Europe is not one of isolation or *Kulturkampf*, but of cooperation. If compared to the Romantic nationalists of the late 1800s, he views are reminiscent of Solov'ev's rather than of Dostoevskiy's. His importance to the Russian debate about Europe is exactly to reinsert these views back into the Romantic nationalist position, thus adding to the pluralism of that position and bringing the number of its proposed relationships with Europe up to what it was a century before, namely, three.

If by far the most numerous and the most successful in penetrating public political space, the Romantic nationalists were not the only ones who painstakingly tried to carve out a niche for themselves at the margin of public political space. As the intense *samizdat* debate of the early 1970s unfolded, Sakharov stopped stressing 'the vitality of the socialist course' as he had done in his manifesto on progress, coexistence and intellectual freedom. Instead, he took steps which can be seen as the embryonic beginning towards resuscitating a liberal position in the Russian debate about Europe. Embryonic, since his writings did not spark enough like-minded reactions in the Russian debate for there to emerge a fully fledged position. The dominance of the

Romantic nationalist position within the *samizdat* literature can be gauged, among other things, by the style employed by Sakharov when he stakes out his turf: 'I am very fond of the landscape and culture of my country and of its people; and I am in no way eager to play the role of a "debunker"', he writes in a piece circulated in 1975, partially in answer to *From Under the Rubble* (Sakharov, 1975: 12). He does, moreover, take up topics which are conspicuously absent in the writings of the Romantic nationalists, such as the Russian 'barbarous race hatred'. Russian race hatred he explains as a vicarious resentment which emerges 'by virtue of tradition', and in order to replace the resentment of the party *nomenklatura* (Sakharov, 1975: 27–8). Finally, he explicitly and at length attacks views held by Solzhenitsyn and associates and central to the Romantic nationalist position:

> The salvation of our country – in its interdependence with all the rest of the world – is impossible without saving all of humanity. The appeal for national repentance on the part of Russia – an appeal born out of long suffering – is noble. It is set in opposition to Great Russian expansion – against national guilt and calamities. But are not both these matters due to one and the same fateful philosophical error – an error that inevitably entails moral harm and tragic consequences? For it is not a matter of accident that religion and life-affirming systems of ethical philosophy (for example, the views of Albert Schweitzer) put their emphasis on the human being and not on the nation. It is specifically the human being who is called upon to acknowledge guilt and succor his neighbor. We must have democratic reform affecting all aspects of life. The future of the Soviet Union lies in an orientation toward progress, science, and a personal and social moral regeneration. The modalities of that regeneration must not be limited to religious or nationalist ideologies, or to patriarchal aspirations in the spirit of Rousseau.
>
> (Sakharov, 1975: 45)[7]

By eschewing the nation in favour of a more cosmopolitan vantage point within a non-Bolshevik framework, Sakharov reinserts views into the Russian debate about Europe which have been absent for five decades. The liberal inclination of his views also emerges in the way he further specifies his views of Europe in direct assessment of the Western liberal intelligentsia, 'this influential and most socially-conscious stratum of Western society' (Sakharov, 1975: 8). While applauding their 'altruism and humanity', he reproaches them for their 'leftist-liberal faddishness', that is, their fear of looking dogmatic and old-fashioned. In the West as everywhere else, he writes, there exist complex social problems that cannot be solved immediately. Only facetious 'radical solutions, with their persuasive, surface simplicity, create the illusion that those problems can be quickly solved' (Sakharov, 1975: 88). The same danger looms in foreign policy, where the most important thing for the West is that it 'must under no circumstances allow the weakening of its stand against totalitarianism'. It must take a firm and united stand against totalitarian regimes, among other things by uniting, 'as in the Common Market', but not in such a way as to alienate the United States (Sakharov, 1975: 94).

In a work from 1980, moreover, Sakharov specifically calls to task 'the anti-Americanism of some European intellectuals' as 'ridiculous' and 'dangerous': 'Europe should fight shoulder by shoulder with the trans-Atlantic democracy, which is born and bred by Europe and constitutes its decisive hope' (Sakharov, 1984c: 84). Sakharov also reproaches those Westerners who do not make a difference between regime and country when they judge the USSR. Things do not go wrong because socialism is to be found in 'benighted Asian countries'. Such theories, which Sakharov denounces as 'inverted Slavophilism', simply do not hold up to historical scrutiny (Sakhrov, 1975: 90–1).

Unlike Russian liberal Westernisers from the period before the First World War, Sakharov looks first and foremost to the US, and not to Europe, when he looks for a Western stronghold which can assist in the Westernisation of Russia which he so much desires. Yet Sakharov shares with the older generations of liberals the dilemma of how to criticise what he sees as a non-European Russian regime while at the same time insisting on Russia's Europeanness *vis-à-vis* domestic opponents and Western sceptics. The coining of the phrase 'Western Slavophilism' to denote both Western European exclusivists and Russian nationalists neatly sums up Sakharov's own stand. Yet Sakharov was not very confident in the possibility of defeating his Russian Romantic nationalist opponents: he held that in wide circles, a feeling of Great Russian nationalism combined with a fear of democratic reform, and that 'Solzhenitsyn's errors' could aggravate this unhappy state of affairs even further (Sakharov, 1977: 301).

Although Sakharov's writings were important in reinserting a number of liberal Westernising ideas into the Russian debate about Europe, they did not spark enough written, like-minded reactions for there to re-emerge a fully fledged liberal Westernising position. That is not to say that there did not appear other writings with a roughly compatible thrust. One case in point is another reaction to Solzhenitsyn's letter to the Soviet leaders, written by Lev Kopolev. 'The "Western world"', Kopolev writes, taking issue with a quote from the letter, 'was never a "united force"', as Solzhenitsyn would have it. A number of Solzhenitsyn's basic attitudes, Kopolev goes on, 'are opposed to reality and are by no means original. There are clear echo[e]s of the "anti-Western" attitudes of the old Slavophiles and recent "Eurasians" and "Young Russians" in them. There is also the rejection of all the tendencies of European secularized human-istic thought' (Kopolev, 1977: 304–6). Solzhenitsyn draws on 'a demonic myth similar to the way the Nazis used the myth of "World Jewry" and the Stalinist and Maoists used the myth of "world imperialism"' in order to show how pre-revolutionary authoritarian Russia was wholly different from what came after (Kopolev, 1977: 336). Solzhenitsyn's juxtaposition of desirable autocracy and dangerous democracy leads him to call on the Kremlin to 'build a closed nationalistic, "authoritarian" state of a kind closest to the ideals of Stalin's autarchy on the "1948–1953 model"', Kopolev charges, and concludes that Solzhenitsyn's writings contain elements of '"inside-out bolshevism"' (1977: 315, 336, 342).

Kopolev's is a reaction which defines itself negatively, by opposing itself to an alleged tradition stretching from the Slavophiles to Solzhenitsyn. At one point he upbraids Solzhenitsyn for 'naively' believing '[t]he shameless claims of the Stalinists to Marxism' (Kopolev, 1977: 339).

This theme receives a rather different slant in Roy Medved'ev's reaction to Solzhenitsyn's open letter to the Soviet leaders. Medved'ev attacks the Marxism-Leninism of Stalin's as 'a faith', and he does so in the name of the 'science' of Marxism, a 'scientific socialism' (Medvedev, 1977: 89, also 87–8). Medved'ev wants a flourishing 'European sector of the USSR' to sustain the development of the rest of the country, a development which must follow the 'socialist path'. '[I]n our conditions', he writes,

> it is unrealistic to seek a way out in the transfer to Soviet soil of those economic and social structures which currently exist in capitalist countries or in the return to the national and religious values of 17th-century Russia. We may only proceed from the possibilities inherent in the society of the U.S.S.R.
>
> (Medvedev, 1977: 84–5)

Medved'ev stresses the Soviet Union's partial geographical presence in Europe, but also the need for a special socialist path necessitated by its different political and economic history. Medved'ev's wish to participate in the debate on the margin of public political space forces him to argue a point which the state and those participating in the tug-of-war over the position of the state treat as granted, namely, the superiority of socialism. If only for this reason, his argumentation is distinct from that of the *mezhdunarodniki*. In a very tentative way, Medved'ev begins to reinsert a theme in the Russian debate about Europe which was also present in the writings of Gertsen and the populists, namely, the search for models which combine the special needs of Russia/the Soviet Union with what is seen as the more advanced parts of contemporary Western practices.

If the foreign policy specialists did not address this theme in particular, they continued their debate about economics for Europe and for Russia's relationship to Europe. Economic intercourse between the two was picking up. Beginning in 1966 with the Soviets granting Fiat a contract to build a car factory in the Volga valley, economic relations between the Soviet Union and Western Europe picked up markedly. That year also saw a change of administration in West Germany that eventually led to Brandt and Scheel's new *Ostpolitik* (Stent, 1981; Sodaro, 1990; van Oudenaren, 1991). American economic strength relative to Western Europe's deteriorated steadily. These themes were taken up in the academic debate, and led to a change in emphasis towards those who stressed Western Europe's relative independence of the United States (Mel'nikov, 1968; Sodaro, 1990: 224; Adomeit, 1986: 506). The most important feature of the debate about Europe during these years is, however, the amazing inertia of the debate. The following quotes from 1975 reiterate the same topics, in the same way, as was done ten years before:

> One of the objectives pursued by the US policy of economic aid to Western Europe was to maintain the unity of the capitalist countries through some form of association. Beginning with the Marshall Plan the US actively peddled the idea of West European integration. A key condition for the implementation of this policy was the establishment of US leadership in any organisation of the West European capitalist countries. Thus, a prior condition for Marshall Plan aid was the creation in Europe of a supervisory committee that would draw up the programme for West European economic recovery under the aegis of the USA.
>
> (Kirsanov, 1975: 43)

And:

> Lenin's brilliant forecast that under capitalism a United States of Europe was possible only as an agreement for the purpose of 'jointly suppressing socialism in Europe' was fully borne out. [...] In theory one cannot rule out the possibility of political integration. Development is possible in the direction of a confederation, which does not infringe upon national sovereignty. But the establishment of a United States of Europe is hardly feasible under capitalism, without the abolition of monopoly rule.
>
> (Kirsanov, 1975: 88, 361–2)

Given the regurgitating character of the *mezhdunarodnik* tug-of-war over the position of the state, it is of little interest to the present concern that the main thrust of this particular book was the argument that contradictions between the US and the EEC had been on the increase throughout the entire postwar era, that the Soviet Union could benefit from exploiting these contradictions, but that it could also be beneficial to work together with the Americans.[8] The balance between views which stressed American predominance in Europe versus those which stressed Western European potential for independent action remained fairly stable. Even the disagreement about whether the EEC was first and foremost an 'objective phenomenon', that is, rooted in firm economic trends, or whether it was a political expedient, remained as an unresolved theme. For example, one writer deemed it necessary to insist on the EEC's 'objective character' in 1978, 1980, 1982 and again in 1983, most strongly perhaps the second time, when she stressed that understanding the EC was the key to understanding Western Europe in the postwar period (Demin and Raskov, 1980; Maksimova, 1978a; Maksimova, 1978b; Maksimova et al., 1982; Anyutin, 1983).

When seen in the context of the Russian debate about Europe taken as a whole, the degree in which *mezhdunarodnik* writings ignored the rest of this debate is remarkable. The immediate explanation of this may be sought in the way the state, through Glavlit and other organs of control, ensured that the limits of academic debate were tight. Yet the *samizdat* debates reviewed above did have an impact on other academic pursuits, notably literary criticism. For example, a 1969 article in *Voprosy literatury* upbraids another in *Molodaya gvardiya* because its author 'approvingly cites Avvakum's words against people who are "fascinated by the brilliance of Europe", which were uttered in a period (the seventeenth century) when Russia's backwardness strongly necessitated its learning from the experience and science of the West' (Pokrovskiy, 1969: 127). The quote in question can be found in Chalmaev (1968: 268): 'It was not the West as such which scared Avvakum', Chalmaev adds (1968: 269–70), 'but the transformation of contingent and obviously imperfect forms and ideas into something absolute and ideal, into the only platform for the development of Russia'.

In these public debates, which took place at the same time as *samizdat* output peaked, epithets like 'Slavophile' were used about political opponents. These public writings also saw the reappearance of themes long out of public circulation. In 1980, writings celebrating the 600-year anniversary of a famous battle against the Mongols at Kulikovo Pole repeatedly stressed 'that the Russian people had saved Europe at Kulikovo, but at a huge cost to themselves' (Duncan, 1989: 443; cf. Likhachev, 1980). This idea of Russia as the often unacknowledged bulwark of Europe against Asiatic chaos was, as noted above, an important ingredient of the Romantic nationalist position as late as the 1920s. Although all these examples are taken from journals specialising in literary criticism, the phenomenon was hardly isolated to this field. The years around 1970 also saw the appearance of articles in natural science journals about the 'bio-geographical conception of ethnic history' which dovetailed with themes floated in the *samizdat* debate (Hauner, 1990: 30–1 particularly singles out the work of Lev N. Gumilev in this regard).

It is commonly argued that themes from that debate surfaced in literary and natural science journals and not in foreign policy ones simply because the latter were subject to even tighter state control. That may well be. Still, the structure of the *mezhdunarodnik* debate itself invites another and complementary reason why what happened elsewhere failed to have an impact. The *mezhdunarodniki*, concentrating as they did on an internal tug-of-war over the position of the state, perhaps also for this reason saw it as counterproductive to allude to developments at the margin of public political space.

There was an exception, however. Sakharov's dictum from 1968 that the possibility of thermonuclear war made the Clausewitzian idea of war as a continuation of politics by other means outdated found an echo in the writings of the political scientist Fedor Burlatskiy. Yet, like Sakharov, Burlatskiy was not able to participate directly in the fully public Russian debate, but published elsewhere. In a 1971 UNESCO paper he held that peace was 'an all-human heritage, *an absolute value*, in contradistinction to relative values which are of significance to particular States, nations and social groups' such as matters of prestige (Shenfield, 1987: 44). Although Burlatskiy was a frequent participant in the fully public Russian debate throughout the 1970s, it was only in 1982 that he was able to insert this idea into the domestic debate, and then his colleague Vadim Zagladin and others had already written about how 'all-human problems' of a military, ecological and economic character necessitated 'a fundamental reconstruction of international relations' (Shenfield, 1987: 63). These were ideas which were to change the state's position in the first half of the next period.

To sum up, the beginning of this period saw a marked change in the Russian debate about Europe, originating in the general political debate. First, the state's position on the West changed. While in the preceding period, 'the camp of imperialism' was presented as a hostile entity trying to penetrate the Soviet Union, the image now shifted towards seeing 'the capitalist system' as an entity which remained morally inferior, but which was not wholly Other. As is evident already in the shift away from the military metaphor of the 'camp' towards the sociological one of the 'system', there was also a shift in emphasis where the proposed relationship with 'the West' was concerned, away from military confrontation and towards ideological confrontation, but also prospects for cooperation. In the Russian debate about Europe, this can be seen by the way the state proposed all-European cooperation as an alternative to the exclusive capitalist cooperation in organs such as the EEC. Much of the debate about Europe focused on the relative merits of treating it as a discrete entity, or as a subordinate part of 'the capitalist system' or 'the West', where American hegemony dominated.

The change in the state's position on the West and the toning down of the existence of internal enemies associated with it went together with an expansion of public political space. The state took steps to vitalise the foreign policy specialist milieu, and allowed them to participate in a reopened but tightly circumscribed public debate about the state's position. As the first part of the period came to a halt with the ousting of Khrushchev, this trend was halted but hardly reversed. The *mezhdunarodnik* debate nevertheless stagnated in the second half of the period. Whereas under Khrushchev, they had provided the Russian debate about Europe with some dynamism simply by resuscitating debate, under Brezhnev it is warranted to follow the lead of the succeeding period and refer their activities as representative of a 'period of stagnation'.

If the fully public part of the debate stagnated, however, developments at the margin of public political space nevertheless infused the Russian debate about Europe with dynamism. The *samizdat* literature provided a hotbed for the reconstitution of a Romantic nationalist position which, in little more than a decade, managed to come up with three different proposed relationships with Europe, one of which made its appearance in a fully public journal. Other *samizdat* writings, often written in response to the Romantic nationalist body of work and thus further attesting to its vitality, tentatively reintroduced themes previously associated with other positions. These writings did not, however, make up the critical mass necessary to reconstitute positions, liberal or otherwise. This development was left to the next period.

8

PERESTROYKA AND AFTER

With Gorbachev's coming to power in 1985, the state's position on the nature of international relations and capitalism changed along the lines staked out by *mezhdunarodnik* thinking on global problems and all-human solutions in the 1970s and especially in the early 1980s. Europe returned as a priority in the Soviet debate about the capitalist West as well as in foreign policy, with the state declaring 1987 'the year of Europe'. From 1987 to 1989, the state's position on the EC and on the US presence in Western Europe took on a much more positive tinge. Yet again, the ground had been prepared by *mezhdunarodnik* writings.

Under Gorbachev's leadership, the state attempted to reform the Bolshevik position, not to abolish it. But as the 1980s drew to a close, so did the reforms. Yet, as the state had also initiated a radical expansion of public political space at the beginning of the period, the Russian debate about Europe did not stop changing. The fully reconstituted liberal position attempted to make the state change even further in a Westernising direction. The Romantic national position, which emerged from the underground complete with a xenophobic and a spiritual wing just as at the beginning of the century, pressed in the opposite direction, protesting against the Westernising and anti-Russian character of *perestroyka*.

When the Soviet Union collapsed at the end of 1991 and the Russian Federation under Boris Yel'tsin donned the mantle of major successor state, the state initially took up an undiluted liberal position, advocating as much integration with Europe as speedily as possible. However, at the very moment of seeming liberal victory, the Romantic nationalist position was making itself ever more strongly felt in the debate. When the weight of the state and its foreign policy landed on the fragile shoulders of the liberal position, moreover, it soon became clear that Russia's relationship to Europe could not simply be one of 'rejoining civilisation by taking Russia into Europe'. Thus, whereas the framework within which liberals saw Europe and the moral judgement they passed on it did not change substantially, the optimism about the possible speed and thoroughness of Russian integration with Europe evaporated. The state's position as well as the main thrust of the liberal position as such shifted in the direction of advocating good foreign relations all around, thus balancing the focus on Europe with a more Eurasian one.

This move by the state also brought it somewhat closer to the spiritual wing of the Romantic nationalist position. However, this wing itself remained weak. At the end of this period, it was the xenophobic wing that was making the running in the debate.

The content of the Romantic nationalist position hardly changed as a result of the collapse of the Soviet Union. Yet by seemingly confirming the xenophobic wing's view of the Russian liberals as the errand-boys of the West, whose dirty deeds could only serve to split the Motherland, the collapse broadened their appeal. Moreover, a number of communists who found themselves without a position in the debate soon took up the Romantic nationalist one.

Throughout 1992 and 1993, the bearers of this position attacked the state's position more and more vigorously. When, in the autumn of 1993, people like Vice-President Rutskoy and the Speaker of Parliament Khasbulatov joined the all-out attack on the state's position, the state moved to redefine public political space. By literally shooting out and closing parliament, putting a new constitution before the electorate and closing down the main printed conduits of the Romantic nationalists, President Yel'tsin's state tried to strengthen the liberal position by weakening the Romantic nationalists. However, since the use of force was not sustained – for example, newspapers were soon allowed to reopen – Romantic nationalists found their way back in parliament after the December elections. They were also able to continue publishing. Thus, the state's attempt to redefine public political space proved to be a failure. The debate continued to be defined by a liberal and a Romantic nationalist position, with the state still sticking to the liberal position but attempting to borrow elements from the spiritual Romantic nationalists.

PERESTROYKA

In the mid-1980s, the state expanded public political space considerably. This policy, which was introduced by the name of glasnost', meant that the parts of the debates which had previously been going on at the margins of political space could now go public. The fully fledged Romantic nationalist position as well as a number of themes which had been developed in *samizdat* became part of one common debate.

This situation also lent a new freshness to the debate about the state's position. By throwing public political space open in the way it did, the state also placed the onus upon itself of relating to developments within it. This meant that, in a much higher degree than before, *all* writings could indirectly impinge on the state's position simply by inserting themes and positions of which the state would have to take note. This indirect pressure on the state to adjust its position in relation to the debate at large was accompanied by pressure of a more direct kind, inasmuch as *glasnost'* also meant that the stakes involved in the tug-of-war between foreign policy specialists and others professionally preoccupied with the state's position were upgraded. Whereas before, these participants in the debate had only been allowed to argue publicly about minor changes of course and peripheral concerns, they now deemed it possible to address central concerns in a more radical manner.

Very soon after he took over as General Secretary of the CPSU, Gorbachev signalled that some change in the state's position on relations with the West was under way. Already in the spring of 1985, he stated that the process of *détente* should be revived, not by returning to the situation of the 1970s, but by 'striving for something much greater'. A new *détente* should serve as a transitional stage on the way to 'a reliable and comprehensive system of international security' (*Pravda*, 9 May 1985).

The very vagueness of such statements serves to underline that reform of the Bolshevik position *as such* rather than change in some specific direction was the main message. The subsequent launching of campaigns in favour of *glasnost'* and new political thinking rather than for some more specified goal, pointed in the same direction. Gorbachev made his appeals for *glasnost'* in terms of means rather than of ends (Goban-Klas and Kolstø, 1994). In July 1986, for example, he held that *glasnost'* was needed to ensure adherence to the line hammered out at the Twenty-seventh Party Congress and 'to include the people in a real way into all aspects of the administration of the state, such as Lenin dreamt about' (*Pravda*, 1 August 1986).

The idea of raising the regime's legitimacy and efficiency by letting people participate in a public debate was not necessarily a Westernising idea; it could equally well be interpreted along Slavophile lines: by giving people an open channel to the leadership in the form of the press, the bureaucracy's dealings became more transparent, the leadership gained an extra means of control, and the 'organic' tie between the 'head' and the 'body' of the nation was strengthened. For this reason, the introduction of *glasnost'* did not in and of itself signal a change in the state's position along the lines which became apparent later in the period. Its importance to that debate was to do primarily with the way in which it expanded public political space.

Gorbachev's insistence on quoting Lenin signalled his continued adherence to a Bolshevik position. The Lenin quotes went together with a denunciation of Stalin's policies as an aberration from Leninism, and with rehabilitations of old Bolsheviks long dead. Politics in the 1920s were re-represented as a fight between Stalinist and Bukharinist 'lines', with Bukharin in the role of the 'true' Bolshevik. The ideal of the law-governed state was emphasised: 'From the very beginning of Soviet rule Lenin and the Party attached paramount importance to the maintenance and consolidation of law', Gorbachev wrote in 1987 (1988: 105–6).

The state declared 1987 to be 'the year of Europe', and gave new emphasis to the old theme of the need for wide-ranging European state-based cooperation. Already in the preceding period, Brezhnev, and also Gorbachev himself, had used the expression of a 'common European home' in debates with foreign statesmen. Brezhnev used the expression 'our common home' about Europe during a visit to Bonn (*Pravda*, 24 and 25 November 1981, article entitled 'Europe – Our Common Home'; Sodaro, 1990: 281). Gorbachev did the same in a speech to the House of Commons (*Pravda*, 19 December 1984).

A tremendous potential for a policy of peace and neigh-
borliness is inherent in the European cultural heritage.
Generally, in Europe the new, salutary outlook knows much
more fertile soil than in any other region where the two
social systems come into contact.

(Gorbachev, 1988: 198)

Although the idea of two social systems was still present in
the book from the one which the above quotation is taken
(*Perestroika*), the stress was no longer on a 'true' Europe as
opposed to a 'false' – as it had always been before within the
Bolshevik position – but on Europe as a cultural whole.

The writings evolving from the state about the 'common
European home' also entailed a shift on the question of Europe's
relative importance within the West. Gorbachev stressed the
importance of changing attitudes so that Europe was seen less
'through the prism of relations with the United States' (*Pravda*,
24 May 1987; Wettig, 1990: 5). Whereas, at the beginning of
the period, the United States was represented as clearly non-
European, by 1987 it was held to be attached to it, but hardly
to be occupying any central part of the building. Russia,
however, was placed squarely within the perimeters of Europe:

Some in the West are trying to 'exclude' the Soviet Union
from Europe. Now and then, as if inadvertently, they equate
'Europe' with 'Western Europe'. Such ploys, however,
cannot change the geographic and historical realities.
Russia's trade, cultural and political links with other
European nations and states have deep roots in history. We
are Europeans. Old Russia was united with Europe by
Christianity. [. . .] The history of Russia is an organic part
of the great European history.

(Gorbachev, 1988: 190)

Statements such as these marked the apex in the change of the
framework within which the state saw Europe during *perestroyka*,
and the nadir in the view of Russia as an entity morally superior to Europe. From 1987 to the end of 1991, changes in the
state's position did not take place at the levels of framework or
moral assessment, but concerned specific aspects of the relationship with Europe. Specifically, the state's position changed
on the two questions which dominated *mezhdunarodnik* debate

in the preceding period: the status of the EC and the assessment of the US role in Europe. And if the foreign policy specialists had introduced the general ideas which were adopted by the state in the first half of this period already in the 1970s, it is equally clear that they precipitated these two specific changes in the state's position with their writings during the first Gorbachev years.

In the early years of *perestroyka*, there was a sharp increase in *mezhdunarodnik* writings affirming international relations as an interdependent concern where the actors did not only have specific, but also mutual interests, and where the use of force and a position of strength may not always be a panacea. For example, in April 1986 the columnist Aleksandr Bovin held that 'Anyone trying to build up his own security will ultimately aggravate his own military-strategic security' (quoted in Hoffman, 1990: 57–8). The month afterwards, young Gromyko and Vladimir Lomeyko wrote that 'while before peaceful coexistence could proceed in various forms of confrontation, now – only and exclusively in the form of peaceful cooperation and peaceful rivalry' (Gromyko and Lomeiko, 1986: 22; cf., Gromyko and Lomeiko, 1984 for the first use of the expression 'new thinking').

The focus of the *mezhdunarodnik* debate rapidly shifted away from the question of the nature of the ties between the entities to the question of which entities were paramount in international relations – classes or states. Already in 1986, Gorbachev had written that 'the interests of societal development and pan-human values take priority over the interests of any particular class' (*Literaturnaya gazeta*, 5 November 1986; see also Malcolm, 1994: 155). In the summer of 1988, this issue became a focal point for the determination of the state's position. Foreign Minister Shevardnadze held that 'We are justified in not understanding [peaceful coexistence] as a specific form of class struggle' (*Pravda*, 26 July 1988). Politburo Member Egor Ligachev, however, held that 'We proceed from the class nature of international relations' (*Pravda*, 6 August 1988). The arguments were fleshed out in a debate between Aleksandr Bovin and foreign policy specialist Vladimir Lukin printed in January 1989. Lukin held that the 'simple' image of two blocs, two systems, and the developing colonial and semi-colonial world in between had been overtaken by events. Bovin, however, countered by still seeing the central drama of present-day international relations in the competition between two social systems (Bovin and Lukin, 1989: 59). By 1989, however, this was no longer the most widespread view in the *mezhdunarodnik* debate. Nor did it coincide with the state's position, which had changed decisively away from seeing international relations as a zero-sum game between classes, towards seeing it as a potential positive-sum game between states.

Where the specific question of the EC was concerned, already in 1986, *mezhdunarodnik* writings began to highlight the 'subjective' sides of EC integration, and especially the role played by the idea that integration of old West European enemies might contribute to the peaceful settlement of conflicts between them.[1] Whereas in the previous period, the moral assessment of West European integration had been negative or neutral, for the first time the suggestion was now made that capitalist integration may actually be a morally positive thing, not only in economic terms but also as a mechanism for conflict resolution. In December 1988, a new set of IMEMO theses on the EC appeared. It stressed how the idea of integration had received broad support from different social forces: having experienced the horrors of two World Wars, the peoples of Western Europe saw in integration a possibility to end armed conflicts, mistrust and, above all, the traditional Franco-German antagonism (IMEMO AN SSSR, 1988: 7). This highlighting of the 'subjective' and 'peace-building' elements in the analysis of the EC mirrored the development of the broader political debate already mentioned, especially the toning down of economic determinism and the more positive moral assessment of capitalist European politics and politicians (which was also granted retrospectively).

Whereas the IMEMO theses also mirrored the upgrading of Europe as a concern to the USSR and stressed its economic independence *vis-à-vis* the US, it qualified this view by explicitly drawing into doubt the possibility of evolving an EC security identity. It was argued that the Community's material ability to direct a more or less independent policy was to a significant extent neutralised by the fact that in the military field, the US remained the unconditional leader of the Western world. Quite often, it was stated, it was dissatisfaction with this subordinated position that served as the point of departure for different projects for military-political integration within the EC. Thus, 'the West European striving to increase its role in the military sphere is one of the factors which undermines American supremacy in the system of Atlantic ties' (IMEMO AN SSSR, 1988: 17).

The state's position changed towards seeing the EC as the institutionalised expression of Western Europe, and an entity which was if not on a par with the US, then at least one which could be mentioned in the same breath. Foreign Minister Shevardnadze remarked in 1989 that if a certain Soviet proposal 'is supported by the European Community, the United States and other great powers, then success should be expected' (official Soviet text quoted in *Financial Times*, 24 February 1989). At the same time, however, the US role in Europe was acknowledged as a legitimate fact. Later during the same year, Gorbachev stated that 'the USSR and the United States constitute a natural part of the European international-political structure' (*Pravda*, 7 July 1989).[2] If this was a significant change on a specific point, however, Gorbachev also used the same speech explicitly to draw up the line which the state's position would never cross as long as he remained at the helm when he warned against thinking that 'the overcoming of the division of Europe is the overcoming of socialism. That is a course for confrontation.' This is where the state's position came to rest for the remaining part of the period.

As the changes in the state's position came to a standstill and the *mezhdunarodnik* writings focused on specific and immediate foreign policy issues like German reunification, the centre stage in the Russian debate about Europe was taken over by what rapidly became a fully fledged liberal position. Within a year, however, they had to share it with a resurgent Romantic nationalist position.

Aspiring liberals emerged from the underground and from the most unlikely places, writing articles, advising new and old politicians, dominating the debate. If there were no further change in the state's position in a liberal direction, it was certainly not for lack of new liberal ideas. The writings of key advisers and foreign policy specialists started to converge with a new spate of writings from the embryonic liberals who had been publishing in *samizdat* since the late 1960s. Together, these two groups were able to re-establish that fully fledged liberal position in the Russian debate which Sakharov and others had started to resuscitate twenty years before. The two groups also drew near to each other in the sense that Sakharov and others emerged from the underground to engage in parliamentary work. So did a number of former political advisers to Gorbachev, after having become impatient with his unwillingness to evolve the state's position even further in the direction they desired.

If some texts written around 1989 were immediately recognisable as liberal, other liberal ideas appeared in texts which were decked out with Marxist markers. For example, the theme that Stalinist policies were negative and 'Asiatic' and a negation of normal and positive 'European' policies re-emerged in an article from 1989 where, following four Lenin quotes, Marx and Engels were quoted to the effect that 'civil society is the real starting point and arena for all history', and Plekhanov as saying that 'a *people* in the European sense of that word is now being formed in Russia in the figure of the working class' (Starikov, 1989: 144, 136). Stalin's collectivisation and 'unaddressed terror', the author wrote, did away with civil society, thus scoring a victory for an Asiatic paternalistic model over a European, civil-society-based one (Starikov, 1989: 136).

The framework within which Europe was seen by these aspiring liberals was a cultural one, stressing humanist ideas about the integrity of the individual and the limited rights of the state *vis-à-vis* the citizen as the common political goals of all mankind. Russia was not held to be morally superior to Europe, but as its potential equal and in certain respects contemporary inferior. For example, building on the state's idea of a 'common European home', already in 1988 Vladimir Lukin wrote that

> The 'Common European House' is the home of a civilization of which we have been on the periphery for a long time. The processes that are going on today in our country and in a number of socialist countries in Eastern Europe have besides everything else a similar historical dimension – the dimension of a movement towards a return to Europe in the civilized meaning of the term.
>
> (*Moscow News*, 25 September 1988)

Becoming more specific, the writer Chingiz Aytmatov told the Congress of People's Deputies meeting in the summer of 1989 that the Soviet Union should learn a new brand of socialism from 'the flourishing law-governed societies of Sweden, Austria, Finland, Norway, the Netherlands, Spain and finally, Canada across the ocean' (*Izvestiya*, 4 June 1989). Moreover, during the session, Gorbachev's top adviser, Aleksandr Yakovlev, told a TV journalist that parliaments in other countries had entirely different and more solid and detailed traditions. Russia, on the other hand, did not, and therefore had to learn: 'Of course, we must learn professionalism in the economy and politics; above all we must learn democratic professionalism. We must learn democracy, tolerance of others' opinions and thoughts' (quoted in Brown, 1990: 61).

In putting forward this agenda for learning from Europe, aspiring liberals were acutely aware of the implications for group identity. For example, in January 1989 the journal *The Twentieth Century and Peace* printed three articles on convergence between capitalism and socialism. This was an old theme of Sakharov's, and with direct reference to his work the journal asked whether, by writing off a special socialist path into the future, Russia would not also have to write off its self-consciousness as a global avant-garde: 'Will not the rapprochement (*sblizhenie*) of the systems lead to loss of originality for all of us? If we lose faith in our own exclusivity, do we not simultaneously lose any kind of faith altogether?' (*Vek XX i mir*, 1989: 14).

As liberals stopped taking the existence of two different social systems as the starting point for their thinking, this question of whether there was not still a need for some separate group identity gave rise to a bifurcation of views within the liberal position. Building on the introduction into the debate of the theme of 'European civilisation', some liberals presented the need to copy and learn from the West as a question of qualifying for membership in 'civilisation'. In formulating an extreme position on the preferred relationship between Russia and Europe, many liberals followed their pre-revolutionary predecessors in seeing the Russian people's *own* lack of 'European democratic consciousness' as perhaps the main problem. 'Civilized democracy never had a good chance in this country', Liliya Shevtsova wrote at the end of 1990 (Shevtsova, 1990: 4; see also Timmermann, 1992: 58). And in the summer of 1991, Andrey Novikov formulated the problem in considerably greater detail:

Today the question of 'Westernisation' (*vesternizatsiya*) is very much in vogue. How can we become Europe in the course of three Five-Year Plans? How can we cover the path which the West spent five hundred years traversing? The answer is self-evident – not in any way. If a liberal consciousness was not able to take hold during the nineteenth century, how should it be able to do so today? And if there is no liberal consciousness, can there be liberal democratic institutions? And if so, what are the chances for a 'return' to the lap of world civilisation envisioned by those who talk about 'new thinking' and the end of the Cold War? Will it take the shape of crowds of wild barbarians who, passports in hand, storm the Soviet–Polish border in order to sell off ikons for a hundred dollars? No, the wall will not be built by us, but by the West, a wall similar to the one which the Americans have built along their border with Mexico. Only today do we begin to understand that warlike confrontation is only a superficial manifestation of a deeper confrontation between West and East. Today, the 'Homo Soveticus' who has emerged from the regime's test-tube is the main carrier of totalitarianism. The problem does not reside in the KGB or the CPSU, and absolutely not in statism as such. The problem resides in society itself, which reproduces totalitarianism in ever new aspects.

(Novikov, 1991: 14)[3]

There is in these writings the same thrust as can be found in pre-revolutionary liberal writings and for that matter in Bolshevik writings: the writers set themselves up as belonging to an endangered species of Russian Europeans, somehow managing to keep aflame the torch of civilisation in the presumed non-European twilight of Russian mass culture. Novikov takes this so far as to propose a relationship between Russia and Europe based on isolation, not because he wills it, but because he holds the non-European parts of Russia to deserve it, and sees the need for Europe to impose it.

The irony of it is of course that 1990–1 was the high tide of Westernisation generally, and the time when discourses about 'Russia and Europe' everywhere were lifted back into the debate in Russia specifically. For example, Haruki Wada participated in a roundtable covered by TV as well as in *Kommunist*. He noted that the debate centred around four 'myths': Russia as the West, Russia as the East, Russia as 'some kind of bridge between the

West and the East', and Russia as a Sphinx-like enigma (Vada et al., 1990: 19). Moreover, the journal *Neva* serialised a book by Alexander Yanov (1987; 1990). It was also in 1990 that a number of texts written by Russians in exile long dead started to be published in Russia, with a number of 'thick' literary and scholarly journals starting to run series on the history of Russian social and political thought (e.g. Berdiaev (1947); Fedotov [1932] 1990). One last example concerns a roundtable of young social scientists on 'Russia and Europe' held in 1991, where Vladimir Malakhov raised 'the question about the place of "the European" in the structure of "Russian identity". That is, the question of the Russian imagination and its Other' (Kara-Mursa et al., 1991: 148). And there we are, with the Russian debate itself incorporating the kind of theoretical insights underlying the present work.

Other liberals, seeing the political dead-end into which Novikov's proposed relationship with Europe would lead, insisted on trying to replace the fading Soviet Russian identity with something else, and came up with the slogan of 'Eurasia'.

For example, the historian Mikhail Gefter in the summer of 1989 pointed out that a Frenchman can have a number of other identities and still be a Frenchman. But are the Soviets (*sovetskie*) 'forever attached to that ethnonym?' Gefter asked. The answer is both yes and no: 'Our Eurasia is not just a geographical given, or a fact of Russian history', he answered himself, but added that in the final analysis, 'we are all the hostages' of such givens and such facts. In his time, Lenin also struggled with this, and wanted to rename the USSR the Union of Soviet Republics of Europe and Asia, Gefter pointed out. Asked whether Russians have not always 'felt themselves to be of Europe, yet disputed everything European', he answered that 'We are not a country. We are a *country of countries* [. . .] a centaur by birth', and therefore dependent on the development of all mankind (Gefter, 1989: 22–7).

The thrust of Gefter's argument is very different from Novikov's, inasmuch as Gefter does not seek to dissolve Russia in Europe, but to carve out a new identity for it in lieu of the identity furnished by the old Soviet communist one. The dichotomy between seeing Russia only in terms of Europe, and of seeing it as somehow bridging Europe and Asia, was highlighted in the title of the piece, which was 'Dom Evrazii' – a

Eurasian home – as opposed to the 'Common European Home' propagated by the state. The dichotomy was made explicit on the front page, where the topic of the article was given as 'Europe or Eurasia? USSR on the Border'.[4]

The emergence of Eurasia as a theme for liberals to ponder caught on and soon became central to the debate. In the autumn of 1990, Viktor Krivorotov published an article starting from the premise that Russia is a Eurasian civilisation. Rather than justifying the epithet, he saw a need to insist on Russia actually *being* a civilisation: 'Civilisation? Doubtlessly. Yet for others our civilisation has a whiff of superciliousness about it, they look at us like one looks at an aristocrat who has fallen on bad times' (Krivorotov, 1990: 141). This situation calls for a particular approach to Russia's problems:

> For example, the Westerners totally ignore fundamental ideological questions when they do not even pose the questions of Russia's future role as a superpower (*sverkhderzhava*), about the traditional messianism of the Russian people etc. Where immediate and long-term national goals are concerned, the Westernisers simply do not take cognizance of them.
>
> (Krivorotov, 1990: 157)

Krivorotov's critique of the failure of the extreme liberals to address the national theme is reminiscent of Herzen's old dictum that Westernisers would be cut off from the people for as long as they ignored the questions posed by the Slavophiles. A number of liberal writers complained about the 'masochism' of the extreme liberals (e.g. Kara-Mursa et al., 1991: 144).

The idea of a 'Eurasian' destiny for the Soviet Union also cropped up in *mezhdunarodnik* writings. In groping for a strategic goal for Soviet foreign policy to take the place of the defunct ideological struggle with the West, Vladimir Lukin came up with an idea for a European community from the Atlantic to the Urals in the west and the joining of the Pacific integration process in the east. This, he thought, would form a bridge between 'two Europes. This may sound utopian today, but this variant seems highly realistic to me, perhaps the only way our country may enter the upcoming Millennium in a worthy manner' (Bovin and Lukin, 1989: 67).

At this juncture, then, the liberal position proposed a relationship with Europe based on two different variants of partnership. Whereas some liberals advocated a 'return to civilisation' – that is, a relationship with Europe where Russia was seen as an apprentice with no clear additional and specific identity – others saw this as a poor way of rallying mass Russian support behind a programme based on individual rights, market economy and political pluralism. Instead, they evolved the slogan of 'Eurasia' as a proposed group identity for a Russian-based state which should secure the electorate's support for closer relations with Europe.

Where the Romantic nationalist position is concerned, it slithered effortlessly out of its underground existence and into public political space. A number of the Romantic nationalist *samizdat* writers of the late 1960s went about reiterating their ideas in public media. For example, Aleksandr Solzhenitsyn published a long Philippic against modernity in two newspapers, reiterating almost verbatim a number of the ideas from *From Under the Rubble*: Russia should not spend its force being a superpower, but on attaining spiritual clarity; free elections and a multiparty system were harmful onslaughts against the organic nation, and so on (Solzhenitsyn, 1990).

Solzhenitsyn's old associate from *From Under the Rubble*, Igor' Shafarevich, published an old manuscript written in the early 1980s. An editorial introduction states that 'The article was written in the beginning of the 1980s; however, the reader may convince himself that it has not lost its actuality'. Thus, *Nash sovremennik* explicitly throws its weight behind the article. The piece was an attack on Russia's detractors, those who see it as an Asiatic slave state, and who hold that communism was only the last in a number of totalitarian reigns. Shafarevich pointed out that the idea of the totalitarian state was developed in the West, by Hobbes and others, and not in Russia. So was the idea of socialism, which 'had no roots at all in Russian tradition before the nineteenth century. Russia did not have any authors of More's and Campanella's type' (Shafarevich, 1989: 171). As a matter of fact, he concluded, the characteristics singled out by Russia's detractors as 'typically Russian' were not Russian at all, but were to the contrary 'the price for Russia's joining the sphere of the new Western culture' (Shafarevich, 1989: 171). But if this is so, Shafarevich asked rhetorically, then why do the detractors go on spreading what they must know are lies? The answer he found in their hatred of the Russian nation. Latching on to and pursuing Solzhenitsyn's attack on cosmopolitans lacking faith in Russia in *From Under the Rubble*, he lashed out against ecumenism, the multiparty system and other long-standing *bêtes noires* of the Romantic nationalists. The 'liberal-ecumenistic' camp, he argued, was simply 'un-national'. And, when the Western multiparty system seems to be 'an outgoing social order', he asks why Russia should bother to copy it. Rather, it should say good riddance to it, since 'it came with a guarantee for civil war, for defence from government terror (but not from "Red brigades") and for increase in material well-being (and the threat of economic crisis)' (Shafarevich, 1989: 174–6).

Nevertheless, Russia's detractors want to impose this system on Russia, and they want to do it in the manner of an 'OCCU-PATION', Shafarevich wrote, using capital letters: they are in cahoots with the West. Like the Russian intelligentsia in the nineteenth century, which brought about communism, Russia's detractors today make up a 'little people', characterised by their 'Russophobia' and living in the midst of the real Russian 'great people' which they hate so much. This 'little people' of Russian detractors consists of part of the intelligentsia, and '[O]bviously, Jewish national feeling is one of the basic forces which keep the "Little People" going today' (Shafarevich, 1989: 189). Shafarevich detailed Jewish ploys to undermine Russia, not stopping short of mentioning a number of Jews by name and, in a case where the name does not sound obviously Jewish, giving the former family name in parentheses in order to press home the point.

As demonstrated above, the term 'Russophobia' had earlier been used by Romantic nationalists such as Danilevskiy and Solzhenitsyn. Solzhenitsyn, incidentally, has never distanced himself from the views of his old associate Shafarevich. By once again wheeling out the figure of the rootless and Westernised Russian Jew as the Russian enemy within, Shafarevich made fully public a theme which had lurked within the Romantic national-ist position since Solzhenitsyn and associates started to resusci-tate it. Despite the state's attempts at keeping this line of argument out of the debate by using anti-discrimination laws to silence leading members of *Pamyat'*, the idea of the Jewish fifth column, so important for the Romantic nationalist position at the beginning of the century, was back. What this *Pamyat'* appeal of 8 December 1987 had not seen fit to spell out, Shafarevich had:

In our country these days the activity of *enemies* is becoming more obvious. They are entrenching themselves in all the sections of the PARTY, the leading force of the USSR. Dark elements in it, speculating with Party slogans and Party phraseology, are in practice carrying out a struggle with *the indigenous population of the country, and annihilating the national face of the peoples*. They are reanimating Trotskyism, in order to discredit socialism, in order to sow chaos in the State, in order to open the sluices of Western capital and Western ideology.

(quoted in Duncan, 1989: 597)

As was the case at the beginning of the century, moreover, there were no watertight compartments between the different circles making up the Romantic nationalist position. Shafarevich was part of a link between anti-modernists like the authors Solzhenitsyn and Valentin Rasputin on the one hand, and more state- and military-minded Romantic nationalists of the variant that was called 'national Bolsheviks' in *From Under the Rubble* – people like the TV journalist Aleksandr Nevzorov and the writer Aleksandr Prokhanov – on the other. To stay with the terminology used throughout this book, there was a confluence between the spiritual and xenophobic variants, with the latter almost eclipsing the former.

The latter were people who now self-consciously set about restructuring a xenophobic nationalist position by emphasising the role of the Russian state as absolutely central to the future of the Motherland, and attempting to bring in at least some of the nationalists who rather concentrated on the ethnic Russian nation as the prime factor (Simonsen, 1993). Moreover, a further attempt to consolidate the Romantic nationalist position overall was made by commencing a dialogue between their own and the spiritual variants of it. Before long, not only Shafarevich but also people like Valentin Rasputin, who had dedicated his entire career to defending the Russian countryside against the town and had clearly been a Romantic nationalist of the spiritual variant, were to be found squarely at the core of the united Romantic nationalist position.

Already at the outset of 1988, Prokhanov – a writer of heroic wartales with a wide military following that has earned him the nickname 'the nightingale of the general staff' – referred to two 'pillars' of contemporary Russian thought. One he held to be '"leftist", of Western-liberal orientation, the other one "rightist", representing traditional Russian values, leading back to "the pre-socialist world", to "the Russian idea"' (*Literaturnaya Rossiya*, 22 January 1988; also Simonsen, 1993: 86–100).

The reference to the pre-socialist world was of the essence. Prokhanov the statist did not try to occupy the terrain previously held by the state and now abandoned. Rather than raising the banner of communism, he emphasised the continuity in Russian history before and after October 1917. The effortlessness with which the Bolshevik position over the next few years was simply subsumed by the Romantic nationalist position, invites speculation as to the structural similarities between the Bolshevik and the national images of the ideal political unit. Both positions are constructed around a clear-cut divide between 'us' and 'them', with those not with 'us' (the class enemy, the un-national) being against us. Both see the ties holding 'us' together to be organic, and thus the 'natural' and indeed only possible formation and aggregation of the body politic to be harmonious. In Lenin's famous phrase, the party was the mind, honour and conscience not only of the state, but of the entire epoch. The 'plans of the party were the plans of the people', to paraphrase a ubiquitous slogan from the Soviet period. If Bolshevism saw the party as the head and the masses as the body of the body politic, in much the same way nationalism sees the state as the head and the nation as the body. The organic metaphor also suggests that any conflict inside the body politic is by its very nature an illness or a disease – an unnatural mode of operation, possibly with external causes.

Bolshevism's structural similarities to nationalism stand out with particular clarity when compared to the liberal position, where the line between 'us' and 'them' is not equally clear-cut, and where the image of the political unit is not organic, but mechanical. Rather than postulating conflictless harmony between the party and the masses or the state and the nation, the liberal position sees politics as a game involving three units – individual, society and state. Each of these may have conflicting interests, and some degree of conflict is legitimate. Moreover, the social contract is not seen only as the starting point of politics, but as the matrix on which it is played out: for communists and nationalists, the leading role of the party/the state is a given, whereas liberals refer to the *Rechtsstaat* as the political master principle. In order to keep the always latent conflicts in check and secure a certain degree of harmony, the state should be a *Rechtsstaat*, where – to use Spinoza's classical formulation – the King's documents should take precedence over the King's will. In other words, the state should guarantee and implement a state of law where written, non-retrospective rules regulate relations between as well as within state and society. The latter should be a civil society, that is, it should to some extent have an existence independent of the state, in the economic as well as in other spheres. The individuals constituting society should have rights guaranteed by the *Rechtsstaat*, and should have the opportunity to participate in the organisation of civil society.

There are of course a number of reasons why people who formerly held key positions in the communist political structure started to support a Romantic nationalist position and not a liberal one. While their respective potentials as ways of hanging on to power are basic, the lower number of conceptual moves it takes to get from a Bolshevik to a xenophobic nationalist position is an important additional explanation.

It is remarkable that the Bolsheviks, who flocked to the Romantic nationalist position, were not even able to rub off some of their former specific ideas on it. If the alliance between old *apparatchiks* deserting the Bolshevik position to take up the nationalist cause and old Romantic nationalists was potentially of enormous political significance, it did not yield any new ideas, but concentrated on attacking the positions of the state and the liberals. 'There is no future for *perestroyka*, because it is too much of a Western idea', Nevzorov stated in 1991. Nevertheless, the West cannot suppress the Russian soul, since Russians are still able to work miracles. Russians fight against the enemy, be they hungry and empty-handed, Nevzorov declared, and acknowledged that this was not appreciated by everybody. Therefore, 'we must protect the culture and the Orthodox church with tanks. Otherwise they will be suppressed. We need to save our beloved Fatherland. We have to do away with the democrats. Otherwise they will rob Russia' (*Rahvalent*, 29 May 1991).

Innovation was left to other nationalists, and the most significant development was perhaps the re-emergence of a 'Eurasianist' line of argument. For example, in an article from

1991, foreign policy specialist El'giz Pozdnyakov's starting point
was that 'The disease of "Europeanism", of "Westernism", came
to Russia' with Peter the Great (Pozdnyakov, 1991: 46).[5] Since
then, he charged, a number of Russians have seen Russia
through the eyes of an outsider, and not of an insider. These
'Westernisers' have either held that Russia's destiny lay with
European civilisation or they have not seen a destiny for it at
all. In either case, they have been wrong, since nations, like
human beings, have their individual destinies. Nobody can
replace their destiny with another and pursue the historical
mission preordained for another nation, he held, and added that
providence indeed paid more attention to Russia than to any
other nation or people. Russia's particular destiny is to maintain
a strong state so that it can act as the holder of the balance
between East and West, a task 'vitally important both for Russia
and the entire planet' (Pozdnyakov, 1991: 47). In performing this
balancing act throughout its history, Russia has given 'the
Eurasian community' a unique experience.

Having thus drawn up a historiosophical framework and filled
it with organic nations, each living out its particular destiny, with
Russia taking pride of place among them, Pozdnyakov proceeded
to elaborate on the differences between Russia and the West. The
Russian empire, he stated, 'may be described as organic and mild
in contrast to other, harsher, world Empires [like] the Roman,
Ottoman, British or French which did not have either an organic
character or a natural geopolitical basis' (Pozdnyakov, 1991: 48).
Quoting Dostoevskiy, he sees the Russian empire as having a civil-
ising mission: for a millennium it has 'been beating off cruel enemies, who but for them would have fallen on Europe. Russians
colonized the further regions of their infinite Motherland,
Russians stood up for their outlying lands and consolidated their
domination, and did that so that we, cultural people, not only
would not succeed in their consolidation, but would on the
contrary probably shake them loose' (Pozdnyakov, 1991: 57).
Commenting on his quotation from Dostoevskiy, Pozdnyakov
(1991: 48) concludes that 'As for the last idea, considering all
that is going on now, one cannot help acknowledging that
Dostoyevsky was right', thus embracing a passus which reads not
unlike Kipling's 'The White Man's Burden'. Yet Pozdnyakov also
strongly insisted that one *cannot* compare Russia and Europe,
since they belong to two different cultural types:

Russia cannot return to Europe because it never belonged
to it. Russia cannot join it because it is part of another type
of civilization, another cultural and religious type. [. . .] Any
attempt to make us common with Western civilization and
even to force us to join it undertaken in the past resulted
in superficial borrowings, deceptive reforms, useless luxury
and moral lapses. [. . .] in nature there does not exist such
a thing as a 'Common Civilization'. The term in fact
denotes the pretention of Western European civilization to
the exclusive rights to universal significance. And it is a
mistake to reduce the basics of every civilizations to only
one type. Moreover, it is impossible, in practice at least,
because the fundamentals of one type of civilization cannot
be transferred to nations belonging to other types. [. . .]
History confirms the impossibility of such a transfer (and
God himself provides evidence through Moses in the
Pentateuch).

(Pozdnyakov, 1991: 49, 54)

Nevertheless, Europe and Russian Westernisers have time and
again tried to 'Europeanise' Russia. Marxism, as one of many
branches of the European civilisation whose common denominator is a rationalism 'totally alien to the Russian spirit', is only
the latest example but one of such a Westernising onslaught on
the Russian nation. According to Pozdnaykov, Marxism as a part
of West European ideology was stamped with an inherent spirit
of violence and aggressive Messianic interventionism that is
largely absent from Orthodox civilisation and its ideology. The
attempts to 'Europeanise' Russia can be compared to the labours
of Sisyphus: 'every attempt to roll the "European stone" up the
"Russian mountain" by the gigantic effort of the whole nation
ended with it rolling back downhill crushing and devastating
everything in its way' (Pozdnyakov, 1991: 50).

Nevertheless, Pozdnyakov complains, the state's policy of *perestroyka* – 'completely based on Western liberal democratic
conceptions' – constitutes yet another attempt at Westernisation,
and in an even more brutal form: 'Never before has
"Westernism" taken such a barefaced aggressive form in this
country, rejecting everything Russian' (Pozdnyakov, 1991: 50).
Perestroyka is a greater evil than Marxism because it encroaches
on the lynchpin of Russia's destiny, namely, the strong state.

Under Gorbachev's leadership, the Russian state acts as the errand-boy of the West, Pozdnyakov charged: 'We are today fulfilling the eternal dream of the West with our own hands, namely, to throw Russia back to Asia, to reduce its role to that of a secondary power, to make it dependent on the mercies of the West' (Pozdnyakov, 1991: 51). And to what avail? The obvious priority given by Western civilisations to 'Reason (*ratio*) above all the other vital characteristics of human nature' means that those peoples and societies which do not share in the worshipping of reason are written off as 'indigenous' or 'barbarian'. Instead of supporting 'the unconditional recognition of equal rights for the nations and peoples existing in this world', the West maintains a 'troublesome preoccupation with human rights in countries belonging to other civilizations', Pozdnyakov concluded (Pozdnyakov, 1991: 53–4).

Pozdnyakov's article attracts attention, not for its originality but for its character as a catalogue of previous Romantic nationalist themes, some of which had been absent from the fully public Russian debate about Europe for a long time. The idea of the strong Russian state as the holder of the balance between Europe and Russia predates the time-span under discussion here and goes back at least to Catherine the Great. Likewise, with the idea that Westernisation is a threat to the integrity of the state – this idea is very much present in Karamzin, but also earlier. The idea of Russia and Europe belonging to different civilisational types which should be treated as analytically discrete is of course Danilevskiy's, and the idea that Europe is masquerading as the keeper of world civilisation to the detriment of all other civilisation was first formulated by Trubetskoy, that great Eurasianist of the 1920s. The idea that the occasional spurt of Russian Westernising zeal devastates society to no avail is also Trubetskoy's.

If both the liberal and the Romantic nationalist positions emphasised the 'Eurasian' character of Russia, they put different meanings into the term and used it for different ends. Whereas old and new Romantic nationalists used the idea of Eurasia to forge a non-European identity for Russia, the liberals used it in an attempt to add a complementary, separate identity for Russia on top of the European identity they so desired for it. Characteristically, Pozdnyakov the Romantic nationalist saw the geographical position between Europe and Asia as making

Russia the dominant power on which all others are dependent. Gefter the liberal, on the contrary, saw it as making Russia dependent on all mankind.

To sum up the debate during *perestroyka*, it started with the state cutting some of the moorings of the Bolshevik position, but without ever leaving all the central tenets of the Bolshevik position behind. The state's expansion of public political space made it possible for the liberal position not only fully to re-establish itself, but to become the dominant position in the Russian debate about Europe. As *perestroyka* and the existence of the Soviet Union drew to a close, however, it had to share centre stage with a Romantic nationalist position which had also gone fully public. The greatest 'liberal moment' in the debate since the spring of 1917 came in the autumn of 1991, when an attempted *coup d'état* became the prelude to downfall for Gorbachev's Soviet Union. As the Soviet Union disintegrated and the former Russian federation took its place as the Russian state, the liberals, having abandoned Gorbachev and regrouped around Russia's president, Boris Yel'tsin, sailed into power and were able decisively to influence the new state position. The Bolshevik position simply disappeared as such. The Gorbachev period spelled an end to the Soviet Union, and also to the idea that Soviet Russia was the caretaker of 'true', socialist Europe.

AFTER *PERESTROYKA*

The *coup* attempt that finished off the Soviet Union was an explicit attempt at saving it, so a good example of a self-negating action. The declaration of the *coup*-makers drew significantly on a xenophobic Romantic nationalist text published a month earlier under the heading 'A Word to the People':

> A great, unheard of disaster is happening. Our MOTHER-LAND, our soil, the great state that history, nature and our renowned forefathers have trusted us with, is going under, is being destroyed, is descending into darkness and nothingness [... Shall we let the betrayers and criminals] take away our past, cut us off from the future and leave us pitifully to vegetate in the Slavery and downtroddenness of our almighty neighbours?
>
> (*Sovetskaya Rossiya*, 23 July 1991)

179

Directing themselves to the army and sundry other institutions and groups, they asked how it was that 'those who do not love their country, those who lovingly serve their foreign masters' were allowed to go on ruining and breaking up the country, leading it into a second civil war. The document, the main author of which was Aleksandr Prokhanov, left little doubt about who they saw as the protagonists in this civil war. It was the very same tendencies – '"leftist", of Western-liberal orientation' and '"rightist", representing traditional Russian values' – about which Prokhanov had written three and a half years earlier. It is very complimentary of the work done since then on consolidating the Romantic nationalist position that the text was signed not only by xenophobic Romantic nationalists, but also by key former communists and spiritual Romantic nationalists. If the attempted *coup* failed to salvage the Soviet Union and spelled a very short period of decline for the Romantic nationalists, it nevertheless established them as serious contenders in the new race to occupy the position of the state.

The immediate fallout was, however, the diametrically opposite. The new Russian state adopted the liberal position as its own. When Yel'tsin and his team took over the leading positions of the state, however, they took with them the liberal position in both its variants. Thus, the cultural framework and the positive moral judgement of Europe on which the liberals agreed by and large remained outside the debate (but cf., below). Yet the fight over whether Russia's relationship with Europe should be one of as much and as rapid integration as possible, or whether Russia should stick to a 'Eurasian' concept and go for good relations all around, now went from being an internal liberal quarrel to a quarrel inside the state structures about the state's position.

The first variant, of a 'return to civilisation', found its most prominent home at the top of the Russian Foreign Ministry. Already in his previous incarnation as the Foreign Minister of the Russian Socialist Federative Soviet Republic, Kozyrev had pursued the line that Russia should join the community of civilised countries that it has traditionally admired, such as France and Britain. This line he reiterated from his new rostrum at the first possible occasion:

> our active foreign policy, our diplomacy, are necessary to guarantee the entry into the world community [. . .] and

thereby to help meet the internal needs of Russia. [. . .] The developed countries of the West are Russia's natural allies. It is time finally to say firmly that we are neither adversaries nor poor little brothers who are following the orders of a rich and malevolent West intending to buy up Russia.

(Izvestiya, 2 January 1992)

However, only two months were to pass before Kozyrev was challenged, and that on his home turf. As journalist Vladimir Razuvae wrote:

At an extremely representative conference on problems of Russian foreign policy organised by the Foreign Ministry, I was astonished to see how many representatives of the democratic current who have switched to a neo-conservative position. Evidently, some people's dreams of a rosy 'return to civilisation' from 'communist barbary' have ended.

(Nezavisimaya gazeta, 5 March 1992)

This indirect report was soon followed by a direct engagement, when the president's adviser Sergey Stankevich maintained that Russia should steer a Eurasian course. Its mission in the world was to initiate and support a multilateral dialogue of cultures, civilisations and states, a task which came to it naturally, since Russia was by nature dialogical. Turning to the Russian debate, he held that the two tendencies of Atlanticism and Eurasianism now made themselves felt in Russian foreign policy.

Atlanticism tends to the following set of ideas and symbols – to become part of Europe, to make a swift and well organised entry into the world economy, to become the eighth member of the Group of Seven, to concentrate on Germany and USA as the two dominant members of the Atlantic alliance.

(Nezavisimaya gazeta, 28 March 1992)

This, Stankevich argued, was rational, practical and natural, since that was where the credits, aid and advanced technology were. 'The opposite tendency – Eurasianism – is not yet so clear-cut, but it is already knocking at the door of the tall building on Smolensk Square', that is, the Foreign Ministry. Stankevich welcomed this tendency as a counterweight to 'the evident distortion created by the authors of the Common European

House concept. [...] In order to broaden its field of political action as much as possible, Russia must quickly become *self-sufficient'* (*Nezavisimaya gazeta*, 28 March 1992; also Stankevich, 1992; Malcolm, 1994).

Kozyrev immediately rose to the challenge, insisting that Russia should not aspire to be a military superpower, but 'a normal great power'. Having named some of the obstacles to Russian foreign policy abroad, he added: 'there is also a real possibility of revenge by the apparatus – consolidating the old nomenklatura in administrative structures, the military-industrial complex, and (let us state it clearly) the foreign policy sphere ... We can go on about the need to do away with the "pro-Western bias" and turn Russian foreign policy in an eastward direction, exploiting our central Eurasian possibility', Kozyrev wrote, but then gave his readers to understand that this was not the most promising course (*Izvestiya*, 1 April 1992).

As a presidential adviser, Stankevich belonged to an institutional structure which was in direct competition with the Foreign Ministry about the making of Russian foreign policy (Crow, 1993). The reference to the other tendency knocking on the Ministry's door is clearly to the one held by himself and other people in the president's entourage. Kozyrev tried to maintain the position of his Ministry by accusing his opponents of 'old thinking': 'One of the favourite methods of old party apparatchiks is to create parallel structures: state councils, etc.' (*Moscow News*, 7 June 1992). These ruses notwithstanding, Kozyrev and the idea of a 'return to civilisation' lost the tug-of-war over the state's position on its relationship with Europe. This became evident already in January 1993, when Yel'tsin remarked that

> Russia's independent foreign policy started with the West. It started with the United States, and we feel that this was justified. We had to lay the main foundation – that is, to prepare a detailed treaty on the global reduction and elimination of strategic nuclear weapons, on the basis of which it would be easier, afterward, to build relations with any country, be it from the West or East, Europe, or Asia.
>
> (quoted in Crow, 1993: 76)

Yet, by distancing the state from the rhetoric of a 'return to civilisation', Yel'tsin did not really leave many liberals behind.

Indeed, at this stage not many people advocated the ideas of 'returning to civilisation' and integrating with Europe in a 'common European home' as closely and as speedily as possible any more. A number of liberals who had taken part in the forging of the idea of a 'common European home' in the first place now opted for a more 'Eurasian' course. For example, Yuriy Borko declared himself the victim of a widespread illusion, and turned his back on the idea of a 'common European home': 'The question should no longer be how Russia should enter such a home. Rather, Russia should concentrate on putting its own home in order' (Borko, 1993: 9). Citing the case of Germany, the Europeanness of which was avidly discussed as recently as in the middle of last century and which has gone through a few rough patches since then, Borko concluded that Russia's looking after its own home may indeed turn out to have similar positive effects on its relationship with Europe. Europe, moreover, is no longer the sole or dominating centre of advanced civilisation, as it was when Russia's reformers looked to it in the eighteenth and nineteenth century. Therefore, Russian foreign policy should head in many different directions. 'Such a judgement is not in the least anti-European', Borko assured his readers (1993: 10).

Thus, the liberal position as well as the position of the state consolidated around the idea that the relationship with Europe should not be allowed to marginalise relations with other parts of the world. The alternative liberal idea, that Russia should go to school with Europe, was pushed to the margins of the debate. This also meant that more specific ideas on the relationship with Europe emanating from the victorious liberal camp, for example, those in a document penned by the *mezhdunarodnik* Sergey Karaganov and presented as a report from the Council for Foreign and Defence Policy of which he was the head, were now inscribed with a new significance. 'In the long run', Karaganov had maintained in the document that may have played a role in swaying Yel'tsin and the position of the state,

> the United States's possibilities and role as partner
> will decrease, while Western Europe's has the potential
> to increase. However, this does not spell a 'Euro-centric'
> model for foreign policy. Cooperating with the United
> States in as high a degree as possible will strengthen

Russia's position in Europe, a position which has grown weaker and will grow weaker still over the next decade. Russia's interest lies with a permanent balancing between an American and a European orientation. Russia's long-term interest is to draw as closely as possible to the EC, with the aim of stepping into the European economic and political space of which the EC is the centre. Yet this does not imply the total identification of Russian interests with those of the Community. Russia will maintain political room for manoeuvre and a multi-polar European politics, and she will limit the military-political functions of the EC. Therefore, there is also a long-term interest in maintaining NATO and developing a partnership with this organisation.

(*Nezavisimaya gazeta*, 19 August 1992)

Kozyrev, while deploring his loss, nevertheless put a brave face on it. Declaring himself worried by Western ideas that a weakened Russia would be better than a strengthened one and also by Russian 'defeatist isolationist' ideas, he insisted that attempts to demote a power that was 'historically doomed to be a great power is not only unrealistic but dangerous, since it fuels aggressive nationalism and confrontational feelings in the world'. This had to be driven home, and so what he termed 'the Romantic period' in the new Russia's relations with the West was definitely over (Kozyrev, 1992: 11, 12).

As Kozyrev was losing the tug-of-war with another variant of liberalism about the specific relationship with Europe, he turned to face the much more fundamental opponent of Romantic nationalism. One notes as a key development that the state's and the liberals' shift in emphasis away from a 'return to civilisation' and towards a 'Eurasian' position seemingly marked a convergence with the Eurasian rhetoric of the Romantic nationalists. However, this convergence was superficial, inasmuch as the Eurasianism of the state and of the liberals continued to be based on an assessment of Europe as being morally equal to Russia. The Eurasianism of the Romantic liberals, on the other hand, still sprang out of a view of Europe as being morally inferior to Russia. Moreover, whereas the relationship proposed by the liberal Eurasianists was one of balanced good relations, the Romantic nationalists saw it as one of clear-cut confrontation, for example, in the formerly Yugoslav theatre. Yugoslavia, it was argued, was Europe in miniature, and Serbia could be seen as its Russia. The priority must be to avoid a situation where Europe would throw itself at Russia like Yugoslavia threw itself at Serbia:

> The international sanctions which threaten Serbia is a warning to the Russians: The [Russian] colossus is temporarily weakened because it has been betrayed from within. The Russians must not leave their former allies viciously to be turned into somebody else's lackeys. They must not leave their compatriots, sons and daughters of the greatest people world history has ever seen, to be derided.
>
> ('Evraziyskiy analiz': 71)

The Romantic nationalists had wasted little time in hibernation after their failed *coup* attempt the year before. Even people like Eduard Volodin, who had been among those who signed the 'Word to the People', were already reiterating their attacks and continuing to consolidate the position by trying to give it a leader. To him, Russian politics was a confrontation between national forces who favoured a strong state and those who favoured an anti-national regime. The 'hysterical anti-Russian and anti-state nihilism of the last seven years have made healthy forces among the people realise that we have reached the final frontier, where we must stand and fight to death, just like during the Great Patriotic War', he argued. Ideological squabbles between communists and non-communists and between religious and anti-religious patriots had to come to a halt so that the regime could be fought effectively. The opposition had to seek the common ground 'which transcend ideologies and doctrines – the survival of the nation and state integrity and independence' (*Sovetskaya Rossiya* [sic], 23 June 1992).

In a conversation with Aleksandr Yanov, the main author of the 'Word to the People', Aleksandr Prokhanov declared himself as 'a traditional imperialist and statist' and took the view that Europe was a stupid and unreal machine, created by a great Germany intent on declaring a Fourth Reich within twenty years: 'I sense the world as a continuous struggle, as an enormous, gigantic conflict, in which thousands of other conflicts are embedded' (*Literaturnaya gazeta*, 2 September 1992).

Prokhanov's solution for Russia was to impose 'authoritarianism, which will make it possible to begin to stabilise chaos, blood and insanity, and then, through strong authoritarian power, the cultivation of democracy will slowly begin, not through the creation of insane parliaments, but corporative democratism'. When his interlocutor protested that this was the programme of Mussolini, Prokhanov shot back that it certainly was the programme of Mussolini and also of Pinochet, but that 'Mussolini did not have the possibility of reaching democracy because it all ended too quickly'.

The Russian parliament soon became the main institutional platform for the Romantic nationalist position. The National Salvation Front, a group consisting of liberals-turned-Romantic nationalists (the so-called moderate right), reorganised communists and Romantic nationalists and defied the state's attempts to ban the organisation. It was able to consolidate as the largest faction and emerged as a united opposition in October 1992. Thus, Kozyrev was right to complain that, since the decline of the Soviet Union, the opposition had couched their rejection of the surrounding world not in communist, but in gung-ho patriotic terms. The emphasis, he argued, was now 'on the loss of superpower status rather than on the defence of socialism against imperialist intrigues' (*Nezavisimaya gazeta*, 20 August 1992).

The opposition, however, continued to assail the state's position as being at the very least naive, possibly treacherous, and more preoccupied with name-calling than with defending Russian interests. For example, Aleksandr Vasil'ev ridiculed Kozyrev for writing that statists and national socialists did not like him because they regarded him and other democrats as secret Jews. Quoting one of the parliamentary leaders, Vasil'ev then went on to assail Kozyrev as a Westernising idealist who held the international environment to be favourable at a time 'when virtually half of our neighbours are trying to cut off a piece of Russian territory'. Invoking various authorities, he held that it was simply impossible to be a Westerniser once in power: 'You can only be a Westerniser when you are in opposition' (*Komsomol'skaya pravda*, 3 September 1992).

The main drama of the Russian debate about Europe from the autumn of 1992 onwards lies exactly here, in the ability of the Romantic nationalists to attract the uncommitted or the lapsed liberals, and how success on this score may force the state to shift its position away from the liberal and further towards the Romantic nationalist. This question, moreover, lies at the heart of most Russian debates about more specific questions of foreign and also internal policy. As should be clear already from the way they came bouncing back after the failed coup attempt in August 1991, the Romantic nationalists do not increase their strength mainly by making new moves, but by sending out siren calls across the expanses of political space between themselves and the liberals.

The model example of how this process works is the case of Vice-President Aleksandr Rutskoy and Speaker of the Russian Parliament Ruslan Khasbulatov. Immediately after the break-up of the Soviet Union, Rutskoy wrote a newspaper article called 'I do not want to live in a "banana republic"' (*Komsomol'skaya pravda*, 17 January 1992). If the disintegration tendencies were not stopped, Rutskoy warned, Russia's days as a great power may soon be over. The danger, he specified soon afterwards, was not least of a spiritual nature. What drove people to wait for hours outside McDonald's was not mainly about food, he argued, but was rather in the order of waiting for holy communion with the Western way of life. Sadly, people wanted to feel part of 'that most civilised world with freedom and plenty galore' (*Izvestiya*, 1 February 1992).

If Rutskoy in his spate of articles gave the specific purpose of wanting to 'enter into a theoretical discussion on the nature of democracy and ways to achieve it' (*Nezavisimaya gazeta*, 13 February 1992), the sentiments expressed were much too vague to serve as the stepping-stone for a separate position. With their regret about Russia's lack of moral vigour *vis-à-vis* the West they were, however, specific enough to signal a dissatisfaction with the liberal position of the state. Consequently, Romantic nationalists immediately saw him as a potential ally inside the state structures, and rushed to congratulate him on his ideas. Little by little, Rutskoy traversed the ground between the liberal and the Romantic nationalist positions, inching ever closer to the latter. The same movement could be spotted in Khasbulatov, who tried to keep abreast of developments inside a parliament where the Romantic nationalist position became ever more pervasive. He hit his stride at the beginning of 1993, and came out more and more strongly against Western influences:

the mighty West will probably be capable of sending 'blue helmets' to Russia's regions to perpetuate in practice the 'patchwork Russia' in its status as the raw material reserve of postindustrial countries. The centuries-old dream of the West – to resolve the 'Russian question' once and for all – will materialise. [...] Of course, a great deal depends on Russia itself, on the population's state of mind and its spirit. But even Dmitriy Merezhkovskiy wrote, already after the revolution: 'Oh, of course Russia destroyed itself: It is to blame for nine-tenths of its own destruction, but nonetheless Europe is to blame for the other one-tenth. A man may be able to carry nine poods on his back, but the tenth will break his back.' This 'tenth pood' represents the 'contribution' made by international financial and industrial circles. They have already divided Russia's economic regions into zones of influence and have elaborated the financial and economic mechanisms for harbouring them inside their own production complexes. And the Kremlin radicals are consciously or unconsciously performing their assigned tasks in this.

(*Rossiyskaya gazeta*, 28 May 1993)

As part of parliament's campaign to eschew the president and represent itself as the core of the state, Khasbulatov explicitly enrolled 'the Russian idea' on his side. In a newspaper article which was printed under this very heading, he represented parliament as the mainstay of the people and the heir to the long Russian tradition of opposing Westernisation and dictatorial rule (*Rossiyskaya gazeta*, 17 June 1993). Thus, when the National Salvation Front went on the attack against President Yel'tsin in September 1993, they had succeeded in enrolling both Rutskoy and Khasbulatov on their side. Having both started out by manoeuvring between the liberal and the Romantic nationalist positions, they finally found themselves squarely among the latter. Indeed, Rutskoy expressed the conviction that this was an historical necessity: 'I have always viewed centrism and centrists [...] as my opponents. I'll have no common road with these people. History will show them for what they are' (quoted in *The Economist*, 9 October 1993).

Thus, when Yel'tsin took it upon himself to root out parliament by armed force in October 1993, Rutskoy and Khasbulatov were literally trapped inside parliament with mainstays of the National Salvation Front. Once again, the state resorted to violence in order to redefine public political space, shooting dead a number of parliamentarians in their offices and meeting rooms, banning newspapers and censoring others. 'There will be no more leniency to communist-fascism in Russia', Yel'tsin concluded in his TV speech to the nation on 6 October. And if the clash itself was part and parcel of the Russian debate about Europe, so were the reasons the state gave for the crackdown. After the October events, Yel'tsin's press spokesman Vyacheslav Kostikov referred to European ideals in order to justify the state's actions. Even in Western Europe with its century-old free press, he argued, 'a blatantly fascist newspaper like DEN' and similar publications would not be tolerated'. If nothing else had, then the bloodshed should now teach Russians what people in the West had known for a long time, 'they must know that unbounded freedom is called anarchy and results in the destruction and discrediting of democracy' (*Rossiyskie vesti*, 19 October 1993).

And in the wake of the October events, Kozyrev went along with Rutskoy's analysis of the impossibility of constructing a centre position when he took to task those he judged to be insufficiently loyal to the state's position:

> Some politicians have again engaged in a search for certain 'centrist leaders' – like Rutskoy and his colleagues in Civic Union, as they were seen in the past. The October drama, however, demonstrated that Russian society is dominated by two sociopolitical forces: the national-communists and the democrats. 'Centrism' in between is at best a swamp [i.e. the unstable centre groups first of the French revolutionary assembly, now of the Russian parliament] and at worst political prostitution. It is not accidental that the 'illusory centre' is disappearing as the situation aggravates while its leaders find themselves either at the head of the red-browns or keep a very low profile and stay silent so as to side with the winners after a showdown.
>
> (Kozyrev, 1993: 8)

However, if Kozyrev thought such representations of the debate would deter anybody from gravitating towards the 'red-brown' alliance of communists and nationalists, he missed the mark. Helped by the results of the parliamentary election in December

1993, the Romantic nationalists came bouncing back much as they had after the attempted *coup* two years before. They came, furthermore, in two gestations – one was the aforementioned alliance, and the other was the Liberal-Democratic Party, headed by Vladimir Vol'fovich Zhirinovskiy. Helped by the good election result, quotes from his autobiography found their way to the Russian media. Again, as was the case with other Romantic nationalist moves, this development was not interesting because these quotes brought in new elements to the position, but because the reiteration of certain core ideas had the effect of strengthening it. The master theme of the autobiography was a geopolitical one – that the South was the cradle of human civilisation, that Russia's salvation therefore lay to the South, and that the twenty-first century could still be Russia's if only the people would do away with the liberals and follow Zhirinovskiy in a southward direction. However, the master theme remained sketchy and contradictory. In certain passages, the US is seen as the centre of the entire North, whereas Russia should establish a 'sphere of influence' in the South. In others, Europe is seen as a centre with an African sphere of influence. At times it is stressed that Russia has a unique mission in world history, at others that Russians are 'citizens of the world' just like everybody else (Zhirinovskiy, 1993: 4, 64, 72, 133). Throughout 1994, Zhirinovskiy and his followers continued to stress these varied themes of the Romantic nationalist position rather than to whittle them down to a more cohesive one. By activating a number of the varied historical strains of the position, they staked their claim to being the natural hearth of *all* Romantic nationalists – which in their eyes included all proper Russians save the liberal traitors and those misguided by them.

Beginning in 1993 and continuing throughout 1994, carriers of the Romantic nationalist position also began to cajole people in power in its direction. The first one to thus resuscitate the attempt made in Solzhenitsyn's open letter to the Soviet leadership in the 1960s was a *mezhdunarodnik*, that is, one coming from a group which has traditionally published texts that do not veer too far away from the state's position. The article by Anatoliy Utkin appeared as the lead in the old house journal of the CPSU, which moved with the state and changed its name from *Communist* to *Free Thought* from its first 1992 issue onwards. The article was called 'Russia and the West', and the editors specifically noted that the West should be understood in its 'narrow sense: as the West European region' (Utkin, 1993: 3). Utkin sees the West as characterised by its will to reach the limits of everything. With a mystical belief in its mission, it treats the world as a manipulable spatial and chronological system. Since Western man sees life as a journey towards an end, his every step must be premeditated so that he can reach his goal. This European world view Utkin refers to as the 'Faustian complex'. During the seventeenth century, Russia and other great countries such as China, India, Japan and the Ottoman Empire faced the choice between resistance and surrender. India surrendered about 1750, China a century later. The Ottoman Empire gave up in 1918, and Russia in 1991. Thus, 'the centres of protracted resistence were the Ottoman empire (throughout her period of decline starting in the seventeenth century) and first of all Russia of the Romanovs'. Thus, Utkin argues, the standard interpretations of Peter's role in Russian history – that he either made Russia part of Europe, or that he destroyed traditional Russia but did not succeed in Europeanising it – are both misplaced. Rather, Peter's reforms did not penetrate all of society, and therefore they neither made Russia a Western country nor did they destroy the Russian heritage. Rather, the reforms served as a shield which allowed Russia to maintain its independence and originality while it was at the same time included in the sphere of European culture. Albeit cruel, Peter's reforms preserved the traditional Russia for almost three centuries, and even consolidated the nation's power and spirit. 'Without Peter the First, Africa's sorry fate would have awaited Russia' (Utkin, 1993: 5).

The three million Eurasians were alright as long as they nursed their stunning skill at copying Western military models, but they landed themselves in a quandary when they wanted to copy the 'Faustian spirit' and drew up programmes for implementing capitalism in five hundred days, Utkin concludes (1993: 5). Yet, unfortunately, this is what a number of Russians today do not understand: 'Is there anything more disgusting and insulting than saying that your own people "somehow does not live up to", somehow does not conform to global (understood as Western) standards?' Utkin asks, adding that the only reason why the West loves Russian literature from the golden age of Dostoevsky and others is because they respect the people who are *not* driven by 'the Faustian spirit' (Utkin, 1993: 7).

Even when Russia copied capitalism around the turn of the century, she did it her own way, Utkin maintained. Citing the example of the Trans-Siberian railway, he commented that

Not in one Western country would it have been possible to build a national railway on the bones of the taxpayers and then pride oneself of it in front of them. It could be done in Africa, in India (or in the United States with workers imported from China). And thus Russian capitalism was exactly Russian – it spoke French during banquets, but with the knout on the construction sites.

(Utkin, 1993: 7)

Utkin's conclusion is that Russia should follow the Romanovs and once again try to salvage its originality and shield itself from the West by borrowing from it. Only in this way can it hope to hit a balance between modernisation and nationalism:

Today, Russia's modernisation is carried out by extreme Westernisers, but objectively it will set the people against the West and capitalism. Yet to refrain from modernisation will objectively place Russia outside the world arena and encourage backwardness. [...] It is impossible to leave Russia's fate in the hands of those who hate her and those of her admirers who only speak of yesterday's Russia.

(Utkin, 1993: 14)

Yet from the beginning of *perestroyka*, and especially during 1993, the rulers have chosen to follow a course which split the country and destroyed its sense of direction, just as had happened, for example, in India, Utkin charged. And this is where he issued his warning: Russian capitalism's great leap forward from 1892 to 1914 brought about the formidable opposition of the great Social Revolutionary Party. 'Many of the developments inside our state are attempts at dressing up in the European clothes that were torn to pieces from 1914 to 1920' (Utkin, 1993: 13). The present rulers, however, do not see this danger of a violent reaction from below, and therefore they are putting themselves and the nation in an extremely unstable situation. '... ruling Russia and seeing it only as a part of the West is like sitting on a volcano', Utkin argued (1993:11), and concluded that the present course could not possibly lead Russia beyond the situation of India, a state which he held to be deeply fractured between an elite and a people unable to withstand the colonialism of the West.

Utkin's warning, then, is that if the state continues its policy of Westernising reform unabated, it will force a reaction from below, which will usher in the only alternative position around, namely, that of the Romantic nationalists. In order to avoid this turn of events, the state must distance itself from Europe and the European heritage and go about its own business. It seems a fair prediction that more texts like this one will appear in the immediate future, and that the state will be tempted to steer in this direction. As 1994 wore on, the enthusiasm about Europe as a model which characterised the state's position upon Yel'tsin's coming to power had clearly dissipated, leaving an insistence on a Russo-European partnership on equal terms.

9

CONCLUSION

The Russian debate about Europe has focused on a tightly limited number of questions, which has been answered by a very limited number of ideas. The preceding chapters have demonstrated how these ideas have been generated and transformed by one another within a public political space controlled by the Russian state. In discussing Europe, the Russians have also clearly been discussing themselves, and so the debate is an example of how Russians have talked themselves into existence.

Having spent the eighteenth century copying contemporary European models, the Russian state went on to offer its citizens two different models to identify with. During the nineteenth century, the Russian state represented itself as 'true Europe' in a situation where the rest of Europe had failed the best in its own tradition by turning away from the past values of the *anciens régimes*. During the twentieth century, the Russian state represented itself as 'true Europe' in a situation where the rest of Europe had failed the best in its own tradition by not turning to the future values of socialism.

What will be the position of the state in the Russian debate about Europe on the threshold of the twenty-first century? There always exists the possibility that some entirely new idea will appear and be adopted by the state – perhaps as a reaction to some unexpected new development in Europe. It seems highly likely, however, that such a new idea would have its roots in European thinking. This prediction is made bearing in mind that *all* the participants in the debate have drawn on European ideas to forge their own. Where the constitutionalists and, later, the liberals are concerned, they have always acknowledged their intellectual debt to Europe. Yet the Romantic nationalists as well as other positions which are not for the time being present in the debate – like populists and Bolsheviks – and who frequently protested their independence of European thinking, were nevertheless also deeply indebted to it. It was demonstrated above how the early Romantic nationalists adopted German Romantic national thinking to their own ends, how the populists paid homage to European thinkers, and how the Bolsheviks predicated their ideas on European ones. When a contemporary antimodern Romantic nationalist like Solzhenitsyn rails against Western civilisation, he does so within European literary genres like the novel and the essay, availing himself of European-developed media like the newspaper, in a public debate upheld by conventions developed in Europe, in a formal language with its roots in Europe, availing himself of linguistic archaisms in the way pioneered by German Romantic nationalists. In short, it has always been the fate of Russians and others who have wanted to forge a non-European, anti-hegemonic debate that such debates cannot fail to maintain ties to Europe, if only inversely so, because of the very fact that they are patterned as attempts to negate the European debate, and therefore remain defined by it.

Given the incremental development of the debate demonstrated above, however, it seems unlikely that some entirely new idea will emerge and then be taken over by the state. It is far more probable that the basic elements of the state's position already exist somewhere in the bowels of the debate. If the genealogy presented in this book does not warrant specific predictions about the position of the state, then it may be used to predict which ideas will dominate the debate in the middle – and perhaps even in the long term (Wæver, Holm and Larsen, forthcoming). This may be done by using the genealogy as a catalogue of the major frameworks, moral assessments and ideas about the Russian relationship to Europe which are in circulation at present, and also previous ideas which are only one step removed from ideas currently in circulation, and which can therefore easily be reinserted into the debate. I sum up the debate by first summarising the Romantic nationalist position, then proceed to the liberal position, making comparisons and predictions as I go along.

One prediction can, however, be made immediately: as the stigma of socialism left by the collapse of the Soviet Union and the Bolshevik position and the fascination of the liberal position to Westernisers start to taper off, some kind of social democratic or socialist position will re-constitute itself. So many of the ideas presented in the past by Russian socialists, populists, Mensheviks and Bolsheviks retain their contemporary relevance that it would indeed be remarkable if, for the first time since the 1840s, the debate about Europe should be without one or even two variants of a socialist position for much more than a few years.

The Romantic nationalist framework gives pride of place to the organic nation, understood as a living being where each part is dependent on the others, and where no basic conflict of interest can therefore exist. The state is seen as the 'head' of the organic nation, embodying its will, defining its interests and defending it against harmful internal microbes and external onslaughts. The well-being and good fortune of nation and state are guaranteed by God or a functional equivalent thereof – for example, the course of history.

At the end of the Gorbachev period, a new alliance between old Bolsheviks and Romantic nationalists began to take shape. The similarities between the frameworks of the old Bolshevik position and the Romantic nationalist position are such that it takes little effort to latch some old Bolshevik ideas on to the Romantic nationalist position: if 'the party' is substituted for 'the nation' in the definition of the Romantic nationalist framework, then it reads like a definition of the old Bolshevik framework. The Bolsheviks also set great store by the organic tie between the party and the people, the absence of conflict and the coincidence of interests: *'Plany partii – plany naroda'* – 'The plans of the party are the plans of the people' – was a ubiquitous slogan in the old Soviet Union. And if most Romantic nationalists see God as supporting their position, then Bolsheviks have always seen History as being on their side.

There exist empirical examples of what such variants of Romantic nationalism might look like in the Eurasianism and *smenovekhovstvo* of the 1920s, and in the writings of Antonov and others in *Veche* during the early 1970s. Whereas these coteries were made up of Romantic nationalists who had to accommodate themselves to the limits of debate laid down by the Bolshevik state, however, the new 'National Bolshevism' will be formulated by old Bolsheviks who attempt to accommodate themselves to a Romantic nationalist position which is already in place, and which aspires to become the state's position.

The Romantic nationalist position incorporates two different moral assessments of Europe, and it is the difference in thinking at this level which defines the two variants of the position – the xenophobic and the spiritual. Since there is no clear-cut line either between the thinking of the two wings or between its carriers, they must be considered parts of a continuum. The most xenophobic elements see Europe as being clearly morally inferior to Russia – an enemy at the gate with its tentacles inside the living Russian nation. During the last two years, this variant has almost crowded out the spiritual nationalists. Two other moral assessments made by Romantic nationalists have therefore been marginalised: Pozdnyakov's drawing on Danilevskiy's that Europe belongs to another civilisational type and therefore defies moral classification by Russian criteria, and Likhachev's drawing on Solov'ev's that Russia and Europe are moral equals.

Different proposals for the relationship between Russia and Europe arise from the different moral assessments. The xeno-phobic Romantic nationalists stress defence or even a national liberation struggle against Western 'occupation'. One possible relationship which has once again begun to be spelled out by Prokhanov and others is Ustryalov's idea that Russia's foreign policy must be unabashedly aggressive and imperialistic, and that only a physically powerful state can possess a great culture. Some Russian Romantic nationalists take these ideas with them when they leave the domestic discourse. For example, when asked by an Italian journalist why Russian nationalism seemed to enjoy a revival, the editor of *Nash sovremennik*, Stanislav Kunaev, answered that 'The question is asked in an incorrect manner. Nationalism is for small peoples who fear extinction. The Russians are a great people [. . .] Russia speaks like Christ used to speak: come to me and share my spirit' (*La Repubblica*, 27 January 1990).

Danilevskiy's and Trubetskoy's suggestion for all-out war is only one move away from that. This idea may re-emerge when the xenophobic Romantic nationalists once again decide to go on the offensive against the state, as they did in September 1993. The marginalised views within the position, which may come back to resuscitate the pluralism of the position, belong to Pozdnyakov and Solzhenitsyn, who want to move in the direction of isolation (although the latter also stress the aspect of *Kulturkampf*), and Likhachev, who wants a spiritual partnership.

If the Romantic nationalist framework stresses nation, state and the harmony of interest between the two, then the liberal framework stresses state, society, individual and the possible conflict of interests between them. In order to keep latent conflicts in check and secure a certain degree of harmony, the state should be a *Rechtsstaat*, where – to use Spinoza's classical formulation once again – the King's documents should take precedence over the King's will. In other words, the state should guarantee and implement a state of law where written, non-retrospective rules regulate relations between as well as within state and society. The latter should be a civil society, that is, it should to some extent have an existence independent of the state, in the economic as well as in other spheres. The individuals constituting society should have rights guaranteed by the *Rechtsstaat*, and should have the opportunity to participate in the organisation of civil society.

The differences between the liberal and the Romantic nationalist frameworks have been much discussed by the participants in the Russian debate. For example, Romantic nationalists, from Odoevskiy, Shevyrev and especially Konstantin Aksakov to Shafarevich, have contrasted their own organic framework to the liberal mechanistic framework. They have seen Russian political life as a struggle between a harmonious Land which embodies their own ideal, and a conflict-ridden city society which demonstrates the horrors of the liberal ideal. When Shafarevich ridicules the multiparty system as the guarantor of civil war, he applies a general Romantic nationalist critique of the liberal position and Europe to one of its contemporary manifestations. In this way he also demonstrates in what sense he and other Romantic nationalists are warranted in seeing Russian 'Westernisers' – today represented by the liberal position – as a 'Westernised' and therefore alien element whose political position dovetails with the one which is dominant in Europe and the West.

Since the liberal and the Romantic nationalist frameworks are incompatible on basic questions like the ontological status of the individual and the state and the nature of the good life, and since they – after two hundred years – show few signs of dialectical potential, the debate about their relative merits seems set to continue in the same tracks. As seen in the moral assessments made by its xenophobic wing, however, the Romantic nationalist framework opens for a *Gleichschaltung* of the nation whereby its organic character is attempted secured by rooting out the carriers of the liberal position. Indeed, if there cannot exist any basic conflict inside the nation and the liberals nevertheless insist on perpetrating one, then they must constitute an *illness* in the body politic. They should therefore be surgically removed before they can contaminate the entire organism. If the xenophobic wing of the Romantic nationalists should succeed in their bid to take over the state apparatus and should spell out this possible implication of their position, it seems likely that they would attempt to redefine public political space in such a way that the Romantic nationalist position would be the only position left in the debate.

The liberal framework gives rise to an even more tightly circumscribed set of moral assessments of Europe than does the Romantic nationalist framework. The Romantic nationalist framework allows for moral comparison to be based on different criteria, and is therefore open to a shifting of the ground of comparison in cases where Europe may be seen to be superior in some fields, but not in others (see Hogg and Abrams, 1988). The Russian debate about Europe furnishes a number of examples of how Romantic nationalists, when confronted with the lower economic output, standard of living or military capability of Russia as in contrast to Europe, have written off such comparisons as insignificant compared to others. For example, faced with the more efficient European economic model of industrialisation, Slavophiles insisted that Europe had paid for it by its spiritual death, while Russians had retained a richer spiritual life and were therefore morally superior to Europe. Furthermore, Slavophiles hinted that the greater European military prowess was due to the inherently violent nature of European states, while the Russian state was peace-loving by comparison and therefore less effective militarily, but more advanced morally. An argument similar to the former is made by Solzhenitsyn, who, following the Slavophiles and Dostoevskiy, argues that the Russians are morally superior to people of the West because they have grown spiritually as they have been faced with hardships such as communism, which have not been present in the West. Shafarevich writes that the West may be richer than Russia, but then again it is more prone to economic crises. The two are at one in insisting that Western economic models are morally inferior to their own vision of a Russian old-style village economy because the latter is ecologically sounder.

Liberals cannot shift the ground of moral comparison in the same way: for them, the moral assessment unequivocally rests on the degree in which the *Rechtsstaat*, civil society and individual rights are in place and are functioning. Consequently, Europe has always been regarded by liberals either as morally superior to Russia if viewed synchronically, or as morally equal to Russia if viewed diachronically. They tend to see Russia as steadily developing along the same lines as Europe, and therefore as being of a kind with it – practically as well as morally. The proposed relationships with Europe are, therefore, those of partnership or apprenticeship.

One classical formulation of this was made by Turgenev when he – in refutation of Gertsen's insistence that Russia was a cousin of Europe who had taken little part in the family chronicle but whose rustic charms were fresher and more commendable than those of her cousins – held that Russia was a girl no different from her older European sisters, 'only a little broader in the beam' (Turgenev, 1963: 65). The anthropomorphisation aside – that was hardly out of character for a nineteenth-century constitutionalist but would, if only for its organic connotations, certainly have been so for a contemporary liberal – this insistence that Russia is just like Europe, only a little slower and a little less subtle, was initially the assessment made by the Russian state under Yel'tsin's leadership. The state took over the liberal position, and tended to see Russia as an apprentice returning to European-based 'civilisation'.

This did not last long, however, before the idea of apprenticeship had to give way to the idea of partnership. The idea of apprenticeship was marginalised as most liberals and also the state rooted their positions not only in a moral assessment of Europe, but also of Asia: if it is true that the liberals cannot shift the *functional* ground of moral comparison, they are as free as are the Romantic nationalists to change the *geographical* ground of comparison. When Dostoevskiy wrote that

In Europe we were hangers-on and Slaves, whereas we shall go to Asia as masters. In Europe we were Asiatics,

whereas in Asia we, too, are European. Our civilizing
mission in Asia will bribe our spirit and drive us thither
(Dostoevskiy, 1954: 1048)

it can be taken as a recommendation to perform just such a
change of the geographical ground of comparison. And indeed,
whereas Eurasianist Romantic nationalists took up this line of
reasoning in the 1920s, today both Romantic nationalists like
Zhirinovskiy and liberals like Stankevich are doing so, and
always to circumvent comparisons with Europe only.

Eurasianist liberals want Russia to copy European models, but
they want it to proceed not at a breakneck pace, and they want
the debate about Europe to be complemented by a debate about
Asia, ostensibly so that Europe will not serve as the only basis
of comparison. In this way, comparisons with neighbouring
countries will not be so demoralising, and the chances that Russia
may keep up Westernising reforms will increase. The Eurasianist
liberals respond to the dilemma formulated by Russian liberals
from Milyukov to Sakharov – that is, how to criticise domestic
opponents who are seen as non-European without compromising Russia's Europeanness in the eyes of Europe itself – by refus-
ing to admit the dilemma and representing Eurasianism simply
as a necessary detour to further Westernisation.

The point of this excavation of different Russian ideas about
Europe was to present a history of the present, and so to bring
to light a variety of international thinking which colours Russian
political process generally, and the state's position specifically.
In addition to being a part of the growing literature on culture
and international relations (Neumann and Eriksen, 1993), it has
presented itself as an addition to two ongoing debates in the
field of international relations. First, it is a complementary
critique of the literature on 'international society'. As previously
noted, an international society was defined by Hedley Bull as 'a
group of states, conscious of certain common interests and
common values', which by dialogue and consent have formed
'a society in the sense that they conceive themselves to be bound
by a common set of rules in their relations with one another,
and share in the working of common institutions' (Bull, 1977:
13; Bull and Watson, 1984: 1). Members of the 'English School'
writing on international society have often drawn attention to
the cultural underpinnings of international society:

all historical international societies have had as one of their foundations a common culture. On the one hand, there has been some element of a common *intellectual* culture – such as a common language, a common philosophical and epistemological outlook, a common literary or artistic tradition – the presence of which served to facilitate communication between the member states of the society. On the other hand, there has been some element of common *values* – such as a common religion or a common moral code – the presence of which served to reinforce the sense of common interests that united the states in question by a sense of common obligation.

(Bull, 1977: 316)

However, although there has been no lack of calls for empirical research into how these underpinnings come about and are reproduced (e.g. Wight, 1977; Vincent, 1980; Buzan, 1993), the attempts to do so have either focused on the expansion of international society itself (Bull and Watson, 1984) or on diplomatic culture (Gong, 1984). By setting out Russian reactions to having been as it were 'expanded upon' by the historical European core of international society, I hope to have demonstrated how in one instance the process of expansion divided the intellectual culture of one particular state. That divide, if it is ever to dissipate, will hardly do so before Russians, Europeans and third parties alike talk about Russia as forming part of the core of international society.

Another and even more wide-ranging debate concerns the status of neo-realist insights. The importance of the system of states for Russian ideas about Europe is striking, and it brings to mind two grand narratives of how European hegemony formats the Russian debate about it. The first is Marx's, of how the capitalist mode of production forces other modes of production out of business. The second is that of the mercantilists and international relations 'realists', of how the anarchical structure of the system of states forces each one of them to copy the most effective models for social organisation around. Invoking this theory and referring to it as no less than the goddess of fate, Kenneth Waltz has formulated the idea in the following manner:

The fate of each state depends on its responses to what other states do. The possibility that conflict will be conducted by force leads to competition in the arts and the instruments of force. Competition produces a tendency toward the sameness of the competitors. [...] It is this 'sameness', as effect of the system, that is so often attributed to the acceptance of so-called rules of state behavior. Chiliastic rulers occasionally come to power. In power, most of them quickly change their ways. They can refuse to do so, and yet hope to survive, only if they rule countries little affected by the competition of states.

(Waltz, 1979: 127–8)

Indeed, the material presented here seems to support the idea that the 'competition' in the states system imposes a certain 'sameness'. But how far does that take us? Waltz's project is to foreground the abstract category of system competition in order to present a parsimonious theory of international relations. One of the many costs of this manoeuvre – and this is a point which has been made time and again since Ruggie (1986) pointed out that Waltz had no ontology of the state and nothing to say about the genesis of the modern states system – is that it discourages enquiry into what competition means. This study shows one instance of how Russians have interpreted this competition, and how they have considered meeting it. Thus, 'competition' does not emerge from this study as a category afloat in time and space, but as a phenomenon which can be clearly situated as part of a social context which one may sweepingly refer to as modernity. It is the social appeal of the different political orders available in this setting to Russians and the competition generated by this which is at issue. Given these constraints, one may conclude from the empirical investigation of two hundred years of debate that *any* regime, no matter how bent it may be initially on following a specifically Russian path of development, is likely to discover that maintaining the position of Russia in its international setting may demand a certain copying of European models. This was the thrust of Minister of Finance Reutern's advice to Tsar Alexander II more than 130 years ago, when he warned that

Without railways and mechanical industries Russia cannot be considered secure in her boundaries. Her influence in Europe will fall to a level inconsistent with her international power and her historical significance.

(quoted in von Laue, 1963: 9)

In other words, if the Russian state should disregard those developments in Western political and economic models which translate into a consolidation of Western hegemony and superior Western military capabilities, and should instead give priority to another path of development, the price may be further international marginalisation. Indeed, the Bolshevik state went for exactly such an anti-hegemonic strategy, and it ended in tears: it was probably the insight that the state's economic base could not sustain the concurrent level of political and military activity which made Gorbachev call off the state's anti-hegemonic strategy and go for some kind of accommodation to Western hegemony.

Among those active in the debate now, Utkin is in the exalted company of Gertsen, Trotskiy and Trubetskoy when he takes the consequence of this pinch and insists that Russia cannot simply disregard Europe's dynamism. Moreover, when I have had the chance to present the material to experts on Ottoman, Persian, Japanese, Chinese or other civilisations which have struggled in coming to terms with European hegemony, they have immediately and invariably spotted a structural similarity between the Russian debate and the debates inside those other states (McNeill, 1963: 605 *passim*). It must be stressed that the similarity is in form, and concerns the questions of whether to accept hegemony or fight it, and of the degree in which to copy European models. Since Ottoman, Persian, Japanese and Chinese orders wary widely, and since the participants in the respective debates have differing ideas about what confrontation entails, a comparison of the debates will of course throw up a number of differences as well. Yet the similarities suggest that the states which possess the most effective economic and political models, and which by this token will in the long term form the core of the states system, exert a structuring influence on the debate about the core in peripheral states.

This question has vexed theoreticians from Hegel to Marx to Gramsci to Gilpin to Fukuyama, and I do not intend to enter that debate in its full historiosophical range. I will limit myself to two crude points. First, although a main conclusion which can be drawn from the material presented above is that developments in the Russian debate about Europe are gradual, and that even discontinuities on the level of the position of the state have deep roots in the debate itself, one cannot for these reasons alone rule out the coming of new anti-hegemonic positions, chiliastic or otherwise. All one can say is that such a new position will to a large extent be made up of elements already present in the debate, and that it will need to be in gestation for some time. Drawing among other things on the present genealogy, an observer should have ample time to spot it even before it has formed into a fully fledged position.

Second, few would argue that a rationalist-style analysis rooted in the exigencies of the system of states will necessarily deter Romantic nationalists or others from trying to impose their position on the state. Indeed, to many carriers of the Romantic nationalist position, rationality is itself part of the European models which one wants to avoid. If what is real is rational, furthermore, it also means that not yet imposed schemes are 'real' to those who hold them. In today's Russian debate, there only exist two models which challenge the Western ones, and they are both equally ill-defined. The main Romantic nationalist model favours a tightly disciplined, militaristic society, while an even more diffuse model turns on resuscitating an idealised version of the pre-Petrine Russian pastorale. Yet the characterisation of these models as 'un-rational', 'diffuse', 'unrealistic' and the like by Russian liberals and other outsiders will hardly deter Russian Romantic nationalists (or future revolutionaries for that matter) from trying to implement them. Whether or not it is a fair prediction that the implementation of these models will only increase the power discrepancy between Russia and Europe and will – if only for this reason – have to be abandoned at some later stage, is immaterial in this regard. The example of the Iranian reaction to the coming of modernity in the late 1970s is a warning against thinking otherwise.[1]

I have persistently stressed how Russians who comment on Europe cannot but implicate themselves in Russo-European relations. Poetic justice seems to demand that, in bringing the book to a close, I should therefore reflect on how this text and the debate of which it is part are implicated in those very relations.

Whereas the debate traced here is one source of Russian foreign policy, it would of course be mistaken to see it in isolation from the dialogue, or rather heterologue, which has gone on between Russia and (the rest of) Europe. One of the epigraphs to this book issues a warning against studying cultures 'rather than their practice of co-existence' (Vincent, 1980: 259). I chose it as a reminder to myself and my implied readers that the Russian debate about Europe is entangled with the European debate about Russia. A book which had encompassed that wider debate would have presented the internal Russian debate about Europe in a rather different light. It would have noted even more strongly that whereas the latter debate has had a solid and continuous presence in the overall Russian debate, it was of particular importance at times when Russia was or had just been at war with Europe: after the Napoleonic Wars, after the Crimean War, at the time leading up to the Congress of Berlin, during and after the First World War, and around the end of the Cold War. Since the occurrence of these wars has been used here as a chapter-dividing device to structure the narrative, it is of course present. When I draw attention to it here, it is because it exemplifies the central point that events at the level of the international system force changes in the way social reality is constructed inside Russia itself.

Furthermore, adding a focus on the European debate about Russia would have been a healthy antidote against the disbelief that I should think must have overwhelmed my implied readers as they read some of the things that have been written about Europe in recent Russian history – Danilevskiy's insistence that Europeans are a violent cultural type, wholly different from the peace-loving Slavs, is a pertinent example. Perhaps readers have found the way Russians have implicated Europe in their construction of identities somewhat unsettling overall. Lest it should be forgotten, then, the opposite also holds true: a plethora of European writers have used Russia as an entity by means of which they could delineate European identities. Whether Russia has been constructed as the Barbarian at the gate, as the ambiguously Christian bulwark against the Barbarians or indeed as the Land of the Future, the overwhelming tendency has been to conduct a European heterologue *about* Russia, rather than a dialogue *with* Russia (Neumann, 1995b). And this European debate about Russia has also been a source of policy. It was mentioned above, for example, how Paul-Henri Spaak (1969) held that a shared fear of the Soviet Union was the main motivation behind the formation of the EEC. Shared fear can hardly be treated as something extraneous to the European debate about Russia.

What we have seen since the beginning of the end of the Soviet

Union has been a European and a Western debate about Russia's transition to the market and democracy – to capitalism and a multiparty system, that is. A corollary, perhaps even subsidiary, theme has been where Russia fits into a European security order. Most participants in the debate may therefore be said to have predicated their moves on the assumption that the degree of sameness of the social orders characterising the constituent parts of the international system may be more fundamental than the abstract competition inherent in the system itself. Some have seen this Western concern as a neo-imperial one, and condemned it as an attempt to foist a Western ideology on to a country for which it is foreign. Yet, as long as some Russians see the adoption of some variant of these models as a question of making their state able to compete in the international system, however, this kind of condemnation remains shallow and gratuitous. It is simply too easy to hold up cultural relativism or all-out revolutionism as political alternatives in a world where a knowledge/power nexus which historically evolved in Europe already imposes itself on almost all political arenas, and where it is more often than not recognised exactly as a hegemonic force which somehow has to be accommodated.

That said, it is nevertheless easy to criticise the oft-employed assumption that post-communist Russia would become a European country just like any other simply by embracing 'the market and democracy'. The level of generality necessary for it to be possible to talk about 'a European country like any other' should already be a warning that this assumption is a misleading one: accommodation to an abstract idea of a hegemonic social order may take many institutional forms. More importantly, the widespread idea that this goal could be furthered by supporting what is at any one time seen as the Westernising guarantors of reform in Russia may have been a misleading one. Granted that a number of Russians saw a need to copy European models, one could and should have allowed oneself to indulge in the smug thought that things were already moving in the desired direction, and so spent more time on broadening the heterologue with Russia and less on overtly assimilating its social order to one's own. By not doing so, one has inadvertently strengthened the perceived need of the Russian state to emphasise its preferred role as a great power.

Whence this lack of European security of self? A lot of it is bound up with questions which fall outside the purview of this book, such as the role of the EU or lack thereof in the former Yugoslavia and the growing number of voices which want to assert Islamicist social orders in the Maghreb. Yet some of it is also bound up with the debate in question here. Could it be that Russia is simply an ontological Other for Europe, an Other which must either be annihilated or assimilated? Hardly. Whereas it is a truism that a human collective needs to delineate itself from others, it would simply be ahistorical to insist that Europe's Others have not changed over time. Furthermore, Spain and Germany may serve as two examples that human collectives whose Europeanness was at one time more negotiable than that of others, are now recognised as European in just as many or even more contexts than is, say, France. There is no reason why present political contexts should not be conducive to expanding the instances in which Russia is counted as part of Europe.

Could triumphalism have something to do with it? It is hard to avoid gloating when an anti-hegemonial power disappears from the scene, even when such gloating may trigger a resentment and so be detrimental to self-interest. Yet, once this is discovered, triumphalism, like other raw material for collective identity formation, may cease to be invoked, and so lose its force. If it has already had the damaging effect of being one of the factors to push the Russian state in the direction of Romantic nationalism, it also seems that one is learning from this and at least in some degree have put an end to it.

A major factor behind the lack of European security of self is perhaps the insistence of former communist states to the West of Russia that they are European. The Soviet Union's disappearance made a greater European security of self possible. Yet, the insistence of these 'Central and East European' states that they were European states threatened by non-European Russia very quickly became a central theme of the debate about European identity at large (Neumann, 1994). The result was to expand the human collective which was most often invoked as politically relevant, and so to perpetuate the lack of a European security of self. It should perhaps be stressed that what is at issue is not the pinning of blame for European ontological insecurities, but rather a reminder that, if the Russian debate about Europe has its fair share of moves which contribute to such insecurities, so do others.

To return now to the point of departure for this study, Russians, in trying to impose ideas of Europe on one another, are also trying to impose their own idea of what *Russia's* social order should look like. After the collapse of the Soviet Union, the new Russian state soon found itself too weak to banish the Romantic nationalists from the debate and keep its own position unchanged. If the state is not to be taken over by the Romantic nationalists, it may either have to accept the use of physical force as a regular technique to keep them from taking over or steer towards their position. There does exist a variant of Romantic nationalism which shares with the liberals a moral assessment of Europe as equal with Russia. True, spiritual nationalism is for the time being marginalised in the debate, and it does not look more promising as a lasting state rhetoric than did the liberal variant of seeing Russia as an apprentice to Europe. It is, therefore, not obvious that the state's moving towards this destination would be sustainable, or that it would dampen the tension in the debate. Xenophobic Romantic nationalists may perhaps even be encouraged to renew their assaults on the state. Nevertheless, it is a possibility for the state to move in this direction. In practical terms, the state would then start to dabble in organic rhetoric and emphasise the unity of people and state. The 'destiny' of Russia in taking the practical and spiritual lead in the former Soviet Union and the Balkans, as Europe's representative, would become an even more pervasive theme. National pride would become a key concern.

There would be an obvious tension between the declared goal of acting as Europe's representative in the traditional Russian sphere of interest on the one hand and maintaining good relations with Europe on the other. This would spell the return of the dilemma faced by tsarist Russia throughout the nineteenth century, and coming to a head at the time of the Crimean War. In the nineteenth century, tensions of this kind made the state evolve a doctrine of 'official nationality'. Should the state continue its present slide in the direction of Romantic nationalism, it may once again evolve a doctrine of this kind. And in doing so, it may come to emphasise that the relationship with Europe is less and less of a partnership, and more and more of a competition. Furthermore, if such a move should be seen by the Russian state itself as failing to secure Russia's standing as a European great power, there may be a further move beyond spiritual Romantic nationalism, in the direction of questioning Europe's moral equality with Russia. If this should occur, the state would have come very close to taking up a xenophobic Romantic nationalist position without having been taken over by any of those who are now carriers of that position.

Thus, either way, in the short term, Russia's future seems to lie in a nationalist direction. The question is to what variant of that position the state will come to adhere. Yet, in the longer term, the pressure on the Russian social order exerted by the competition inherent in the international system will not simply evaporate. The Russian state may dabble with Romantic nationalism, but it will not be able to ignore the nagging presence of outside social orders, and it may choose not to silence Russian Westernisers completely. The debate will continue. Whether people like Count Trubetskoy were right in predicting that Russia would never be able to 'catch up with Europe', or whether Russia can emulate Japan and certain other Asian countries and generally see itself as having developed a fully competitive economic base is a question which seems certain to remain a focal point of the Russian debate about Europe for years to come, and which – as long as it is not resolved by the realisation of the latter alternative – remains a question of faith. Even if Russia should accomplish this feat, however, the debate about Europe is so central to the formation of Russian identity that it would hardly disappear, but would merely undergo yet another transformation.

NOTES

3 OFFICIAL NATIONALITY, 'SLAVOPHILES', 'WESTERNISERS'

1 This issue has a tangled historiography. Shevyrev owed his chair at Moscow University to a recommendation from the father of the doctrine of official nationality, Uvarov, and this was only one example of the closeness of the Slavophiles to government elements. Thus, Walicki (1975: 47) writes about 'The doctrine of Official Nationality propagated by Pogodin and his fellow ideologist, the literary historian S. Shevyrev'. Soviet historiography, moreover, latched on to these ties to equal the two positions. Leonard Schapiro duly takes issue with this point of view when he writes that 'Unless we ourselves wish to become the victims of propaganda, there is every reason, in our pursuit of Russian intellectual history, to distinguish between such sincere and relatively independent-minded scholars and publicists as Shevyrev and Pogodin, on the one hand, and government hacks like Grech or Bulgarin on the other – even though all of them supported certain basic views on the Russian state' (Schapiro, 1967a: 62; also Dowler, 1977).

2 Elsewhere, Belinskiy insists that cosmopolitans are not worthy of the 'sacred name of human being' (quoted in Zen'kovskiy, 1955: 40).

4 FROM THE SPRINGTIME OF NATIONS TO THE ASSASSINATION OF TSAR ALEXANDER II

1 von Schelting (1948: 190) maintains that the 'anti-revolutionary, militant-Orthodox and even pan-Slav' reasons the state gave for waging war found 'a full-bodied resonance' among the Russian people, but this remains an under-studied topic.

2 In the field of foreign policy, Nesselrode, who had been Russia's Foreign Minister since 1816, significantly improved relations with France. Russia, the lynchpin of the old coalition against Napoleon and of the old order, now had to turn to Napoleon III's France as the only safeguard against a hostile coalition of European powers

211

against itself. Spurred by considerations of the balance of power, this move was not without relevance to the reassessment of the European scene which was now being made in St Petersburg. The pertinence of Russian domestic affairs to the liaison became utterly clear in 1863, when the newfound friendship foundered on the fate of the Polish rebels against Russian rule.

3 Herzen (1968: 1680–1749; 1693–7, 1716–18). The criticism emerges as part of a homage to Mazzini, the man of whom Cavour is 'the prose translation of his poem'. The stress on social relations also emerges in Herzen's criticism of the events of Magenta and Solferino and the way he stresses the domestic causes of war: 'It would have been the less easy for any amphictyonic Councils [that is, for the Concert of Europe] to avert the Italian war that there was no international cause for it, since there was no subject in dispute. Napoleon waged this war as a remedial measure to calm down the French by the gymnastics of liberation and the shocks of victory. What Grotius or Vattel could have solved such a question? How was it possible to avert a war which was essential for domestic interests?', he asks. International lawyers may inveigle against war, he continues, but they do not see 'that their opponent is nature itself, history itself'. Still, nature seems in Herzen's view to be changeable, since he grants that the international lawyers are right in theory, but that 'under the present political *régime*' their thought is useless.

4 Not everybody would share this assessment. Danilevskiy's biographer Robert MacMaster, from whose work the present analysis borrows, holds that he did not stop at seeing a coming clash as a likely necessity. Rather, as an eschatologist, he actively willed it: 'he wanted the Pan-Slav Union not so much as a protected political base for a cultural flowering, but more because its institution would bring on a war with Europe – a war that was providential in origin and liturgical in function. Slavic practice of *Realpolitik*, including war, was per se more important to Danilevskiy than the Pan-Slav Union; the union seems to have been proposed as a means of intensifying this practice even more than as its goal' (MacMaster, 1967: 245–6, also 183–97; Petrovich, 1956: 281).

5 FROM THE ASSASSINATION OF TSAR ALEXANDER II TO THE FIRST WORLD WAR

1 'To Pobedonostsev', his American biographer writes, 'the West meant that part of Western Europe, including the British Isles, where four significant ideas were widely accepted: the concept of the excellence of natural man and the belief that man was a rational being, which he thought fundamental to Catholicism and to Protestantism and which he considered the basis of Western political institutions; the idea that the individual was important, perhaps even more important than the state or society; the belief in the effectiveness and propriety of government by law and parliamentary democracy; and the

emphasis on freedom and diversity. Pobedonostsev thought that none of these ideas could or should be adopted in Russia' (Byrnes, 1962: 134). Of course, a lack of faith in 'the excellence of natural man' was the main charge Romantic nationalists of all hues brought against official nationality and its bureaucratisation of the relations between tsar and people. Moreover, there were still people within the state itself who favoured a reformist turn. In 1900, for example, Sergei Witte wrote to Tsar Nicholas II that 'The experience of all peoples shows that only the economically independent countries are fully able to assert their political power [. . .] If we do not take energetic and decisive measures so that in the course of the next decades our industry will be able to satisfy the needs of Russia and of the Asiatic countries which are – or should be – under our influence, then the rapidly growing foreign industries will break through our tariff barriers and establish themselves in our Fatherland and in the Asiatic countries mentioned above and drive their roots into the depths of our economy. This may gradually clear the way also for triumphant political penetration by foreign powers. It is possible that the slow growth of our industries will endanger the fulfillment of the great political tasks of the monarchy. Our economic backwardness may lead to political and cultural backwardness as well' (quoted in von Laue, 1963: 2–3). The Minister of Finance argues within a framework dominated by what he sees as the exigencies of the states system.

2   Marx and Engels' own positions were in constant flux. In 1875, Engels held that Tkachev had still 'to learn the ABC of socialism', and that he was full of 'hot air' (Shanin, 1984: 24). Marx, who in the last phase of his life taught himself Russian, in the early 1870s wrote off a representative Russian populist pamphlet as 'rubbish' (Wada, 1984: 45). After the assassination of Alexander II, however, he was full of praise for the populists. 'They are sterling people through and through', he wrote in 1881, '*without a melodramatic pose*, simple, businesslike, heroic. Shouting and dying are irreconcilable opposites [. . .] They try to teach Europe that their *modus operandi* is a specifically Russian and historically inevitable method about which there is no more reason to moralize – for or against – than there is about the earthquake of Chios' (Baron, 1963: 67). When the majority of *Zemlya i volya* set up The Social Revolutionary Party of the People's Will, one of the first things they did was to write to Marx as follows: 'Citizen, The educated and progressive classes in Russia, always attentive to the development of ideas in Europe and always ready to respond to them, received the appearance of your scientific works with delight' (Shanin, 1984: 256–7). Then there was Marx's letter to Vera Zasulikh, drafted no less than four times (and not made public by the addressee), where he famously held that stages are not completely fixed.

3   This was also part of a debate about the extent to which the workers should aim for what Axelrod dubbed 'hegemony' over the bourgeoisie. Laclau and Mouffe (1985) erroneously hold that Plekhanov, and not Axelrod, was the first to do this.

4 Although Martov and others saw some revolutionary potential in the proletariat, others, notably the 'economists' Prokopovich and Kuskova, saw none: 'Judged by Western standards, the Russian workers were still politically immature. This was no reflection on their honour; it was a plain fact which it would be unwise for the party to ignore. Their backwardness was primarily due to the heritage of absolutism: the lack of constitutional rights or democratic institutions hindered the mass of Russians from becoming properly aware of the values of political liberties. Nor did they have the traditions of organized association that had been built up by the artisans of Western Europe from medieval times onwards.' This is the premise of 'economist' thinking as summed up by Keep (1963: 58–9). The epithet 'economist' was used to denote their tactical conclusion; since Russian 'objective' conditions made political gains hard to come by, social democrats should concentrate on winning economic improvements. It was this conclusion, not the description preceding it, with which Lenin took exception in *What is to be Done?* and elsewhere.

5 The word 'man', however, was still most often taken to refer to the gender, and not to humanity, although female suffrage was already just around the corner. Moreover, whereas there were still a number of different restrictions on the right to vote, the principle that voting should be carried out by the entire electorate as one entity was already firmly established. By implication, the principle of voting by estate was largely abandoned.

6 This point is echoed in other contributions. 'Our consciousness has not worked out its own essential values and gradually re-evaluated them, as happened in the West; therefore, there has not been so much as a trace among us of our own national evolution of thought', writes Gershenzon ([1909] 1967: 81). 'The socialist idea that dominates the minds of the intelligentsia, had been borrowed whole, without criticism or verification, in the form in which it had crystallised in the West as a result of a century of intellectual ferment', writes Frank ([1909] 1967: 209). Bulgakov, incidentally, makes an interesting illustration of the intellectual trek made by many of the *vekhovtsy*. In 1897, during his legal Marxist phase, his sight had rested on rather different aspects of the problem: 'Every new factory, every new industrial concern leads us forwards, increasing the number capable of intellectual Europeanization. [. . .] For Russia, there is only one way of development, inevitable and undeniable: it is the way from East to West. It is high time!' (quoted in Kindersley, 1962: 218). The generalisation of the *vekhovtsy* as Romantic nationalists is not a frictionless one; Kistyakovskiy's contribution, for example, holds up the rule of law as practised in the West as morally superior to indigenous Russian tradition, and criticises the Russian intelligentsia for not being able to grasp this. Thus, he can hardly be said to have broken with the liberal position. It is, moreover, plainly wrong to pigeonhole for example Struve as a Romantic nationalist. When the generalisation is nevertheless made, it is because my main concern

is the impact certain ideas had on the debate as a whole, rather than the intentions of any one given writer. In this perspective, *Vekhi* was important to the debate on Russia and Europe not because of the remnants of liberalism, but because of the turn towards organic thinking.

7 In the original Russian, the last sentence is '*Kapitalizm kazhetsya detishchem gosudarstva*'; the uncertainty conveyed by the verb is of the essence. Interestingly, Deutscher (1954) gives part of this quote in his treatment of '*Itogy i perspektivy*', but leaves out the last sentence, with its crucial ambiguity.

8 Cf., also the discussion in Knei-Paz (1978: esp. 77*ff*.). Trotskiy's formulations closely resemble those used by Engels in a letter to a Russian comrade: 'in a country like yours', Engels wrote, 'where modern large-scale industry has been grafted onto the primitive peasant commune and where, at the same time, all the intermediate stages of civilisation coexist with each other, in a country which, in addition to this, has been enclosed by a Chinese wall, in the case of such a country one should not wonder at the emergence of the most incredible and bizarre combinations of ideas' (quoted in McAuley, 1984: 17).

6 FROM THE FIRST WORLD WAR TO DE-STALINISATION

1 The Bolsheviks saw to it that the book, *Iz glubiny*, was not distributed, however. In a number of later books, Berdiaev addressed the debate about Europe. In his book about the intellectual roots of Bolshevism, for example, he held that 'the ancient Russian messianic idea goes on living in the deep spiritual layers of the Russian people. But in the conscious mind its formula changes, the thing "in the name" of which it acts; the messianic idea raises out of the collective unconsciousness of the people's life and takes on another name. Instead of the monk Philothey's Third Rome we get Lenin's Third International. It takes on Marxist clothes and Marxist symbolism, and adopts the characteristics of the Russian messianic idea' (Berdiaev, 1961: 41). In a book written explicitly 'to show Westerners' that a non-individualist humanism need not be anti-personalist, Berdiaev repeated that 'all great peoples have their own "idea"' (Berdiaev, 1949: 107) and that 'Universalism is more suited to the Russian than to other peoples' (Berdiaev, 1949: 68). 'The Russian Idea includes the synthesis of East and West, of two currents in world history' (Berdiaev, 1949: 69). '*Personality*', he adds in an italicised sentence, '*has always been more pronounced in Russia than in the depersonalised, mechanized and levelled-out civilization of the modern West*' (Berdiaev, 1949: 53). All these themes come together in his book (Berdiaev, 1947), which declares its intention as follows: 'What will interest me in the following pages is not so much the question: what has Russia been from the empirical point of view, as the question:

what was the thought of the Creator about Russia' (Berdiaev, 1947: 1). The answer is given in terms of Russian universalism, and is reached through observations like the following: 'Among the Russians there is a different feeling for the soil and the very soil itself is different from soil in the West' (Berdiaev, 1947: 255). Where other exiles are concerned, 'Miliukov went from seeing the revolution as regression to seeing it as a perhaps necessary step, a "violent overthrow of obsolete political and social institutions [...] very likely to come in every civilized community capable of evolving from medievalism to modern democracy"', Burbank (1986: 163) writes, quoting from a book published by Milyukov in English in 1922. Where the left social revolutionaries are concerned, Agursky (1987: 165) stresses their Messianic internationalism, giving the following 1918 quote from Roman Petkovich as an example: 'Each nation creates its own particular and individual modes and methods of social struggle which are characteristic of that nation only. The French and Italians are anarcho-syndicalists, the English are more inclined toward the trade unions, and the social democratism of the Germans, patterned after their military establishment, is the clearest possible reflection of their lack of talent. We, on the other hand, according to the prophecy of our great teachers – for instance, Dostoevsky and Tolstoy – are a messianic people entrusted with the task of outpacing and outdistancing all others.'

2 Some of the contributors to *Vekhi* saw this as an abomination. Yet, as the quotes from Berdyaev the exile given above should indicate, the ideas of the two groups were hardly far apart, although the attitude to Soviet power varied. Burbank (1986: 309, note 182) notes how Ustryalov, in a 1920 letter to Struve, one of the contributors to *Vekhi*, writes that he 'had taken a position [...] of national Bolshevism (the use of Bolshevism for national ends ...)'. In academic literature, the term 'national bolshevism' is sometimes used to refer only to the *smenovekhovtsy*, sometimes to all the bearers of the Romantic nationalist position who did not actively distance themselves from Soviet power. Ustryalov was a member of the Cadet Party at the time. The treatment of the *smenovekhovtsy* is based on secondary literature and on a collection of articles (Ustryalov, 1927), which was kindly put at my disposal by Pål Kolstø. Mikhail Agursky, in a rambling yet periodically stimulating volume already referred to, seems to argue that national bolshevism – 'the Russian etatist ideology that legitimizes the Soviet political system from the Russian etatist point of view, contrary to its exclusive Marxist legitimacy' (Agursky, 1987: xv) – far from being an isolated and inimical phenomenon to the Bolsheviks, actually proved to be historically productive. Stalin's 'socialism in one country' was the 'triumph of Russian etatist nationalism' (Agursky, 1987: 305). Lenin, more specifically, is seen as the 'principal "shadow" advocate' of smenovekhism (Agursky, 1987: 260). The main problem with the book is that this interesting hypothesis receives little systematic attention, but is bogged down in a welter of biographical trivia and underdetermined

generalisations like the following: 'The conflict between Marx and Engels on the one hand and Bakunin on the other is very often interpreted as the ideological confrontation between anarchism and Marxism, but it was only a rationalization of a greater conflict between German and Russian socialism' (Agursky, 1987: 24).

3 According to Carr (1959: 32 note), Stalin maintained that the resolution was drafted by Zinov'ev, who, in an article in *Izvestiya*, 13 January 1925, had bamboozled 'the "European" theories of Trotskyism'. Trotskiy, on the other hand, bracketed Stalin, Bukharin and the other proponents of socialism in a separate (in the sense of cut off, *otdel'nyy*) country with the old *narodniks*. '[T]he promotion of the idea of a closed national economy, a closed building of socialism', Trotskiy commented privately in December 1925, contained 'elements of Soviet *narodnichestvo*' (quoted in Carr, 1959: 168).

4 The ambiguity at stake here can also be seen in a text which has not been published in the original Russian but only in a revised translation, and which may for this reason be somewhat misleading, namely, Khrushchev (1971). Khrushchev (1971: 516) refers to 'Our potential enemy – our principal, our most powerful, our most dangerous enemy – was so far away from us that we couldn't have reached him with our air force'; this is obviously a reference to the US. Yet on the succeeding page, he writes that 'Adenauer was absolutely right' in saying that West Germany would be the first country to perish in another world war, and that 'I was pleased to hear this, and Adenauer was absolutely right in what he said. For him to be making public statements like that was a great achievement on our part. Not only were we keeping our number one enemy in line, but Adenauer was helping us to keep our other enemies in line, too'. It is at least arguable that Khrushchev is actually referring to West Germany when he talks about our 'number one enemy' here. The text also contains numerous references to 'imperialism', 'monopoly capital' and so on as the principal enemy. It is a general and hardly surprising point that one author may use the same designation to denote different human collectives in different contexts. Yet this particular instance seems to indicate the analytical fruitfulness of simply acknowledging and tracing this ambiguity where terms like 'the West', 'the capitalist countries' and so on are concerned, rather than imposing logical stringency and consequence where none seems to exist.

7 FROM DE-STALINISATION TO *PERESTROYKA*

1 This in itself does not mean that the foreign affairs specialists necessarily played any direct or important role in the decision-making process. For discussions of this point, which remains outside the purview of this work, cf., Eran (1979); Malcolm (1989b); Neumann (1989: 7–35). For a view which goes far in denying any role to the *mezhdunarodniki* in the Russian political debate whatsoever, cf., Staar

(1985). Staar rather sees their function in terms of waylaying people like himself. A view which rests on the presuppositions that the Soviet Union employed thousands of their best brains, incurred wide-reaching expenses and cluttered their decision-making process with a lot of useless paperwork in order to disinform a handful of Western researchers seems to demand rather more substantiation than what is given in Staar's work. The point made by Malcolm (1984: 154) that the *mezhdunarodniki*, simply by gathering new information about Europe and introducing it into the Soviet debate, had a 'Westernising' function, is more to the point: 'a large part of the work of the foreign affairs specialists can be interpreted quite simply as a continuation of the long Russian tradition of Westernising journalism, in which the passing on of information is far more important than superficial critical elements which may occur in the presentation'; see also Malcolm (1989a: 32), where he refers to 'the predominantly internationalist and Westernist specialist world'.

2 Thus, Sodaro (1990: 85–6) is wrong when he singles out Bunkina (1966: esp. 67–70) as the work which introduced the 'new theme' of power centres into the debate.

3 'On September 11 [1964] *Kommunist* published an unsigned article criticizing the Chinese leadership for holding the view that Western Europe, spurred on by the "French and West German monopolies," was becoming increasingly independent of the United States. It was precisely this image of US–West European "contradictions," of course, that Khrushchev and advocates of a more Europeanist orientation in the secondary elite had been projecting when they justified talks with Bonn. The author accused proponents of this view of moving toward "dubious political combinations"'(Sodaro, 1990: 65). Following Sodaro's lead, one may point to two articles in *MEiMO* for further evidence of the two different thrusts. Beglov, Zhurkin and Sturua's situation report (1963: 63–85) stresses the predominance of the US, whereas the importance of the French line and the French–German axis is stressed in Madzoevskiy [Donald Maclean], Mel'nikov and Molchanov (1963: 73–81).

4 This is a constant theme with Solzhenitsyn. In exile in the US, he had this to say: 'But should I be asked, instead, whether I would propose the West, such as it is today, as a model to my country, I would frankly have to answer negatively. No. [...] A fact which cannot be disputed is the weakening of human personality in the West while in the East it has become firmer and stronger'(Solzhenitsyn, 1980a: 57). Borisov (in Solzhenitsyn et al., 1975a: 210) quotes from the Bible in support of the idea that God instituted nations: 'If the *nation* is a corporate personality endowed with its being by God, then it cannot be defined as a "historical community of people" or a "force of nature and history" (Vladimir Solovyov). The nation is a level in the hierarchy of the Christian cosmos, a part of God's immutable purpose. Nations are not created by a people's history. Rather, the nation's personality realizes itself through that history or, to put it another way, the people in their

history fulfill God's design for them'. Shafarevich (in Solzhenitsyn et al., 1975a: 101) writes that 'I do not think Russians suffer from the national arrogance that Western Europeans display in their relations with their Eastern neighbors and even more toward non-Europeans. Russians mix easily with other peoples and often place too low a value on their own culture.'

5 For a rather more far-reaching discussion of the interrelationship between these two variants of Romantic nationalism, cf., Yanov (esp. 1978: 1–20; 1987: 78–81), where he postulates that any variant of 'the Russian Idea', independently of attached intentions and political expression, will go through a political transformation and end up as an expression of fascism. Duncan (1989: 519) criticises Yanov on empirical grounds, writing that 'The movement from loyal nationalism to the human rights movement was precisely the opposite of that predicted by Ianov'. Dunlop (1984: 256ff.) notes the intertwining of the two variants, but stops short of any historiosophical discussion. The original editor of *Veche*, Vladimir Nikolaevich Osipov, was able to put out nine issues over a period of three years, aspiring to the status of an 'apolitical', 'Russian patriotic' 'typed journal'. In an editorial to the second issue (1973: 2) he insists that the journal is not 'subterranean'. However, at the last page of the last issue to appear under his editorship (issue 9, 1973: 237), he insists that any typing of an entire issue must be done *'bez propuskov'*, that is, without admission from official organs. Where Solzhenitsyn is concerned, the way he latches his scepticism of the West and of modernity on to the views of the Slavophiles could hardly be more explicit. 'How they laughed, how they tormented those reactionary "Slavophiles"', he writes in his 'Letter to the Soviet Leaders' (Solzhenitsyn, 1980d: 94). 'They hounded the men who said that it was perfectly feasible for a colossus like Russia, with all its spiritual peculiarities and folk traditions, to find its own peculiar path; and that it could not be that the whole of mankind should follow a single, absolutely identical pattern of development.' In his Harvard Address (1980d: 42–3, 48), he once again reiterated a central Slavophile move, arguing that 'the persisting blindness of superiority continues to hold that all the vast regions of our planet should seek the level of development of contemporary Western systems, the best in theory and the most attractive in practice; that all these other worlds [that is, the former colonies] are but temporarily prevented (by wicked leaders or by severe crises or by their own barbarity and incomprehension) from pursuing Western pluralistic democracy and adopting the Western way of life. Countries are judged according to their progress in that direction. But in fact such a conception is a fruit of Western incomprehension of the essence of other worlds, a result of mistakenly measuring them all with a Western yardstick. The real picture of our planet's development bears little resemblance to all this. [. . .] A society based on the letter of the law and never reaching any higher fails to take advantage of the full range of human possibilities.'

6 The reference to 'our great Union' suggests a statist perspective, but

219

not necessarily a regime-supporting one. Again modelling himself on Dostoevskiy, Likhachev (1980: 34) writes that Russia has not only consisted of Karamozovs, but also of 'Smerdyakovs'. But when the leaders – 'Sometimes an Arakcheev, sometimes a Pobedonostsev, sometimes others . . . ' have not been the best, the Russian people has not always been to blame. The juxtaposition of bad leaders and a good people is a typical Romantic nationalist trait, and a rarity in a fully public source at this time. It is, moreover, hardly an overinterpretation to see a reference to contemporary leaders here.

7 For the sake of completeness, it should be noted that the attack does come with the caveat that he is 'not arguing with anyone in particular'. Still, the addressees are unmistakable given context and phrasing. In another piece Sakharov (1977: 294) is equally clear: 'I also find myself far from Solzhenitsyn's views on the role of Marxism as an allegedly "Western" and anti-religious teaching which perverted a healthy Russian course of development. In general I cannot comprehend this very separation of ideas into Western and Russian. In my opinion the only division of ideas and concepts in a scientific, rational approach to social and natural phenomena can be in categories of right and wrong. And just where is this healthy Russian course of development? Has there in fact ever been even one moment in Russia's, as well as any country's history, when she was capable of developing without contradictions and cataclysms? [. . .] I object primarily to the attempts to partition off our country from the supposedly pernicious influence of the West.'

8 That Western analysts have differed about the relative importance of these themes is quite another matter. Western adherents of the view that the USSR saw it in its interest to preserve the American military presence in Europe routinely use the circumstances surrounding the Senate's vote on the Mansfield resolution as their showcase. In the spring of 1971, the Senate was widely expected to vote in favour of Mansfield's suggestion to halve the number of American servicemen in Europe. On 14 May, however, five days before the vote was to take place, Brezhnev held a speech in Tbilisi where he suggested that a conference be held to discuss multilateral troop cuts (these later materialised as MBFR). For the view that this is decisive evidence of a perceived Soviet interest in keeping the American military presence in Europe, cf., Freedman (1984: 87–8); Garthoff (1985: esp. 116 note 24) where he explicitly disagrees with Kissinger's interpretation. For a typical example of pre-Tbilisi analysis, cf., Wolfe (1970: 462–3), who, with specific reference to Mansfield, argues that 'the Soviet leaders may have thought that by simply sitting tight they could watch their relative military position vis-à-vis West Europe grow stronger without having to offer a major quid pro quo.' For a rearguard defence of Wolfe's position, cf., his fellow RAND analyst van Oudenaren (1991: esp. 423 note 223); also Adomeit (1994: 36–7).

8 *PERESTROYKA* AND AFTER

1 Knyazhinskiy et al. (1986: 21) mentions that socialists in Belgium and France and a number of Resistance groups in France and Italy went in for building a post-war European federation. A comparison of this source and Knyazhinskiy (1958) reveals either a change of thrust, or it may be interpreted as support for the idea that criticism of Western ideas during the preceding period was a way of disseminating those very ideas in the Soviet Union. Borko (1988: 40) is quite explicit about the 'subjective' factor in EC integration. He charges fellow *mezhdunarodniki* with having forgotten 'the idea, solidly rooted in the public conscience for a long time, of the historical fates of the European peoples being inextricably intertwined; of the unity of European culture and European civilisation. As a phenomenon of spiritual life, "Europeanism" has a centuries long tradition.'

2 Gorbachev's Strasbourg speech before the Council of Europe, printed in *Pravda*, 7 July 1989. Not long afterwards, the *mezhdunarodnik* Sergey Karaganov (1989: 17–26) called for the continued 'stabilizing' military American presence in Europe. Malcolm (1991: 45–82) discusses the question of attempted exclusion of the US, arguing that it constituted 'Anti-American Europeanism' (Malcolm, 1991: 51). 'Towards the end of 1990, even TASS releases were implying the need to accept not just Bush's Europe without walls, but Thatcher's Europe of democracy, the rule of law, and free enterprise', he writes on p. 73. Elsewhere (Malcolm, 1989a: 80) he holds that 'Yet the impression persists from the days of earlier Soviet all-European campaigning that the "European home" is essentially a device for shutting out the United States'. This is a very British view. Another question which comes to mind is to what extent the Soviet acceptance of the US presence in Europe was presented because international diplomatic debate evolved in such a fashion that this seemed a necessary prerequisite for the Soviet Union itself to secure a legitimate place in European affairs.

3 By calling his article 'I am a Russophobe', Novikov cocks a snook at Igor' Shafarevich, whose article 'Rusofobia' will be discussed below. The title is presumably an attempt to defuse an intendedly stigmatising term by adopting it, much in the same way as the Slavophiles adopted a term which originated with their political opponents.

4 'Évropa ili Evraziya? SSSR na rubezhe'. Afanas'ev (1990: 13) echoes the idea of the USSR straddling the two world cultures by calling it 'a world of worlds'. After this, *Vek XX i mir* took to using 'a world of worlds' as a subheading in the table of contents when presenting articles on the USSR. Similarly, an article in no. 6, 1990 (27–31) of the same journal carried the title 'Vooruzhennye sily SSSR: v kontse puti' – 'The End of the Road for USSR's Armed Forces' – but was announced on the front page as 'Vooruzhennye sily Evrazii' – 'The Armed Forces of Eurasia'. Some authors, notably Karaganov (1990: 75) wanted the Soviet Union to renounce the role of a superpower

in order 'to reassign our country its natural Russian role, the role of a great European power having interests in Asia'.

5 The article was originally presented at a conference at the Moscow State Institute for International Relations (MGIMO) in April 1991 (inconsistent English spelling retained). There exists a link between the Eurasians of the 1920s and those of the 1990s in the person of Lev Gumilev, who was a fellow prisoner of Savitskiy's in a Mordovian labour camp at the beginning of the 1950s, who was able to publish a few articles after his release, and who recently published a book on Russia and geopolitics (Torbakov, 1992: 13; Hauner, 1990; Malashenko, 1990).

9   CONCLUSION

1 A last intrusion into the international relations family quarrel. One notes that arguments such as these move at the level of states, which means that neorealists like Waltz would label them reductionist and programmatically leave them out of their accounts (Waltz, 1979; see also Hollis and Smith, 1991a: 68–91; 1991b). If it is conceivable that this study may be recognised as a quarrelsome affine of the literature on international society, then, from a neorealist perspective it may not even be counted as an illegitimate relation, but only as an irredeemable stranger. Yet, as Simmel (1970) points out, the stranger is part of the group inasmuch as he serves as an ambiguous point in relation to which it can find its identity, 'an element whose membership within the group involves both being outside it and confronting it', be that a professional group or otherwise.

BIBLIOGRAPHY

Despite, or perhaps because, of the topic's pervasiveness, there are few monographs which address the question of Russia and Europe *in toto*. Those which do, are often of little analytical value for students of international relations. They may be interesting for other reasons, for example, as carriers of the Cold War, as is Keller, 1963. Since history must wittingly or unwittingly be comparative, with the society from which the author has his or her main experiences serving as a baseline, the topic is present as a more or less acknowledged rider in all 'Western' historiography. The immediacy of Europe for Russian identity formation also inscribes it in Russian historiography. Where Russian debates about Europe before the First World War are concerned, there exist four interesting monographs, none of them in English: Koyré, 1929; Krag, 1932; Zen'kovskiy, [1929] 1955; von Schelting, 1948. The first three concern tsarist Russian nationalist thinkers, whereas the last is a work of historiosophy. The first half of Jelavich, 1974 (also Seton-Watson, 1988) covers the much understudied topic of Russian tsarist foreign policy. Historians of ideas such as Nicholas Riasanovsky and Andrzej Walicki have written magisterially on a number of topics with a bearing on the present undertaking. Masaryk, 1931; Rogger, 1960 and Treadgold, 1973 sketch in some of the wider cultural background. E.H. Carr's much maligned but still central *History of Soviet Russia* covers the early interwar period, as does Burbank, 1986. Ulam, 1974 has yet to be overtaken as a standard work on Soviet foreign policy. Yanov, esp. 1978 and Duncan, 1989 are good on Russian nationalism in the 1960s and 1970s, while Adomeit, esp. 1990, Malcolm, esp. 1994 and Neumann, 1989 cover other aspects from the Cold War period. Finally, mention should be made of a number of shorter, stimulating think-pieces with titles like 'Russia and Europe' and 'Russia and the West', written by historians who often use them to synthesise a lifetime of scholarship: Carr, 1956, 1958: 3–22; Gerschenkron, 1962; Raeff, 1964; Sumner, 1951; also Dawisha, 1984; Roberts, 1964; Wittram, 1973. The US Government's *Foreign Broadcast Information Service* issues a daily report on 'Central Eurasia' which is useful. The freshest volumes of the latter were of particular use for the present undertaking, as were the bibliographies in the other sources just listed.

Adomeit, Hannes (1979) 'Soviet Perceptions of Western European Integration: Ideological Distortion or Realistic Assessment?' in *Millennium*, 8, 1: 1–24.

Adomeit, Hannes (1986) [1984] 'Capitalist Contradictions and Soviet Policy' in Robbin F. Laird and Erik P. Hoffman (eds), *Soviet Foreign Policy in a Changing World*, New York, NY: Aldine, 503–27.

Adomeit, Hannes (1990) 'The Impact of Perestroika on Soviet European Policy' in Hasegawa and Pravda 1990, 242–66.

Adomeit, Hannes (1994) 'The Atlantic Alliance in Soviet and Russian Perspective' in Neil Malcolm (ed.), *Russia and Europe: An End to Confrontation?*, London: Pinter, 31–58.

Afanas'ev, Yuriy (1990) 'Chto pozhinaem' in *Vek XX i mir*, 33, 5: 10–14, 48.

Agursky, Mikhail (1987) *The Third Rome: National Bolshevism in the USSR*, Boulder, CO: Westview.

Allen, Robert V. (1988) *Russia Looks at America: The View to 1917*, Washington, DC: Library of Congress.

Anderson, Benedict (1983) *Imagined Communities: Reflections on the Origin and Spread of Nationalism*, London: Verso.

Anderson, M.S. (1970) 'Eighteenth Century Theories of the Balance of Power' in Ragnhild Hutton and M.S. Anderson (eds), *Studies in Diplomatic History: Essays in Honour of David Bayne Horne*, London: Longman, 183–98.

Antonov, M. (1971) 'Uchenie Slavyanofilov – vysshiy vzlet narodnogo samosoznaniya v Rossii v doleninskiy period' in *Veche*, no. 1, 1971, 13–44; part two in no. 2, May 1971 (AS no. 1020), 4–27; part three in no. 3, September 1971 (AS no. 1108), 5–49.

Anyutin, P. (1983) 'Ekonomicheskaya integratsiya v mire kapitala' in *Mirovaya ekonomika i mezhdunarodnye otnosheniya* (hereafter *MEiMO*), 26, 3: 130–40.

Ashley, Richard (1987) 'The Geopolitics of Geopolitical Space: Toward a Critical Social Theory of International Politics' in *Alternatives*, 12, 4: 403–34.

Baron, Samuel H. (1963) *Plekhanov: Father of Russian Marxism*, Stanford: Stanford University Press.

Bassin, Mark (1991) 'Russia between Europe and Asia: The Ideological Construction of Geographical Space' in *Slavic Review*, 50, 1: 1–17.

Baudrillard, Jean (1977) *Oublier Foucault*, Paris: Galilée.

Beglov, S., Zhurkin, V. and Sturua, M. (1963) 'Tekushchie problemy mirovoy politiki' in *MEiMO*, 7, 7: 63–85 .

Belinskiy, Vissarion Grigor'evich (1956) [1847] 'Vzglyad na russkuyu literaturu 1846 goda' in *Polnoe sobranie sochineniy*, 10, Moscow: Akademiya nauk, 7–50.

Berdiaev, Nicolas (1947) *The Russian Idea*, London: Geoffrey Bles; Russian original reprinted as 'Russkaya ideya' in *Voprosy filosofii*, 1, 2, 1990.

Berdiaev, Nicolas (1949) *Towards a New Epoch*, London: Geoffrey Bles.

Berdiaev, Nicolas (1960) [1937] *The Origins of Russian Communism*, Ann Arbor, MI: University of Michigan Press.

Berdiaev, Nicolas (1961) [1931] *The Russian Revolution*, Ann Arbor, MI: University of Michigan Press.

Berdyaev, Nikolay (1923) *Filosofiya neravenstvo. Pis'ma k nedrugam no sotsial'noy filosofii*, Berlin: Obelisk.

Berdyaev, Nikolay (1924) *Novoe srednevekov'e*, Berlin: Obelisk.

Berdyaev, Nikolay (1967) [1909] 'Filosofskaya istina i intelligentskaya pravda' in *Vekhi*, 1–22.

Berlin, Isaiah (1963) 'The Silence in Russian Culture' in Philip E. Mosely (ed.), *The Soviet Union, 1922–1962: A Foreign Affairs Reader*, New York, NY: Praeger for the Council on Foreign Relations, 337–59.

Berlin, Isaiah (1978) 'A Remarkable Decade' in Henry Hardy and Aileen Kelly (eds), *Russian Thinkers*, Harmondsworth: Penguin, 114–209.

Billington, James H. (1958) *Mikhailovskiy and Russian Populism*, New York, NY: Oxford University Press.

Binns, Christopher A. P. (1978) 'From *USE* to *EEC*: The Soviet Analysis of European Integration under Capitalism' in *Soviet Studies*, 30, 2: 237–61.

Borisov, Vadim (1975) 'Personality and National Awareness' in Solzhenitsyn et al., 194–228.

Borko, Yu (1988) 'O nekotorykh aspektakh izucheniya protsessov zapad-noevropeyskoy integratsii' in *MEiMO*, 32, 2: 35–50.

Borko, Yuriy (1993) 'Esli ne "obshchiy dom", to chto zhe?' in *Svobodnaya mysl'*, 70, 3: 5–11.

Bourdieu, Pierre (1977) *Outline of a Theory of Practice*, Cambridge: Cambridge University Press.

Bovin, A.E. and Lukin, V.P. (1989) 'perestroyka mezhdunarodnykh otnosheniy – puti i podkhody' in *MEiMO*, 33, 1: 58–70.

Brown, Archie (1990) 'Perestroyka and the Political System' in Hasegawa and Pravda, 56–87.

Bukharin, Nikolai (1972) [1917] *Imperialism and World Economy*, New York, NY: Merlin.

Bulgakov, Sergey (1967) [1909] 'Geroizm i podvizhnichestvo (Iz razmyshleniy o religioznoy prirode russkoy intelligentsii)' in *Vekhi*, 23–69.

Bull, Hedley (1977) *The Anarchical Society: A Study of Order in World Politics*, London: Macmillan.

Bull, Hedley and Watson, Adam (eds) (1984) *The Expansion of International Society*, Oxford: Clarendon.

Bunkina, M.K. (1966) *Razvitie mezhimperiàlisticheskikh protivorechiy v usloviyakh borby dvukh sistem*, Moscow: Moscow University Press.

Burbank, Jane (1986) *Intelligentsia and Revolution: Russian Views of Bolshevism 1917–1922*, New York, NY: Oxford University Press.

Buzan, Barry (1993) 'From International System to International Society: Structural Realism and Regime Theory Meet the English School' in *International Organization*, 47, 3: 327–52.

Byrnes, Robert F. (1962) 'Attitudes toward the West' in Ivo J. Lederer (ed.), *Russian Foreign Policy. Essays in Historical Perspective*, New Haven, NJ: Yale University Press, 109–41.

Carr, E.H. (1950) *A History of Soviet Russia: The Bolshevik Revolution 1917–1923*, vol. 1, London: Macmillan.

Carr, E.H. (1953) *A History of Soviet Russia: The Bolshevik Revolution 1917–1923*, vol. 3, London: Macmillan.

Carr, E.H. (1954) *A History of Soviet Russia: The Interregnum 1923–1924*, London: Macmillan.

Carr, E.H. (1956) ' "Russia and Europe" as a Theme of Russian History' in Richard Pares and A.J.P. Taylor (eds) *Essays Presented to Sir Lewis Namier*, London: Macmillan.

Carr, E.H. (1958) *A History of Soviet Russia: Socialism in One Country 1924–1926*, vol. 1, London: Macmillan.

Carr, E.H. (1959) *A History of Soviet Russia: Socialism in One Country 1924–1926* , vol. 2, London: Macmillan.

Carr, E.H. (1979) *The Russian Revolution from Lenin to Stalin (1917–1929)*, London: Macmillan.

Chaadayev, Petr Iakovlevich (1978) [1836] 'Letters on the Philosophy of History: First Letter' in Marc Raeff (ed.), *Russian Intellectual History: An Anthology*, Sussex: Harvester Press, 160–73.

Chalmaev, V. (1968) 'Neizbezhnost'' in *Molodaya gvardiya*, 47, 9: 259–89.

Chelnokov, I. (1957) 'The European Coal and Steel Community' in *International Affairs*, 3, 2: 94–104.

Cherniavsky, Michael (1958) '"Holy Russia": A Study in the History of an Idea', in *American History Review*, 63, 3: 617–37.

Chernyshevskiy, Nikolay Gavrilovich (1987) [1861] 'O prichinakh padeniya Rima (Podrazhanie Montesk'e)' in *Sochineniya v dvukh tomakh*, 2, Moscow: Mysl', 249–77.

Clark, Ian (1989) *The Hierarchy of States: Reform and Resistance in the International Order*, Cambridge: Cambridge University Press.

Cohen, Stephen F. (1974) *Bukharin and the Bolshevik Revolution: A Political Biography 1888–1938*, London: Wildwood.

Cornwell, Neil (1986) *The Life, Times and Milieu of V.F. Odoyevsky*, London: Athlone.

Crow, Suzanne (1993) *The Making of Foreign Policy in Russia under Yeltsin*, Munich: Radio Free Europe/Radio Liberty.

Dalby, Simon (1990) *Creating the Second Cold War*, London: Pinter.

Danilevskiy, Nikolay Jakovlevich (1888) [1869] *Rossiya i Evropa. Vzglyad na kul'turnyya i politicheskiya otnosheniya Slavyanskago mira k Germano-Romanskomy*, St Petersburg: Strakhov, third edn.

Dawisha, Karen (1984) 'Soviet Ideology and Western Europe' in Moreton and Segal, 19–38.

Day, Richard B. (1973) *Leon Trotsky and the Politics of Economic Isolation*, Cambridge: Cambridge University Press.

Degras, Jane (ed.) (1952) *Soviet Documents on Foreign Policy*, 2, Oxford: Oxford University Press.

Demin, A. and Raskov, N. (1980) 'Zapadnaya Evropa v sovremennom mire' in *MEiMO*, 24, 2.

Der Derian, James (1986) 'Hedley Bull and the Idea of Diplomatic Culture', paper presented to the annual meeting of the British International Studies Association.

Der Derian, James (1987) *On Diplomacy: A Genealogy of Western Estrangement*, Oxford: Blackwell.

Deutscher, Isaac (1954) *The Prophet Armed: Trotsky: 1879–1921*, London: Oxford University Press.

Dillon, G.M. (1989) 'Modernity, Discourse and Deterrence', in *Current Research on Peace and Violence*, 12, 2: 90–104.

Dostoevskiy, Fedor Mikhaylovich (1954) [1881] *The Diary of a Writer*, New York, NY: George Braziller.

Dostoevskiy, Fedor Mikhaylovich (1986) Letter to Maykov from Dresden, 9–21 October 1870 in *Polnoe sobranie sochineniy v tridtsati tomakh*, 29, book 1, Leningrad: Nauka, 144–7.

Dowler, Wayne (1977) 'The "Young Editors" of *Moskvityanin* and the Origins of Intelligentsia Conservatism in Russia' in *Slavonic and East European Studies*, 55, 3: 310–27.

Duncan, Peter John Stuart (1989) 'Russian Messianism: A Historical and Political Analysis', Glasgow: Ph.D. thesis, University of Glasgow, mimeo.

Dunlop, John B. (1984) *The Faces of Contemporary Russian Nationalism*, Princeton, NJ: Princeton University Press.

Durkheim, Emile (1964) *The Division of Labour in Society*, New York, NY: Free Press.

Elster, Jon (1985) *Making Sense of Marx*, Cambridge: Cambridge University Press.

Eran, Oded (1979) *Mezhdunarodniki:. An Assessment of Professional Expertise in the Making of Soviet Foreign Policy*, Ramat Gan: Turtledove.

'Evraziyskiy analiz: Geopolitika yugoslavskogo konflikta' in *Elementy. Evraziyskoe obozrenie*, no. 2, 1992, abridged text reprinted in *Osteuropa* (1994) 44, 2: A70–A71.

Faminskiy, I., Kostyukhin, D., Solodkin, R., Vetlanin, V., Chernikov, G., Vasil'kov, N., Vasil'ev, A., Zagorskiy, V. and Frey, L. (1959) '"Obshchiy rynok" i ego rol' v ekonomike i politike sovremennogo imperializma. Nauchnaya konferentsiya' in *MEiMO*, 3, 9: 86–106.

Fedotov, Georgy (1990) [Paris, 1932] 'Russia, Europe and We', originally published in *Novyy grad*, abridged version reprinted in *New Times*, 27 November 1990.

Fischer, George (1958) *Russian Liberalism: From Gentry to Intelligentsia*, Cambridge, MA: Harvard University Press.

Forte, David F.P. (1968) 'The Response of Soviet Foreign Policy to the Common Market, 1957–63' in *Soviet Studies*, 19, 3: 373–86.

Foucault, Michel (1974) *The Archaeology of Knowledge*, London: Tavistock.

Foucault, Michel (1977) 'Nietzsche, Genealogy, History' in Michel Foucault (ed. David Bouchard), *Language, Counter-Memory, Practice: Selected Essays and Interviews*, Oxford: Basil Blackwell, 137–64.

Frank, André Gunder (1969) [1966] 'The Development of Underdevelopment' in Frank (ed.) *Latin America: Underdevelopment or Revolution. Essays on Underdevelopment and the Immediate Enemy*, New York, NY: Monthly Review Press, 3–17.

Frank, Semen A. (1967) [1909] 'Etika nigilizma' in *Vekhi*, 175–210.

Freedman, Lawrence (1984) 'The United States Factor' in Moreton and Segal, 87–109.

Gaganov, A. (1973a) 'Chto takoe "Entsiklopediya liberal'nogo renegatovtsa?"' in *Veche*, no. 7, February (AS no. 1775): 36–77.

Gaganov, A. (1973b) 'Iz glubiny' in *Veche*, no. 9, December (AS no. 2040): 36–66.

Galtung, Johan (1990) 'Cultural Violence' in *Journal of Peace Research*, 27, 3: 291–305.

Garthoff, Raymond L. (1985) *Détente and Confrontation: American–Soviet Relations from Nixon to Reagan*, Washington, DC: Brookings.

Geertz, Clifford (1973) *The Interpretation of Cultures*, New York, NY: Basic.

Gefter, Mikhail in conversation with Pavlovskiy, Gleb (1989) 'Dom Evraziya' in *Vek XX i mir*, 32, 6: 22–7.

Gerschenkron, Alexander (1962) 'Economic Development in Russian Intellectual History of the Nineteenth Century' in Gerschenkron (ed.), *Economic Backwardness in Historical Perspective: A Book of Essays*, Cambridge, MA: Harvard University Press.

Gershenzon, M.O. (1967) [1909] 'Tvorcheskoe samosoznanie' in *Vekhi*, 70–96.

Gertsen, A.N. (cf. also under Herzen) (1919) [1849, Geneva] 'Rossiya' in *Polnoe sobranie sochineniy i pisem*, 5, Petrograd: Narodnyy komissariat po prosveshcheniyu, 330–65.

Goban-Klas, Tomasz and Kolstø, Pål (1994) 'East European Mass Media: The Soviet Role' in Odd Arne Westad, Sven Holtsmark and Iver B. Neumann. (eds) *The Soviet Union in Eastern Europe, 1945–1989*, Basingstoke: Macmillan, 110–36.

Goerdt, Wilhelm (1984) 'Vorsicht vor den Wörtern "Westler" – "Slavophile"! Ein unvermeidlicher historiographischer Exkurs' in *Russische Philosophie. Band 1: Zugänge und Durchblicke*, Freiburg: Alber, 262–71.

Gol'denberg, E. (1929) 'Germanskaya problema' in *Bol'shevik*, 5, 5: 27–40.

Gong, Gerrit W. (1984) *The Standard of 'Civilization' in International Society*, Oxford: Clarendon.

Goodman, Elliot R. (1960) *The Soviet Design for a World State*, New York, NY: Columbia University Press.

Gorbachev, Mikhail (1988) [1987] *Perestroika: New Thinking for Our Country and the World*, London: Fontana, second edn.

Gourevitch, Peter (1978) 'The Second Image Reversed: The International Sources of Domestic Politics' in *International Organization*, 32, 4: 881–911.

Grader, Sheila (1988) 'The English School of International Relations: Evidence and Evaluation' in *Review of International Relations*, 14, 1: 29–44.

Gromyko, Anatoliy and Lomeyko, Vladimir (1984) *Novoe myshlenie v yadernyy vek*, Moscow: Mezhdunarodnye otnosheniya.

Gromyko, Anatoli and Lomeiko, Vladimir (1986) 'New Ways of Thinking and "New Globalism"' in *International Affairs*, 5: 15–27.

Harding, Neil (1977) *Lenin's Political Thought. Vol. 1: Theory and Practice in the Democratic Revolution*, London: Macmillan.

Harding, Neil (1981) *Lenin's Political Thought. Vol. 2: Theory and Practice in the Socialist Revolution*, London: Macmillan.

Hasegawa, Tsuyoshi and Pravda, Alex (eds) (1990) *Perestroika: Soviet Domestic and Foreign Policies*, London: SAGE, Royal Institute of International Affairs.

Haslam, Jonathan (1983) *Soviet Foreign Policy, 1930–33: The Impact of the Depression*, London: Macmillan.

Haslam, Jonathan (1984) *The Soviet Union and the Struggle for Collective Security in Europe, 1933–39*, London: Macmillan.

Hauner, Milan (1990) *What Is Asia to Us? Russia's Asian Heartland Yesterday and Today*, Boston: Unwin Hyman.

Herzen, Alexander (cf., also under Gertsen) (1968) [1862] 'Ends and Beginnings: Letters to I.S. Turgenev (1862–1863)' in *My Past and Thoughts: The Memoirs of Alexander Herzen*, London: Chatto & Windus, 1680–749.

History of the Communist Party of the Soviet Union (Bolsheviks): Short Course (1948) [1938] (ed. by a Commission of the Central Committee of the CPSU (b), authorised by the CC of the CPSU (b) 1938), Moscow: Foreign Languages Publishing House.

Hoffman, Erik P. (1990) 'Gorbachev and the Western Alliance: Reassessing the Anticoalition Strategy' in Robbin F. Laird and Susan L. Clark (eds), *The USSR and the Western Alliance*, Boston: Unwin Hyman, 51–88.

Hogg, Michael A. and Abrams, Dominic (1988) *Social Identifications: A Social Psychology of Intergroup Relations and Group Processes*, London: Routledge.

Holburn, Hajjo (1962) 'Russia and the European Political System' in Ivo J. Lederer (ed.), *Russian Foreign Policy: Essays in Historical Perspective*, New Haven, CN: Yale University Press, 377–415.

Hollis, Martin and Smith, Steve (1991a) *Explaining and Understanding International Relations*, Oxford: Clarendon.

Hollis, Martin and Smith, Steve (1991b) 'Beware of Gurus: Structure and Action in International Relations', in *Review of International Studies*, 17, 4: 393–410.

Hough, Jerry (1986) *The Struggle for the Third World: Soviet Debates and American Options*, Washington, DC: Brookings.

Ignatow, Assen (1992) *Die 'russische Idee' in der gegenwärtigen Diskussion. Die russische Identität und die 'Neuen Ideologien'*, Cologne: Bundesinstitut für ostwissenschaftliche und internationale Studien, report no. 42.

IMEMO AN SSSR (1957) 'O sozdanii "obshchego rynka" i Evratom (Tezisy)' in *MEiMO*, 1, 1: 83–96.

IMEMO AN SSSR (1962) 'Ob imperialisticheskoy "integratsii" v Zapadnoy Evrope ("Obshchiy rynok"). Tezisy'. Supplement to *MEiMO*, 6, 9.

IMEMO AN SSSR (1988) 'Evropeyskoe soobshchestvo segodnya. Tezisy Instituta mirovoy ekonomiki i mezhdunarodnykh otnosheniy AN SSSR' in *MEiMO*, 32, 12: 5–18.

Jarvis, Anthony (1989) 'Societies, States and Geopolitics: Challenges from Historical Sociology' in *Review of International Studies*, 15, 3: 281–93.

Jelavich, Barbara (1974) *St. Petersburg and Moscow: Tsarist and Soviet Foreign Policy, 1814–1974*, Bloomington, IN: Indiana University Press.

Jones, Roy E. (1981) 'The English School of International Relations: A Case for Closure' in *Review of International Studies*, 7, 1: 1–12:

Kara-Mursa, Aleksey, Lyubomirova, Natal'ya, Malakhov, Vladimir, Perevalov, Valeriy and Polyakov, Leonid (1991) 'Filosofiya "russkoy idei": Russia i Evropa. "Kruglyy stol" molodykh uchenykh' in *Obshchestvennye nauki i sovremennost'*, 16, 5: 143–54.

Karaganov, Sergei (1990) 'The Problems of the USSR's European Policy' in *International Affairs*, Moscow, 37, 7: 72–80.

Karaganov, Sergey (1989) 'The USA and Common European Home' in *International Affairs*, 8: 17–26.

Karamzin, Nikolay M. (ed. Richard Pipes) (1969) *Karamzin's Memoir on Ancient and Modern Russia: A Translation and Analysis*, New York, NY: Atheneum.

Keep, J.L.H. (1963) *The Rise of Social Democracy in Russia*, Oxford: Clarendon.

Keller, Werner (1963) [1960] *Ost minus West = Null: Der Aufbau Russlands durch den Westen*, Munich: Knaur.

Kennan, George F. (1960) *Russia and the West under Lenin and Stalin*, New York, NY: Mentor.

Kennan, George F. (1979) *The Decline of Bismarck's European Order: Franco-Russian Relations, 1875–1890*, Princeton, NJ: Princeton University Press.

Keohane, Robert O. and Nye Jr., Joseph S. (1977) *Power and Interdependence: World Politics in Transition*, Boston, MA: Little, Brown.

Khomyakov, Aleksey Stepanovivch (1900) 'Po povodu Gumbol'dta' in *Polnoe sobranie sochineniy*, 1, Moscow: Universitetskaya tipografiya, third edn., 143–74.

Khrushchev, Nikolay Sergeevich (1962) 'Nasushchnye voprosy razvitiya mirovoy sotsialisticheskoy sistemy' in *Problemy mira i sotsializma*, reprinted in *Kommunist*, 39, 12: 3–26.

Khrushchev, Nikita Sergeevich (ed. Strobe Talbott) (1971) *Khrushchev Remembers*, London: André Deutsch.

Kibal'chich, Nikolay Ivanovich (1984) [1881] 'Political Revolution and the Economic Question' in Shanin, 212–18.

Kindersley, Richard (1962) *The First Russian Revisionists: A Study of 'Legal Marxism' in Russia*, Oxford: Clarendon.

Kireevskiy, Ivan Vasil'evich (ed. M. Gershenzon) (1911a) [1832] 'Devyatnadtsatyy vek' in *Polnoe sobranie sochineniy*, 1, Moscow: Tipografiya imperatorskago moskovskago universiteta, 85–108.

Kireevskiy, Ivam Vasil'evich (1911b) [1852] 'O kharaktere prosveshcheniya Evropy i o ego otnoshenii k prosveshcheniyu Rossii', letter to E.E. Komarovskiy in op. cit., 174–222.

Kirsanov, Aleksandr V. (1975) *The USA and Western Europe: Economic Relations after World War II*, Moscow: Progress.

Kiss, Csaba G. (1989) 'Central European Writers about Central Europe: Introduction to a Non-Existent Book of Reading' in George Schöpflin and Nancy Wood (eds), *In Search of Central Europe*, Cambridge: Polity, 125–36.

Kissinger, Henry (1957) *A World Restored: Metternich, Castlereagh and the Problem of Peace 1812–22*, London: Weidenfeld & Nicholson.

Knei-Paz, Baruch (1978) *The Social and Political Thought of Leon Trotsky*, Oxford: Clarendon.

Knyazhinskiy, Vsevolod Borisovich (1958) *Proval planov 'obedineniya Evropy'. Ocherk istorii imperialisticheskikh popytok antisovetskogo 'obedineniya Evropy' mezhdu pervoy i vtoroy mirovymi voynami*, Moscow: Gospolizdat.

Knyazhinskiy, V.B. et al. (1986) *Zapadno-Evropeyskaya Integratsiya: proekty i real'nost'*, Moscow: Mezhdunarodnye otnosheniya.

Kolstø, Pål (1988) *An Appeal to the People: Glasnost – Aims and Means*, Oslo: Institute for Defence Studies.

Kommisrud, Arne (1991) 'Russland før 1917 – patrimonielt imperium eller kolonimakt?', Oslo: Oslo University, mimeo.

Kopolev, Lev (1977) 'The Lie can be Defeated only by the Truth' in Meerson-Aksenor and Shragin, 302–42.

Koyré, Alexandre (1929) *La Philosophie et le problème national en Russie au début du XIXe siècle*, Paris: Honoré Champion.

Kozyrev, Andrey (1992) Newspaper article in *Moskovskie novosti*, 25 October, signed to press 20 October, reprinted in *FBIS*, 21 October 1992.

Kozyrev, Andrey (1993) Newspaper article in *Moskovskie novosti*, 24 October, signed to press 19 October, reprinted in *FBIS*, 21 October 1993.

Krag, Erik (1932) *Kampen mot Vesten i russisk åndsliv*, Oslo: Gyldendal.

Krivorotov, Viktor (1990) 'Russkiy put'' in *Znamya*, 60, 8: 140–64; 9: 184–200.

Kruschev, Nikita Sereevich (1962) 'Nasushchnye voprosy vazvitiya mirovoysotsialisticheskoy sistemy' in *Problemy mira i sotsializma*, reprinted in and quoted from *Kommunist*, 39, 12: 3–26.

Kruschev, Nikita Sereevich (ed. Strobe Talbott) (1971) *Kruschev Remembers*, London: André Deutsh.

Kubálková, Vendulka and Cruickshank, Arthur A. (1980) *Marxism-Leninism and Theory of International Relations*, London: Routledge & Kegan Paul.

Kubálková, V. and Cruickshank, A.A. (1989) *Thinking New about Soviet 'New Thinking'*, Berkeley, CA: Institute of International Studies.

Kuznetsov, B., Panov, N., Sysoev, N., Fituni, L., Aust, Hans V. and Kirsanov, A. (1959) '"Obshchiy rynok" i ego rol' v ekonomike i politike sovremennogo imperializma. Nauchnaya konferentsiya' in MEiMO, 3, 10: 73–83.

Laclau, Ernesto and Mouffe, Chantal (1985) Hegemony and Socialist Strategy: Towards a Radical Democratic Politics, London: Verso.

Lampert, E. (1965) Sons against Fathers: Studies in Russian Radicalism and Revolution, Oxford: Oxford at the Clarendon.

von Laue, Theodore H. (1963) Sergei Witte and the Industrialization of Russia, New York, NY: Columbia University Press.

Lednicki, Wacław (1966) 'Europe in Dostoevsky's Ideological Novels' in Russia, Poland and the West: Essays in Literary and Cultural History, Port Washington, NY: Kennikat, 133–79.

Lenin, Vladimir Il'ich (1958) [1899] 'Razvitie kapitalizma v Rossii. Protsess obrazovaniya vnutrennego rynka dlya krupnoy promyshlennosti' in Polnoe sobranie sochineniy, Moscow: Gosudarstvennoe izdatel'stvo politicheskoy literatury, 1958–1965, vol. 3, 1–609.

Lenin (1960a) [August 1905, Geneva] 'Dve taktiki sotsialdemokratii v demokraticheskoy revolyutsii' in op. cit., vol. 8, 1–131.

Lenin (1960b) [1924] 'O karikature na marksizm i ob "imperialisticheskom ekonomizme"' in op. cit., vol. 30, 77–130.

Lenin (1960c) [1926] 'Etapy, napravlenie i perspektivy revolyutsii' in op. cit., vol. 12, 154–157.

Lenin (1960d) [1926] 'Etapy, napravlenie i perspektivy revolyutsii' in op. cit., vol. 12, 154–7.

Lenin [V. Il'in] (1961a) [1909] 'O "vekhakh"' in op. cit., vol. 19, 167–75.

Lenin (1961b) [1913] 'Otstalaya Evropa i peredovaya Aziya' in op. cit., vol. 23, 166–7.

Lenin (1961c) [1913] 'Probuzhdenie Azii' in op. cit., vol. 23, 145–6.

Lenin (1961d) [1915] 'O lozunge Soedinennykh Shtatov Evropy' in op. cit., vol. 26, 351–5.

Lenin (1962a) [1916] 'Sotsialisticheskaya revolyutsiya i pravo natsii na samoopredelenie' in op. cit., vol. 27, 252–66.

Lenin (1962b) [1917] 'Groznaya katastrofa i kak s ney borot'sya' in op. cit., vol. 34, 151–99.

Lenin [N. Lenin] (1962c) [1918] 'O "levom" rebyachestve i o melkoburzhuaznosti' in op. cit., vol. 36, 283–314.

Lenin (1962d) [1917] 'Imperializm, kak vysshaya stadiya kapitalizma (populyarnyy ocherk)' in op. cit., vol. 27, 299–426.

Lenin (1962e) [1918] 'Tyazhelyy, no neobkhodimyy urok' in op. cit., vol. 25, 393–7.

Lenin (1962f) [1928] 'Porazhenie Rossii i revolutsionnyy krizis' in op. cit., vol. 27, 26–30.

Lenin (1963a) [1919] 'Otchet Tsentral'nogo Komiteta 18 marta' in op. cit., vol. 38, 131–50.

Lenin (1963b) [1921] 'Rech' po zakrytii konferentsii 28 maya' in op. cit., vol. 43, 340–1.

Lenin (1963c) [1929] 'O gosudarstve. Lektsiya v Sverdlovskom universitete 11 iyulya 1919 g.' in op. cit., vol. 39, 64–84.

Lenin (1965) [1922] 'Politicheskiy otchet Tsentral'nogo Komiteta RKP (b) 27 marta' in op. cit., vol. 45, 69–116.

Leont'ev, Konstantin Nikolaevich (1912a) 'Vizantinizm i Slavyanstvo' in *Sobranie sochineniy*, vol. 5, Moscow: V.M. Sablin, 110–260.

Leont'ev, Konstantin Nikolaevich (1912b) 'Pis'ma o vostochnykh delakh' in op. cit., vol. 5, 379–468.

Leont'ev, Konstantin Nikolaevich (1912c) 'Sredniy evropeets, kak ideal i orudie vsemirnago pazrusheniya' in op. cit., vol. 6, 1–79.

Leont'ev, Konstantin Nikolaevich (1912d) 'Zapiski otshel'nika' in op. cit., vol. 6, 81–144.

Leont'ev, Konstantin Nikolaevich (1913) 'Peredovyya stat'i "Varshavskago dnevnika" 1880 g.' in op. cit., vol. 7, 'Vostok, Rossiya i Slavyanstvo', 57–158, entry for 1 March, 120–4.

Lévi-Strauss, Claude (1978) 'Race and History' in *Structural Anthropology*, vol. 2, Harmondsworth: Penguin, 323–62.

Lider, Julian (1986) *Correlation of Forces: An Analysis of Marxist-Leninist Concepts*, Aldershot: Gower.

Lieven, Dominic C.B. (1983) *Russia and the Origins of the First World War*, London: Macmillan.

Light, Margot (1988) *The Soviet Theory of International Relations*, Brighton: Wheatsheaf.

Likhachev, D.S. (1980) 'Zametki o russkom. Priroda, rodnik, prosto dobrota' in *Novyy mir*, 56, 3: 10–38.

Linklater, Andrew (1990) *Men and Citizens in the Theory of International Relations*, London: Macmillan, The London School of Economics and Political Science, second edn.

Ljunggren, Magnus (1992) 'Rysslands rödbruna författare' in *Internationelle studier*, 24, 2: 15–23.

Lotman, Yuri M. (1990) *Universe of the Mind: A Semiotic Theory of Culture*, London: I.B. Tauris.

Lukin, V.P. interviewed by Razuvayev, Vladimir (1991) 'The Axioms of Russia' in *New Times*, 2: 24–6.

Lynch, Allen (1987) *The Soviet Study of International Relations*, Cambridge: Cambridge University Press.

Lyotard, Jean François (1984) [1979] *The Postmodern Condition: A Report on Knowledge*, Minneapolis, MN, University of Minnesota Press.

McAuley, Mary (1984) 'Political Culture and Communist Politics: One Step Forward, Two Steps Back' in Archie Brown (ed.), *Political Culture and Communist Studies*, Houndmills: Macmillan, St Antony's College, Oxford, 13–39.

MacMaster, Robert E. (1967) *Danilevsky: A Russian Totalitarian Philosopher*, Cambridge, MA: Harvard University Press.

McNeill, William H. (1963) *The Rise of the West: A History of the Human Community*, Chicago, IL: University of Chicago Press.

Madzoevskiy, S. [Donald Maclean], Mel'nikov, D. and Molchanov, N. (1963) 'Evropeyskiy uzel' mezhimperialisticheskikh protivorechiy' in *MEiMO*, 7, 8: 73–81.

Maier, L. (GDR), Mel'nikov, D. and Shenaev, B. (1978) 'Zapadnoevropeyskiy tsentr imperialisticheskogo sopernichestva' in *MEiMO*, 22, 12: 22–32.

Maksimova, M. (1978a) 'Kapitalisticheskaya integratsiya i mirovoe razvitie. Stat'ya pervaya' in *MEiMO*, 22, 3: 12–23.

Maksimova, M. (1978b) 'Kapitalisticheskaya integratsiya i mirovoe razvitie. Stat'ya vtoraya' in *MEiMO*, 22, 4: 14–24.

Maksimova, M., Timoshnik, T., Borko, Yu., Velyugo, I., Shishkov, Yu., Korolev, I., Krichigina, N. and Zuev, V. (1982) 'Problemy zapadno-evropeyskoy integratsii' in *MEiMO*, 26, 11: 107–33.

Malashenko, A. (1990) 'Russia: The Earth's Heartland' in *International Affairs*, 36, 7: 46–54.

Malcolm, Neil (1984) *Soviet Political Scientists and American Politics*, London: Macmillan.

Malcolm, Neil (1989a) *Soviet Policy Perspectives on Western Europe*, London: Routledge, Royal Institute of International Affairs.

Malcolm, Neil (1989b) 'Foreign Affairs Specialists and Decision Makers' in David Lane (ed.), *Elites and Political Power in the USSR*, Aldershot: Edward Elgar, 205–24.

Malcolm, Neil (1991) 'The Soviet Concept of a Common European House' in Jyrki Iivonen (ed.), *The Changing Soviet Union in the New Europe*, Aldershot: Edward Elgar, 45–82.

Malcolm, Neil (1994) 'New Thinking and After: Debate in Moscow about Europe' in Neil Malcolm (ed.), *Russia and Europe: An End to Confrontation?*, London: Pinter/RIIA, 151–81.

Malia, Martin (1961) *Alexander Herzen and the Birth of Russian Socialism, 1812–1855*, Cambridge, MA: Harvard University Press.

Marsh, Peter (1978) 'The Development of Relations between the EEC and the CMEA' in Avi Shlaim and George N. Yannopoulos (eds), *The EEC and Eastern Europe*, Cambridge: Cambridge University Press, 25–69.

Marx, Karl (1972) [1867] 'Author's Preface to the First German Edition' in *Capital*, vol. 1, London: Everyman, xlvii-li.

Masaryk, Tomas G. (1931)*Russland and Europa. Studien über die geistigen Strömungen in Russland. Zur russischen Gesichts – und Religionsphilosophie: soziologische Skizzen*, two vols, Jena: Eugen Diederich.

Medvedev, Roy (1977) [1974] 'What Awaits Us in the Future? (Regarding A.I. Solzhenitsyn's letter)' in Meerson-Aksenov and Shragin, 76–94.

Meerson-Aksenov, Michael (1977) 'The Dissident Movement and Samizdat' in Meerson-Aksenov and Shragin, 19–43.

Meerson-Aksenov, Michael and Shragin, Boris (eds) (1977) *The Political, Social and Religious Thought of Russian 'Samizdat' – An Anthology*, Belmont, MA: Nordland.

Mel'nikov, D.E. (ed.) (1968) *Zapadnaya Evropa i SShA*, Moscow: Mysl'.

Melograni, Piero (1989) *Lenin and the Myth of World Revolution: Ideology and Reasons of State, 1917–1920*, Atlantic Highlands, NJ: Humanities.

Mendras, Marie (1990) 'The Soviet Union and its Rival Self' in *The Journal of Communist Studies*, 6, 1: 1–23.

Meyman, E.A. (1975) 'Vladimir Odoevskiy i ego roman "Russkie nochi"' in Odoevskiy, 247–76.

Moreton, Edwina and Segal, Gerald (eds) (1984) *Soviet Strategy toward Western Europe*, London: George Allen & Unwin.

Moser, Charles A. (1972) 'Turgenev: The Cosmopolitan Nationalist' in *Review of National Literatures*, 3, 1: 56–88.

Na putyakh: Utverzhdenie evraziytsev, kniga 2 (1922) Moscow–Berlin: Gelikon.

Nestor (ed. V.P. Adrianova-Peretc) (1950) *Povest' vremmenykh let*, Moscow: Akademiya navk, literaturnye pamyatniki.

Neumann, Iver B. (1989) *Soviet Perceptions of the European Community, 1950–1988*, Oslo: Norwegian Institute of International Affairs, report no. 131.

Neumann, Iver B. (1993) 'Russia as Central Europe's Constituting Other' in *East European Politics and Society*, 7, 2: 349–69.

Neumann, Iver B. (1994) 'A Region-Building Approach to Northern Europe' in *Review of International Studies*, 20, 1: 53–74.

Neumann, Iver B. (1995a) 'Collective Identity Formation and the Other in International Relations' forthcoming in *European Journal of International Relations*.

Neumann, Iver B. (1995b) 'Russia: Barbarian at the Gate, Imperfect European or Land of the Future?' Paper presented to the European Consortium of Political Research second pan-European conference, Paris, September 1995.

Neumann, Iver B. and Eriksen, Thomas Hylland (1993) 'International Relations as a Cultural System: An Agenda for Research' in *Cooperation and Conflict*, 28, 3: 233–64.

Neumann, Iver B. and Radøy, Sverre Tom (1989) 'The Soviet Union and CMEA's Road towards Recognition of the EC' in *Coexistence*, 26, 2: 121–45.

Neumann, Iver B. and Welsh, Jennifer M. (1991) 'The Other in European Self-Definition: A Critical Addendum to the Literature on International Society' in *Review of International Studies*, 17, 4: 327–48.

Norton, Anne (1988) *Reflections on Political Identity*, Baltimore, MD: The Johns Hopkins University Press.

Novikov, Andrey (1991) 'Ya – rusofob' in *Vek XX i mir*, 33, 7: 12–14.

Odoevskiy, Vladimir Fedorovich (1975) [1844] *Russkie nochi*, Leningrad: Nauka.

Offord, Derek (1986) *The Russian Revolutionary Movement in the 1880s*, Cambridge: Cambridge University Press.

Osipov, Vladimir Nikolaevich (1973) 'Zayavlenie redaktsii zhurnala "Veche"', no. 2, May 1971, reprinted as document AS no. 1020 in *Arkhiv Samizdata. Sobranie dokumentov samizdata*, vol. 21, Munich: Radio Liberty.

van Oudenaren, John (1991) *Détente in Europe. The Soviet Union and the West since 1953*, Durham, NC: Duke University Press.

Palmer, Alan (1974) *Alexander I: Tsar of War and Peace*, London: Weidenfeld & Nicolson.

Parthé, Kathleen quoted in 'Russkost' and the Russian Right', *Kennan Meeting Report*, 2, 11, October 1993.

Parvus [Alexandr I. Gel'fand] (1904) [n.d.] *Rossiya I revolyutsiya*, St Petersburg: Glagolev.

Petrovich, Michael Boro (1956) *The Emergence of Russian Panslavism 1856–1870*, New York, NY: Columbia University Press.

Pintner, Walter (1986) 'Russian Military Thought: The Western Model and the Shadow of Suvorov' in Peter Paret (ed.), *Makers of Modern Strategy from Machiavelli to the Nuclear Age*, Oxford: Clarendon, 354–75.

Pipes, Richard (1964) 'Narodnichestvo: A Semantic Inquiry' in *Slavic Review*, 23, 3: 441–58.

Platonov, Sergei F. (1972) [1925] *Russia and the West*, Hattiesburg, MI: Academic International.

Pokrovskiy, S. (1969) 'Mnimaya zagadka' in *Voprosy literatury*, 13, 5: 117–28.

Popov, K., Varga, E., Khmelnitskaya, E. and Makov, M. (1959) '"Obshchiy rynok" i ego rol' v ekonomike i politike sovremennogo imperializma. Nauchnaya konferentsiya' in *MEiMO*, 3, 7: 108–16.

Pozdnyakov, Elgiz (1991) 'The Soviet Union: The Problem of Coming Back to European Civilisation' in *Paradigms*, 5, 1–2: 45–57.

Raeff, Marc (1964) 'Russia's Perception of her Relationship with the West' in *Slavic Review*, 23, 1: 13–19.

Read, Christopher (1979) *Religion, Revolution and the Russian Intelligentsia 1900–1912: The Vekhi Debate and Its Intellectual Background*, London: Macmillan.

Riasanovsky, Nicholas V. (1959) *Nicholas I and Official Nationality in Russia, 1825–1855*, Berkeley, CA: University of California Press.

Riasanovsky, Nikolas V. (1965) *Russia and the West in the Teachings of the Slavophiles: A Study of Romantic Ideology*, Gloucester, MA: Peter Smith.

Riasanovsky, Nicholas V. (1976) *A Parting of Ways: Government and the Educated Public in Russia 1801–1855*, Oxford: Clarendon.

Riasanovsky, Nicholas V. (1985) *The Image of Peter the Great in Russian History and Thought*, Oxford: Oxford University Press.

Riha, Thomas (1969) *A Russian European: Paul Miliukov in Russian Politics*, Notre Dame, IN: University of Notre Dame Press.

Roberts, Henry L. (1964) 'Russia and the West: A Comparison and Contrast' in Donald W. Treadgold (ed.), *The Development of the USSR. An Exchange of Views*, Seattle, WA: University of Washington Press, 359–70.

Rogger, Hans (1960) *National Consciousness in Eighteenth-Century Russia*, Cambridge, MA: Harvard University Press.

'Rol' N. Ya. Danilevskogo v mirovoy istoriosofii'(1972) in *Veche*, no. 5, May, AS no. 1230: 5–32.

Ruggie, John Gerard (1986) 'Continuity and Transformation in the World Polity: Toward a Neorealist Synthesis' in Robert O. Keohane (ed.), *Neorealism and Its Critics*, New York, NY: Columbia University Press.

Sakharov, Andrei D. (1968) *Progress, Coexistence, and Intellectual Freedom*, New York, NY: Norton.

Sakharov, Andrei D. (1975) *My Country and the World*, New York, NY: Vintage.

Sakharov, Andrei D. (1977) [1974] 'On Alexander Solzhenitsyn's *Letter to the Soviet Leaders'* in Meerson-Aksenov and Shragin, 291–301.

Sakharov, Andrey D. (ed. Bent Jensen) (1984a) [1977] *Sakharovs stemme. Fredens forudsætninger. Udvalgte artikler 1975–83*, Viby: Centrum.

Sakharov, Andrey D. (1984b) 'Nobelpris-forelæsning, 1. desember 1975' in Sakharov, 1984a: 20–33.

Sakharov, Andrey D. (1984c) [1980] 'Foruroligende tider, maj 1980' in Sakharov, 1984a: 77–96.

Schafly, Daniel L. (1988) 'The Popular Image of the West in Russia at the Time of Peter the Great' in R.P. Bartlett, A.G. Cross and Karen Rasmussen (eds), *Russia and the World of the Eighteenth Century*, Columbus, OH: Slavica, 2–21.

Schapiro, Leonard B. (1967a) *Rationalism and Nationalism in Russian Nineteenth-Century Political Thought*, New Haven, CN: Yale University Press.

Schapiro, Leonard B. (1967b) 'Lenin after Fifty Years' in Leonard Schapiro and Peter Reddaway (eds), *Lenin: The Man, the Theorist, the Leader*, London: Pall Mall, Hoover Institution, 3–22.

von Schelting, Alexander (1948) *Russland und Europa in Russischen Geschichtsdenken*, Berne: A. Francke.

Schmitt, Carl (1936) [1932] *Der Begriff des Politischen*, Munich: Duncker & Humblot.

Schulz, Eberhard (1975) *Moskau und die Europäische Integration*, Munich: R. Oldenbourg.

Service, Robert (1991) *Lenin: A Political Life: Worlds in Collision*, vol. 2, Basingstoke: Macmillan.

Seton-Watson, Hugh (1988) [1967] *The Russian Empire, 1801–1917*, Oxford: Clarendon.

Shafarevich, Igor (1975) 'Separation or Reconciliation? – The Nationalities Question in the USSR' in Solzhenitsyn et al., 88–104.

Shafarevich, Igor' (1989) 'Rusofobiya' in *Nash sovremennik*, 57, 6: 167–92.

Shanin, Teodor (ed.) (1984a) *Late Marx and the Russian Road: Marx and the 'Peripheries of Capitalism'*, London: Routledge & Kegan Paul.

Shanin, Teodor (1984b) 'Late Marx: Gods and Craftsmen' in Shanin, 3–39.

Shapiro, Michael J. (1981) *Language and Political Understanding: The Politics of Discursive Practice*, New Haven, CN: Yale University Press.

Shapiro, Michael J. (1988) *The Politics of Representation*, Madison, WI: University of Wisconsin Press.

Shenfield, Stephen (1987) *The Nuclear Predicament: Explorations in Soviet Ideology*, London: Routledge & Kegan Paul, Royal Institute of International Affairs.

Shevtsova, Lilia (1990) 'The Chances of Democracy' in *New Times*, 52: 4–6.

Simmel, Georg (ed. David N. Levine) (1970) [1906] *On Individuality and Social Forces. Selected Writings*, Chicago, IL: University of Chicago Press, 1970, 143–9.

Simonsen, Sven Gunnar (1993) 'Dilemma of Dominance: Nation and Empire in Russian Nationalist Ideology', Oslo: MA thesis, Oslo University, mimeo.

Skocpol, Theda (1979) *States and Social Revolutions: A Comparative Analysis of France, Russia and China*, London: Cambridge University Press.

Sodaro, Michael J. (1990) *Moscow, Germany, and the West from Khrushchev to Gorbachev*, Ithaca, NY: Cornell University Press.

Solov'ev, Vladimir Sergeevich (n.d., probably 1905) [1888/1891] 'Natsional'nyy vopros v Rossii' in *Sobranie sochineniy*, 5, (St Petersburg: Obshchestvennaya pol'za), 1–368.

Solov'ev, Vladimir Sergeevich (1990) 'Natsional'nyy vopros v Rossii' (abridged version) in *Literaturnaya kritika*, Moscow: Sovremennik, 292–353.

Solzhenitsyn Alexander (1975b) 'As Breathing and Consciousness Return' in Solzhenitsyn, Alexander et al., 3–25.

Solzhenitsyn (1975c) 'Repentance and Self-Limitation in the Life of the Nations' in Solzhenitsyn et al., 105–43.

Solzhenitsyn (1975d) 'The Smatterers' in Solzhenitsyn et al., 229–78.

Solzhenitsyn (1980a) *East and West*, New York, NY: Harper & Row.

Solzhenitsyn (1980b) [1972] 'The Nobel Lecture on Literature' in op. cit., Solzhenitsyn, 3–36.

Solzhenitsyn (1980c) [1973] 'Letter to the Soviet Leaders' in op.cit., Solzhenitsyn, 75–142.

Solzhenitsyn (1980d) 'A World Split Apart: Commencement Address Delivered at Harvard University June 8, 1978' in op.cit., 39–71.

Solzhenitsyn, Aleksandr (1990) 'Kak nam obustroit' Rossiyu. Posil'nye soobrazheniya'. Enclosure to *Literaturnaya gazeta*, 19 September 1990.

Solzhenitsyn, Alexander et al. (1975a) [1974] *From Under the Rubble*, London: Collins & Harvill.

'Soviet Proposals for All-European Economic Cooperation' (1957) *International Affairs*, 3, 5: 156–60.

Spaak, Paul-Henri (1969) *Combats Inachevés. De l'Indépendance à l'Alliance*, Paris: Fayard.

Spechler, Dina R. (1982) *Permitted Dissent in the USSR. Novy mir and the Soviet Regime*, New York, NY: Praeger.

Staar, Richard F. (1985) *USSR Foreign Policies after Détente*, Stanford, CA: Hoover Institution Press.

Stalin, Iosif Vissarionovich (1947a) [1924] 'Ob osnovakh Leninizma. Lektsii, chitannye v Sverdlovskom universitete' in *Sochineniya*, Moscow: Gosardstvennoe izdatel'stvo politicheskoy literatury, 1946–51, vol. 6, 69–188.

Stalin (1947b) [1924] 'Oktyabr'skaya revolyutsiya i taktika russkikh kommunistov. Predislovie k knige "Na putyakh k Oktyabryu"' in op. cit., vol. 6, 358–401.

Stalin (1949a) 'Ob"edinennyy plenum TsK i TsKK VKP (b) 29 iyulya– 9 avgusta 1927 g.' in op. cit., vol. 10, 1–91.

Stalin (1949b) [1927] 'Politicheskiy otchet Tsentral'nogo Komiteta 3 dekabrya' in op. cit., vol. 10, 271–353.

Stalin (1950a) 'Vystupleniya na VI s"ezde RSDRP (bol'sheviki). 26 iyunya–3 avgusta 1917' in op.cit., vol. 3, 156–87.

Stalin (1950b) 'Rech' na zasedanii TsK. 16 oktyabrya 1917 g.' in op. cit., vol. 3, 381–2.

Stalin (1950c) 'Vystuplenie na zasedanii Tsentral'nogo Komiteta RSDRP (b) po voprosu o mire c nemtsami. 11 yanvarya 1918 g. (kratkaya protokol'naya zapis')' in op. cit., vol. 4, 27.

Stalin (1950d) 'Politika sovetskoy vlasti po natsional'nomu voprosu v Rossii' in op. cit., vol. 4, 351–63.

Stalin (1950e) [1925] 'Politicheskiy otchet Tsentral'nogo Komiteta 18 dekabrya' in op. cit., vol. 7, 261–352.

Stalin (1951) 'O zadachakh kozyastvennikov. Rech' na Vsesoyuznoy konferentsii rabotnikov sotsialisticheskoy promyshlennosti 4 fevralya 1931 g.' in op. cit., vol. 13, 29–42.

Starikov, Evgeniy (1989) 'Marginaly, ili razmyshleniya na staruyu temu: "Chto s nami proiskhodit?"' in Znamya, 59, 10: 133–62.

Starr, S. Frederick (1972) Decentralization and Self-Government in Russia, 1830–1870, Princeton, NJ: Princeton University Press.

Stent, Angela (1981) From Embargo to Ostpolitik: The Political Economy of West German–Soviet Relations 1955–1980, New York, NY: Cambridge University Press.

Stone, Norman (1983) 'Grim Eminence' in The London Review of Books, 20 January: 3–8.

Strémooukhoff, Dimitri (1953) 'Moscow the Third Rome: Sources of the Doctrine' in Speculum, 28, 1: 84–101.

Struve, P. (1894) Kriticheskie zametki k voprosu ob ekonomicheskom razvitii Rossii, St Petersburg: I.N. Skorokhodov.

Suganami, Hidemi (1989) The Domestic Analogy and World Order Proposals, Cambridge: Cambridge University Press.

Sumner, B.H. (1951) 'Russia and Europe' in Oxford Slavonic Papers, 2, 1–16.

Suslin, P., Blishchenko, I., Lyubimova, V., Gantman, V., Novikov, R. and Knyazhinskiy, V. (1959) '"Obshchiy rynok" i ego rol' v ekonomike i politike sovremennogo imperializma. Nauchnaya konferentsiya' in MEiMO, 3, 8: 104–18.

Szamuely, Tibor (1988) [1974] The Russian Tradition, London: Fontana.

Taylor, A.J.P. (1987) [1954] The Struggle for Mastery in Europe, Oxford: Oxford University Press.

Thaden, Edward C. (1990a) 'The Beginnings of Romantic Nationalism in Russia' in Interpreting History: Collected Essays on Russia's Relations with Europe, Boulder, CO: Social Science Monographs, 179–201.

Thaden, Edward C. (1990b) 'The Vocabulary of Russian Historicism' in op. cit., 83–91.

Thomsen, Vilhelm (1877) The Relations between Ancient Russia and Scandinavia and the Origin of the Russian State, Oxford: Parker.

Timmermann, Heinz (1992) 'Opening to the West: Crucial Points in Soviet Policy toward Europe' in The Soviet Union 1990/91: Crisis – Disintegration – New Orientation, Cologne: Bundesinstitut für ostwissenschaftliche und internationale Studien, 48–63.

Todorov, Tzvetan (1991) [1982] The Conquest of America: The Question of the Other, New York, NY: Harper Perennial.

Torbakov, Igor (1992) 'The "Statists" and the Ideology of Russian Imperial Nationalism' in RFE/RL Research Report, 1, 49: 10–16.

Törnudd, Klaus (1963) *Soviet Attitudes to Regional Non-military Cooperation*, Helsinki: Societas Scientiarum Fennica.

Treadgold, Donald W. (1973) *The West in Russia and China: Religions and Secular Thought in Modern Times: Russia, 1472–1917*, vol.1, Cambridge, MA: Harvard University Press.

Trotskiy, L.N. (1924) [*Pravda*, 30 June 1923] 'O sovremennosti lozunga "Soedinennye Shtaty Evropy"' in *Sochineniya*, vol. 12, Moscow: Gosudarstvennoe izdatel'stvo, 367–72.

Trotskiy, N. [sic] (1904) *Nashi politicheskie zadachi. Takticheskie i organizatsionnye voprosy*, Geneva: Izdanie Rossiyskoy Sotsial'demokraticheskoy Rabochey Partii.

Trotskiy, N. [sic] (n.d., 1906) *Nasha revolyutsiya*, St Petersburg: Glagolev.

Trotsky, Leon (1926) *Towards Socialism or Capitalism*, London: Methuen.

Trotsky, Leon (1971) *1905*, Harmondsworth: Penguin.

Trubetskoy, Prince N.S. (1920) *Evropa i chelovechestvo*, Sofia: Rossiysko-bolgarskoe knigoizdatel'stvo.

Tucker, Robert C. (1990) *Stalin in Power. The Revolution from Above 1928–1941*, New York, NY: Norton.

Turgenev, I.S. (1963) Letter to A. I. Gertsen of 23 October/4 November 1862 in *Polnoe sobranie sochineniy i pisem v dvadtsati vos'mi tomakh. Pis'ma v trinadtsati tomakh*, vol. 5, Moscow: Akademiya nauk, 64–5.

Ulam, Adam B. (1974) *Expansion and Coexistence: Soviet Foreign Policy 1917–73*, New York: Holt, Rinehart & Winston, second edn.

Ustryalov, N. (1927) *Pod znakom revolyutsii*, Harbin: Poligraf, second edn.

Utkin, Anatoliy (1993): 'Rossiya i zapad' in *Svobodnaya mysl'*, 70, 13: 3–14.

Vada, Kharuki et al. (1990) 'Rossiya v sovremennom mire' in *Kommunist*, 67, 11: 16–31 [cf., also Wada].

Vek XX i mir (1989), editorial matter, 32, 1: 14.

Vekhi. Sbornik statey o russkoy intelligentsii (1967) [1909] Frankfurt: Posev.

Venturi, Franco (1960) [1952] *Roots of Revolution: A History of the Populist and Socialist Movements in Nineteenth Century Russia*, London: Weidenfeld & Nicolson.

Vincent, R.J. (1980) 'The Factor of Culture in the Global International Order' in *The Year Book of World Affairs*, vol. 34, London: Stevens & Sons, 252–64.

Waage, Peter Normann (1988) *Det usynlige kontinent. Vladimir Solovjov som Europas filosof*, Oslo: Dreyer.

Wada, Haruki (1984) 'Marx and Revolutionary Russia' in Shanin, 40–75 (cf., also Vada).

Wæver, Ole, Holm, Ulla and Larsen, Henrik (forthcoming) *The Struggle for 'Europe': French and German Concepts of State, Nation and European Union*, Cambridge: Cambridge University Press.

Walicki, Andrzej (1969) *The Controversy over Capitalism: Studies in the Social Philosophy of the Russian Populists*, Oxford: Clarendon.

Walicki, Andrzej (1975) *The Slavophile Controversy: History of a Conservative Utopia in Nineteenth-Century Thought*, Oxford: Clarendon.

Walicki, Andrzej (1988) *A History of Russian Thought: From the Enlightenment to Marxism*, Oxford: Clarendon.

Walker, R.B.J. (1987) 'Realism, Change, and International Political Theory', in *International Studies Quarterly*, 31, 1: 65–86.

Walker, R.B.J. (1988) 'Genealogy, Geopolitics and Political Community: Richard K. Ashley and the Critical Social Theory of International Relations', in *Alternatives*, 13, 1: 84–8.

Walker, R.B.J. (1991) 'The Concept of Culture in the Theory of International Relations' in Jongsuk Chay (ed.), *Culture and International Relations*, New York, NY: Praeger, 3–17.

Waltz, Kenneth N. (1979) *Theory of International Politics*, Reading, MA: Addison-Wesley.

Walzer, Michael (1986) 'The Politics of Michel Foucault' in David Couzens Hoy (ed.), *Foucault: A Critical Reader*, Oxford: Basil Blackwell, 51–68.

Wandycz, Piotr S. (1969) *Soviet–Polish Relations, 1917–1921*, Cambridge, MA: Harvard University Press.

Watson, Adam (1984) 'Russia and the European States System' in Bull and Watson, 61–74.

Weber, Max (1906) 'Russlands übergang zum Scheinkonstitutionalismus' in *Archiv für Sozialwissenschaft und Sozialpolitik*, 23, 1: 165–401, Beilage.

Welsh, Jennifer M. (1992) 'Edmund Burke and International Relations: The Commonwealth of Europe and the Crusade against the French Revolution', Oxford: D.Phil. thesis, Oxford University, mimeo.

Wettig, Gerhard (1990) *West European Integration and pan-Europeanism in Soviet Foreign Policy*, Cologne: Bundesinstitut für ostwissenschaftliche und internationale Studien, report no. 10.

White, Stephen (1985) *The Origins of Detente: The Genoa Conference and Soviet–Western Relations, 1921–1922*, Cambridge: Cambridge University Press.

Wight, Martin (ed. Hedley Bull) (1977) *Systems of States*, Leicester: Leicester University Press.

Wight, Martin (eds. Gabriele Wight and Brian Porter) (1991) *International Theory: The Three Traditions*, Leicester: Leicester University Press for the Royal Institute of International Affairs.

Wilson, Peter (1989) 'The English School of International Relations: A Reply to Sheila Grader' in *Review of International Studies*, 15, 1: 49–58.

Wittram, Reinhard (1973) *Russia and Europe*, London: Thames & Hudson.

Wolfe, Bertram D. (ed. Leonard D. Gerson) (1984) *Lenin and the Twentieth Century*, Stanford, CA: Hoover Institution Press.

Wolfe, Thomas W. (1970) *Soviet Power and Europe 1945–1970*, Baltimore, MD: Johns Hopkins University Press.

Yanov, Alexander (1978) *The Russian New Right: Right-Wing Ideology in the Contemporary USSR*, Berkeley, CA: Institute of International Studies, University of California.

Yanov, Alexander (1987) *The Russian Challenge and the Year 2000*, Oxford: Basil Blackwell.

Yanov, Aleksandr (1990) 'Russkaya ideya i 2000–y god' in *Neva*, 36, 9: 143–64; 10: 151–75; 11: 150–75; 12: 163–71.

'Zadachi sovetskikh istorikov v oblasti novoy i noveyshey istorii' (1949) in *Voprosy istorii*, 5, 3: 3–13.

Zeman, Z.A.B. and Scharlan, W.B. (1965) *The Merchant of Revolution: The Life of Alexander Israel Helphand (Parvus), 1867–1924*, London: Oxford University Press.

Zen'kovskiy, Vasiliy Vasil'evich (1955) [1929] *Russkie mysliteli i Evropa. Kritika evropeyskoy kul'tury u russkikh mysliteli*, Paris: YMCA Press.

Zernov, Nicolas (1963) *The Russian Religious Renaissance of the Twentieth Century*, London: Darton, Longman & Todd.

Zhirinovskiy, Vladimir Vol'fovich (1993) *Posledniy brosok na yug*, Moscow: Liberal'no-demokraticheskaya partiya.

INDEX